To Eric,

dear and val

Alma, August 1995.

MANAGING CHANGE

To Jervis and to my family,
for ceaseless inspiration

ALMA WHITELEY
Associate Professor and MBA Director
Graduate School of Business
Curtin University of Technology, Perth

MANAGING CHANGE
A CORE VALUES APPROACH

First published 1995 by
MACMILLAN EDUCATION AUSTRALIA PTY LTD
107 Moray Street, South Melbourne 3205

Associated companies and representatives
throughout the world

National Library of Australia
cataloguing in publication data

Whiteley, Alma (Alma Mary).
Managing change : a core values approach.

Bibliography.
Includes index.
ISBN 0 7329 2801 X (pbk.).
ISBN 0 7329 2802 8.

1. Corporate culture. 2. Organizational change — Management. 3. Corporate culture — Australia — Case studies. 4. Organizational change — Australia — Management — Case studies. I. Title.

658.406

Typeset in Joanna and Gill Sans by
Superskill Graphics, Singapore

Printed in Hong Kong

Designed by The Incredible Sons of Hawaii Five-O
Cover design by Dimitrios Frangoulis
Index by Kathleen Gray

Contents

Preface vii
Acknowledgments x

Part I Concepts and theory

1 Management and corporate culture **3**
Modernism 5
Postmodernism 7
Scientific management 9
The Hawthorne Effect 11
Culture building 14
2 What is corporate culture? **18**
Corporate culture defined 18
Culture as negotiated reality 22
3 Changing corporate values **34**
Change 34
The role of values 36
4 The core values model **42**
Core values 42
Values, strategy, structure and systems 47
Traditional mindsets 49
Changing mindsets 55
Prescribed and negotiated realities 59
5 The core values method **66**
Employee as customer 66
Manager as facilitator 70
6 Culture building and binding, and learning concepts **81**
Culture building and culture binding 81
Matching organisational design to culture building 97
Useful concepts for the agent of organisational change 109
Learning concepts 116

Part II The cases

7 Introduction to the cases **129**
Case study method 130
Tips for using the cases 133
8 BHP Iron Ore **142**
9 Underground Chemicals Limited **151**
10 The Commonwealth Industrial Gases Ltd **158**
11 DuPont (Australia) Ltd **177**
12 Kellogg (Aust) Pty Ltd **191**
13 A new regional bank **208**
14 The Xerox journey **221**
15 Tubemakers of Australia Ltd **233**
16 P.I.C.S.(WA) **242**
17 The Mass Transit Railway Corporation **250**

References 262
Index 268

Preface

The beginning of the quest to understand the complexities of the relationship between the managing and the managed began in 1962 in a shipyard setting. Around two hundred technicians, labourers and workers stood before a foreman who 'recruited' labour from his 'office', a wooden crate, upon which he raised himself from the crowd. He importantly pointed first to one person and then another, signifying selection for work. He was, you may say, breaking the rules of human respect and dignity, not out of malice but because in those days this was the way things were done. This was the labour market. The feelings of violation of the human condition embedded in that early morning experience gave me the determination to make sense of the situation and, if humanly possible, seek the knowledge and skills to understand and change such things. Of course, the labour market in the crude form of the sixties seems to be with us no longer, but metaphorically this may not be the case. The managing and the managed are still very much in evidence. The challenge facing all of us is to find ways to tap into the great heart and spirit of employees and management alike. The question is how can we release the energy and courage needed to face the confusing and complex challenges of the 2000s?

One learns that 'making sense' is not easy. It is a multidisciplinary task. In the organisational contexts, the following disciplines are particularly relevant.

Education alerts us to concepts such as learned helplessness, self-fulfilling prophecy and the inevitability of low/high expectations others have of us. Studying education shows the absolute power of the educator, trainer and manager to shape the realities of those they 'manage' (a term which, with any luck, will become redundant as organisations equalise their resources).

Marketing reminds us of the very sophisticated and well-developed decision-making and negotiation skills of consumers. It recognises that we are skilled decision makers by the time we are a few years old — and so much more skilled by the time we are wage earners. Manager-as-representative of the employment product is no different. He/she has product to sell. This is mainly the management style, supported by organisational culture, company benefits, conditions and work climate. The work experience is the product to be packaged, promoted and personalised for each human being. The marketer would tell us that if we, as managers, want to 'sell' ourselves as products we need to sense, serve and satisfy our consumers' needs. History tells us that we need to proceed gradually, by making employees aware of new 'products', for example organisational change. A marketing approach to change would favour informing employees of important aspects of change and persuading them to 'buy in' to the new situation. Marketing tells us that we need to penetrate the very 'reality' of our consumers not just once but as often as possible, continuously reinforcing our messages in ways they understand.

Anthropology tells us that nature — biological evolution — has not designed humans for any specific environment in the sense of special wings, limbs, beaks, tails or physical tools, but there again, nor has it trapped us into any one environment. We can use our imagination, our vision and our values to create specific adaptive designs — cultures. These cultures are unique worlds of meaning that are home designed and home controlled, and they are prescribed ways of 'seeing' the world and protecting the cultural groups placed in it.

Human resource management puts the other disciplines to work. Building cultures, satisfying 'consumers', negotiating realities, and creating self-fulfilling prophecies of enablement or helplessness are all possible within the organisational context. After all, organisations really are societies. That first labour market experience tells much about the legitimacy of hierarchical power, masculine individualism and unambiguous settle-things-here-and-now rules. What was the labour market in the 1962 cultural context? A ritual, a symbol of perpetuated power, a ceremony to remind labour market members of whose prerogative it is to hire, fire, select, reject (and in consequence to control the very lives, bread and butter, and aspirations of the job seekers). By asking the philosophical question 'why', human resource managers are able to look beneath the prescribed reality of scientific management for ways to incorporate natural justice for all employees into the work setting. Managers' ability to prescribe the reality of others will give way to the need to negotiate reality with them and to manage shared worlds of meaning on an individual basis.

The cases and ideas in this book demonstrate the ground swell of support for other, more human and liberated ways of managing. Things are seen differently because the old ways have produced consequences which competitive organisations are ready to reject. The value of employees' 'ownership' of decisions concerning their lives has become recognised more and more as disciplines such as marketing, anthropology, social psychology and philosophy have become accessible to us. In every case presented here, the organisation has been dissatisfied with some aspect of organisational performance. As each has pursued its own methodology for investigating what will lead to success and competitiveness, a pattern has emerged. It has become realised that ownership of, and commitment to, the organisational development endeavour by *all* employees is the key to ongoing prosperity. The case organisations have given generously of their time and expertise. They have willingly shared their methodologies for continuous change and each would say that it is necessary to go through the investigative and change design processes to produce a custom-built organisational design.

The feeling that comes across when researching these organisations is that of a deep and abiding faith in the untapped abilities and potential of the non-managerial class of worker. The liberation offered by taking away systems for offering taught solutions, removing ways of working dictated by others, and emphasising the need for personal accountability has been recognised in the way employees have been brought into the decision-making process. It is possible to 'see' the subtleties, nuances, psychological consequences and opportunities that will result from the new ways in which we can design our organisational societies. We live at the crossroads. We can accept the gift of 'new tools' absently, and apply them episodically or reactively. Or we can fire them with our imagination, and use them to mould adaptive environments, going from the valleys of scientific management to the cultural peaks of spirits shared, with hearts and energies harnessed in unison to meet the goals and challenges of the future.

Acknowledgments

Many people have directly and indirectly contributed to this book. In particular, I thank the people, colleagues and those whose paths I have crossed in forty years of working life for the chance to learn and experience so many good, bad and indifferent ways of managing and being managed; Peter Frost from the University of British Columbia and those such as Richard Semler from Semco who share an enabling philosophy and faith in the humanness of working life; Peter Senge whose idea of mental models is so seminal; and my mentors at Curtin University: Geoff Soutar and Margaret Nowak.

Grateful thanks are due to the case organisations which were so willing to contribute to the body of knowledge and practice that is fast growing in Australia: David Stringfellow from Fuji Xerox Australia; Bill Richards from Kellogg (Aust) Pty Ltd; Richard McBurney and Peter Lee from the Commonwealth Industrial Gases Ltd; Graeme Longe and Kathy Wiedner from DuPont Australia Ltd; and Robin Buckham from Tubemakers of Australia Ltd, Kembla Grange.

Thanks to the case authors: Sara Tang and Patrick Maule from the Mass Transit Railway Corporation in Hong Kong; Peter Bell from BHP Iron Ore; Joe Garcia from Western Washington University, USA; David Napoli from David Napoli Associates; and John Kelmar from Curtin University.

Thanks also to Peter Debus from Macmillan Education Australia for guiding the book through to completion; to Deborah Lord and Jan Dyball for desktop publishing; and to Valerie Marlborough and Elizabeth Gibson for professional editing.

When I ask, in my seminars, 'how many of you would agree that the vast majority of the workforce possess far more capability, creativity, talent, initiative and resourcefulness than their present jobs allow them to use?' the affirmative response is about 99 per cent. In other words, we all admit that our greatest resources are being wasted and that poor human resource management hurts our bottom lines.

Covey (1992:15)

So it has come to this: You've automated the factory, decimated the inventory, eliminated the unnecessary from the organisational chart, and the company still isn't hitting on all cylinders — and you've got an awful feeling you know why. It's the culture. It's the values, heroes, myths, symbols that have been in the organisation forever, the attitudes which say, Don't disagree with the boss, or don't make waves or Just do enough to get by or For God's sake, don't take chances. And how on earth are you going to change all that? If your company is like a great many others, it will have to step up this challenge. The changes businesses are forced to make merely to stay competitive — improving quality, increasing speed, adopting a customer orientation — are so fundamental that they must take root in a company's very essence, which means its culture.

Dumaine (1992:443)

Part I

Concepts and theory

1
Management and corporate culture

> Management is a mixture of thinking and doing. It is about motivating people to use their knowledge and skills. It is about developing technical and people systems which have an 'enabling' effect on people involved with the company.
>
> Tang and Whiteley 1991:1

This book is about culture building in the face of the fundamental change facing tomorrow's competitive organisations. It is about celebrating the personal power and strategic contribution of *every* employee in an organisation. It is about helping managers to embrace the potential of the individual and also to appreciate that every individual worker as well as his/her manager has an 'internal image' or 'mental model' of the organisation (Senge 1992a:5; 1992b:140). The notion of management belongs with the notion of mindsets. The notion of change requires a concern with changing mindsets. It is conceivable, for example, that in the not too distant future the term 'manager', with the connotations it currently holds, will be inappropriate to describe the relationships between internal members of a customer-orientated organisation. A real change in mindset about the manager/subordinate relationship should mean a change in the very ways of speaking and using language, as well as thinking about the new relationship. In particular, language which labels positions and people can unwittingly cause traditions to linger and be perpetuated. Compare the language in the following two accounts of management:

> Those who occupy directing roles must have an active value system — this is what top leadership is all about. In practice, the principle extends right down the hierarchy; all managers make decisions of principle which profoundly influence the part of the community which they govern.
>
> Woodcock and Francis 1989:vii

> For truly big decisions, such as buying another company, everyone at Semco gets a vote. A few years ago when we wanted to relocate a factory, we closed down for a day and everyone piled into buses to inspect possible new sites. Then the workers decided.
>
> Semler 1993:2

In the spirit of this book, the term 'manager' will be used to represent a partnership relationship. This is on the basis that it is becoming recognised more and more that hierarchical status boundaries can result in a waste of talent as contributions are matched to 'levels'.

Today's effective managers anywhere in the world face an oncoming tide of change as their skills, or lack of them, become a competitive factor for success or failure in the global marketplace. 'After decades of drifting, managers have recognised their tough task of leading, controlling and winning. With global competition there are many more threats. Only the fittest will survive' (Woodcock and Francis 1989: xix). On the Asia Pacific rim, this is especially the case as developing countries take advantage of others' learning at an accelerated pace (Krugman 1994). In Australia, IBIS (1993) gives some idea of the extent of change facing managers today. IBIS says that traditionally we have had an 'exclusive reliance' on the idea of organisations as machines. These mechanistic organisations require 'hard', logical structures

Aspects that have dominated		**Now to include or replace**
The 'machine' ethic with *concrete* structures, strategies and a systems approach	→	The 'organic' ethic with *pliable* structures, strategies to match values, and 'soft' systems which include the people element
Managers think, workers do	→	Managers as facilitators and workers empowered to think, plan and initiate change
Military model of obedience	→	Co-operative model of commitment
Content and outcomes: narrow use of tools and techniques	→	The 'how' processes overall use of tools and techniques
Taught solutions	→	Seeking out problems and issues, and working out solutions which harmonise
'Truth' based on organisational 'laws' and proven principles	→	Interpreting 'reality' to embrace realities of others

Figure 1.1 *Changes facing managers* (adapted from Pascale 1990:32)

(often hierarchical). They require systems which fit the machine concept such as two-tier operations: management systems for thinking and worker systems for doing. Machine organisations would characteristically have down-up-down communication and authority lines. Managers would be keen on finished products, definitively solving problems and eliminating wherever possible malfunctions such as tensions and disharmony. The organisational 'truth' would be that embodied in the organisation's laws and principles. The model of contextual shifts in management (Figure 1.1) gives some idea of the extent of change facing managers today (Pascale 1990:32).

Modernism

The bureaucratic, mechanistic, organisational world, which has held the dominating aspects of workplace relations and management systems for so long, has become known as 'modernism' (Bergquist 1993; Clegg 1992:154). Clegg captures the spirit of modernism when he talks about Weber who typified organisations as bureaucratised, mechanistic structures of control, built on a 'rational' base of divided and deskilled labour. He talks about sections of the labour force being integrated through machinery, conveyer belts and semiautomatic assembly lines and workers being fixed into jobs according to the needs of the machine system. 'Fordism', a term often connected to modernism refers to the system of mass production based on a 'legal contract of employment'. According to Etzioni's (1971) work, there is another contract — the psychological contract — which is a set of expectations the individual has of the organisation and vice versa. We can see that this idea appeared to be totally discounted under Taylorist and Fordist organisational design principles. Investigating expectations were not seen as necessary activities for management to incorporate into recruitment and selection, socialisation, job design or performance appraisal. Etzioni (1971) found it possible to categorise organisations according to the psychological contracts which were evident in the way organisations operated. These contracts are:

- *Coercive contract* — At its extreme, the organisational members are bound to the organisation either against their will, or through forces beyond their control. Immediately, we think of prisons, concentration camps, psychiatric hospitals. However, labour market forces, such as those in an economic depression, often render people powerless to leave their jobs. The coercive contract is characterised by control through punishment (for example docking wages), power in the hands of a few, and effort and energy called in by fear of punishment.

- *Calculative contract* — The expectations are that there is an explicit exchange of money and conditions for services rendered. Control is still in the hands of the organisation but is dependent on its ability to keep the money and conditions (social opportunities, promotion, appropriately enriched jobs and status) flowing in. If an organisation tries to get more effort and work without a corresponding increase in 'pay' the contract is broken. If the organisation subsequently threatens (or appears to threaten) the employee, then the contract will probably become perceived as a coercive contract — the power and control scenario. Here you can have what you can buy. This usually includes time, compliance, full value for money and the notion of fixed conditions.
- *Co-operative contract* — The expectations are that the individual and organisation will co-operate in setting and achieving goals. There is a sense of mutuality in this psychological contract. In order for a set of expectations to be co-operative, the individual enters into the contract (or not) freely, and shares responsibility (and accountability) for goals and decisions. Imposed goals immediately change the contract and the organisation cannot assume that its goals, or senior management goals, will be real or desirable to individuals. Co-operative expectations bring what money cannot buy. Most people express this as loyalty, trust, commitment and the willingness to go beyond what is officially set. Often they include such things as creativity, initiative, risk taking and learning rather than being taught.

Psychological contract setting was probably not a part of modernist management because to do this the organisation has to:

- recognise that the employee has a valid set of expectations from the organisation;
- be prepared to enter the employee's world of meaning in order to find out what the expectations are; and
- be prepared to substantiate the mutuality of the work exchange transaction by allowing individuals some say in their organisation's goal setting and design principles.

Psychological contract setting provides a useful framework for working out the sets of expectations actually designed into working life through organisational design, structures, power and control systems. From the following quotation, it is not too difficult to imagine which contract predominated in the modern era.

> Stretching above the organisational base of Fordist enterprises was a pyramid of control, designed in a classically bureaucratic fashion. At its apex this radiated from the product division to the central organs of calculation and control; according to both the formal theory and the practical application of it in organisational design, authority would reside in individuals by virtue of their incumbency in jobs and/or their expertise. These offices would be organised hierarchically, with compliance being to superordinate instructions expressed in universal fixed rules. The day-to-day principles of control, derived from the hierarchy of offices, would reside in direct surveillance and supervision as well as the standardised rules and sanctions.
>
> Clegg (1992:157)

Postmodernism

And what of the future? From modernism we will move to 'postmodernism' (Bergquist 1993). The postmodern organisation will have to deal with as much chaos as order. It will have often confusing elements of stability and accelerated, even unpredicted, change. The organisations which will not only survive but also thrive will have a 'core of being', portable across a range of situations. They will know who they are and what they are. They will rely on their internal resources to provide a communal front of intellect, energy and creativity. Change will be a constant dynamic and there will be no preoccupation with 'unfreezing' behaviour (Lewin 1947) because there will not be a culture where freezing is a value. The aim of a manager will be to see that every human resource is celebrated and optimised.

Pascale (1990) says that as managers come out of the machine era, organisations will *feel* as well as *think*. Hard logic will run alongside soft management dimensions such as shared values and acceptable management styles. Managers of the future, says Pascale, will be facilitators whose job will be to empower workers to *initiate* improvements and change. Gone will be the merit in being a superworker with some rather annoying administrative tasks that get in the way of the real job, which is to show workers how a superworker does it. Instead there will be a heavy emphasis on helping workers to make sense of their environment. This goes right down the line from helping them understand the organisational philosophy and culture to enabling them to develop problem-solving skills on their particular job. Managers can no longer afford the restrictions which the machine mentality places on developing an employee's ability to see the bigger picture. Developing the 'making sense of' abilities of employees will be one of a manager's prime functions in years to come.

Peter Drucker (1992:128) tells us that the organisation of the future will have fewer than half the management levels and less than a third of the managers, and will differ greatly from the 'manufacturing model' of today. He talks about the information-based organisation and this will be dominated by service organisations of 'specialists who direct their own performance through organised feedback from colleagues, customers, and headquarters'.

All around us, too, 'alternative' management approaches are making their voices heard. The Total Quality Management people say 'Good enough just isn't good enough'. They say that everyone at work is someone else's customer. When marketers want to sell a product, they find out as much as possible about customers — who they are, how they live, what makes them enthusiastic, what they think they need and, as importantly, what they think they don't need.

What has this marketing idea to do with human resource managers? Human resource managers *are* internal marketers. Like external marketers, people are their customers, but very special customers, because it is recognised worldwide that '. . . people make businesses work. And we need to relearn old lessons about how culture ties people together and gives meaning and purpose to their day-to-day lives' (Deal and Kennedy 1982:5). This book captures the very special link between business success, people at work and organisational culture. In particular, it helps managers to recognise the importance of culture building and suggests some practical ways to make a start.

The argument for engaging with behavioural work is powerful (even though it is much less comfortable than technical, accounting and procedural work). Primarily, the reason is that people are emotional as well as logical. People are not a static commodity. It is a sobering thought that, depending on the way people are managed, they can either work to minimal specifications or unleash the sort of enthusiasm, energy, tenacity and synergy which makes one marvel at human capacity and creativity.

Scientific management

Imagine you are a young worker, say in your twenties, going to work somewhere. It could be in an engineering organisation, the service industry or a small enterprise — anywhere in fact. The way you are treated in work makes you feel that your managers follow F. W. Taylor's scientific management principles and methods, which in turn were coloured by his view that 'Hardly a competent workman can be found who does not devote a considerable amount of his time to studying just how slowly he can work and still convince his employer that he is going at a good pace. Under our system a worker is told what to do and how he is to do it. Any improvement he makes upon the orders given is fatal to his success' (Taylor 1929). Briefly, Taylor's four principles were: there was one (management) best way of work organisation based on engineering methods; people should be scientifically matched to tasks; a formula for managing was to 'supervise, reward and punish'; and managers would plan, co-ordinate and control.

Under Taylorism, the work of people like your imagined self is broken down into specialised, standardised, simplified components. You, the worker, keep pace with assembly line-like machines. You work on a need-to-know basis and your job description is designed accordingly. Authority and decision making rest with upper levels. *Thinking, controlling and co-ordinating* are done by managers. *Doing* is what you are paid for and that is made very clear. You are part of modern management of your day, the ultimate in management with tight controls, centralised top-down decision making, and carefully programmed and prescribed tasks. You will never have to worry about thinking, in fact it will be a worry if you do. Thinking belongs with the decision-making and information-gathering activities which are the prerogative of management. This is what management is paid to do.

As this young worker in scientific management days, then, you would expect to find that your world is prescribed for you. You are matched so closely to the job and its tools that you could see yourself as a machine's extra arms and legs. Imagine this drawing board approach to human beings. The most important lesson to learn from

Taylor or any other influential management practitioner/theorist (such as McGregor 1960, Peters and Austin 1985, Kanter 1984, Senge 1992) is that their theories and recommended practices rest upon *a personal view of what human beings are and how they should be treated*. Taylor is of use to us not only to explain our management heritage but also as a working model of how a manager's view of the world dictates his/her blueprint for managing. This personal view has a knock-on effect all the way down to the daily shop-floor management practices. So we can say that managing people begins with a manager's view of humans in the work setting. This influences the underlying management philosophy, which will find its way ultimately into work-design decisions. From these almost every aspect of work will be affected. Figure 1.2 shows how two contrasting world views result in management's different supervisory styles. From this table, you can work out how Taylor might have viewed your work life.

View A	**View B**
Humans are intelligent and able.	Humans are compliant and obedient.
Humans are responsible.	Humans are not responsible.
Humans are self-manageable.	Humans need to be controlled/supervised.
Humans can think.	Humans can do.
Style A	**Style B**
Supervisory style is enabling.	Supervisory style is controlling.
Information is shared.	Information is screened.
Atmosphere is open/trusting.	Atmosphere is closed/suspicious.
This style organises around process.	This style organises around task.
Hierarchy is flatter.	Hierarchy is pyramidal.
Teams are used to manage.	Managers are used to manage.
Customers drive performance.	Profitability drives performance.
Team results are rewarded.	Individual performance is rewarded.
Multiskills are rewarded.	Prescribed skills are rewarded.
Supplier/Customer contact is maximised.	Supplier/Customer contact is minimised.
This style teaches people to think and learn.	This style teaches people to follow taught solutions.

Figure 1.2 *Two contrasting views of humans in the work setting as indicated by supervisory styles* (adapted from an idea in *Business Week*, Dec. 1993, p. 46, using McKinsey & Co data)

According to Taylor's philosophy, which would correspond to View B, supervisors prescribe the skills they want you to use — no decision making there for you. You are closely watched and timed. Your movements are monitored for precision and obedience. You report to the level above you — in fact you're not sure what happens above that except by grapevine gossip. Your supervisor and his/her manager control information about scheduling, performance, who else is doing what and other interesting facts. He/she chooses what you need to know and communicates job-specific requirements plus the odd dark warning about the insecure future to keep you on your toes. You have learned not to trust anyone, especially your bosses, even though you keep checking out the trust situation. Hints, such as the 'Broken Promises' poem put up by the workers on the canteen noticeboard, draw no responses from management; they're just not listening. On Friday afternoons, you don't know whether you will have money or a redundancy notice thrown at you. If management are out of credit with you and need your productivity, you'll find money. If they don't need you, it could be your notice. You would not be too far off the track if you thought that to scientific managers you were an item for sale.

Scientific managers would take it for granted that you would sell your personal choice about how, when and with whom you work. To them, you would simply sell your effort for money in a rational equation.

More effort = more money. Less effort = less money.

And so you would be asked to put your skills but not your spirit into the job. Very soon, there would be a collusion between you and management (maybe not intended, maybe not recognised) to make money become the symbol of excellence. Under this principle, when raw materials or downtime interfere with your bonus-making capacities, your status, prestige and self-esteem suffer as well as your pocket. Money-making capacity becomes an indicator of all these things, which we could term 'personal profit'. If safety first clashes with personal profit, which will win and which will you risk? Would anything be powerful enough to overcome the effects of a rational/economic management philosophy such as Taylor's, you may ask.

The Hawthorne Effect

For a long time the answer was 'no' until a dramatic piece of research commonly called the 'Hawthorne experiments' entered the scene.

Here, in anecdotal form, is the story of the Hawthorne experiments and the Hawthorne Effect as it came to be known (Mayo 1945; Roethlisberger and Dickson 1939).

A research team from Harvard University in the USA began to research illumination experiments with various groups of workers at the Hawthorne Plant of the Western Electric Co., a large organisation. Following the needs of scientific management (which managers and researchers were doing almost universally at that time), the research set out to investigate lighting conditions with a view to matching them to human needs without any wastage and inefficiency. However, the efficiency aspects were not straightforward. Indeed, strange and, at that time, inexplicable things happened.

- Lighting was raised and productivity went up.
- Lighting was lowered and productivity went up.
- Lighting was lowered even further than before and productivity went up.
- Lighting was raised even further than before and productivity went up.

Although results varied across experiments, it was clear that the change in output was not in proportion to the change in illumination either up or down.

What could have caused the change? The individuals in the groups studied were given attention of a particular sort by their supervisors and the researchers. They were listened to. They were asked their advice about productivity matters, thus being allowed to participate in aspects of work which were important to them. The result? Absences and sickness became around one-third in relation to their production colleagues. A reason? Clearly human and social behaviour, not money, was responsible for the increased productivity and decreased absence/sickness. This became known as a 'Hawthorne Effect'. The results of this realisation of the human as decision maker led to the many motivation theories based on the needs of individuals with which you are familiar, including those of managers (Maslow 1970; Herzberg, Mausner and Snyderman 1959; McGregor 1960).

Another example in the same set of studies once more surprised the scientific researchers. The bank-wiring room was studied to gauge the effects of a sophisticated wage-incentive plan. Remember that under the Taylorist assumptions one would automatically expect individual workers to maximise their output when matched with economic rewards. ('Workers are rational and economic people,' said the scientific managers.) This did not happen. Instead, a sort of organisation within an organisation was discovered. In theory, management dictated productivity figures, but in practice, the work group developed its own rules on the matter. A group norm (normal standard of behaviour as agreed by the group) determined what constituted a proper day's work. Individual workers would give erroneous reports on the daily output even though the weekly figures matched. Interviews determined that the group was operating well below its estimated capacity and was levelling out to meet group expectations. Why? Guessing, it could have been group logic about incentive systems, such that if you show your best too often it will be taken as your normal and won't attract an incentive rate. Also, slower workers would show up. They may be reprimanded or even laid off. The group management solution was to work out a felt-fair rate. This was managed by a set of principles, described by Robbins.

> *Don't* be a ratebuster, turning out too much work. *Don't* be a chiseler, turning out too little work. *Don't* be a squealer on any of your peers.
>
> Robbins (1992:97)

How did the group enforce these principles (or norms)? As Robbins says, their methods were neither gentle nor subtle. They included sarcasm, name calling, ridicule and even physical punches on the upper arm of members who violated the norms.

There was no avoiding the evidence. Workers had more control over their working lives than had ever been thought by management. In the illumination experiments, it became evident that individuals had psychological needs of recognition and participation that were an unrecognised part of the 'effort and money' equation. As group members, individuals had needs to belong and to be accepted. In the bank-wiring situation, the work group developed an alternative and informal management strategy to the formal one imposed down the hierarchy. This demonstrates that if management aren't trusted to make rules which are more flexible than those allowed under the 'rational economic' logic, then the workers are quite capable of providing their own management prerogatives. This propensity for the group to manage itself is another Hawthorne Effect. From these foundations, the deep study of group behaviours developed (Emery 1993; Tyson 1989). The many evolutions have resulted in management acceptance of self-directed groups (Robbins 1992; Wellins, Byham and Wilson 1991).

Such groups even legitimately design their own work, under what Emery (1993) calls 'Participative Design'.

The message carried in the Hawthorne evidence is that people will respond to practices which recognise and celebrate who they are, how they can help others and how they can be helped. Cash will satisfy physical needs. Personal recognition and liberation will satisfy the needs of workers to contribute, solve problems, and produce the disagreements and tensions which lead to creative problem solving — all of which in turn lead to higher productivity. The change in mindset from *controlling* to *enabling* entails encouraging workers to put their personal stamp on the job. It is the very thing Fordist/modernist managers did not want. Unfortunately, the modernist habit has stuck, in Australia as well as elsewhere in the world. But was it ever really possible, never mind desirable, to control people's natural abilities? Is it not a tragedy that Taylor's evident genius at matching skills and tasks did not take into account that humans are whole people who can see whole pictures? They have a spirit which defies scientific explanation. Human determination can result in unbelievable feats of effort, stamina, creativity and courage. Nevertheless, Taylor and other scientific managers succeeded in building a durable and widely accepted *work culture*, described in more detail in Chapter 2. Modernist values were expressed as beliefs across the Western world. The idea that money was *the* symbol of recognition and reward was held without question. A whole edifice of management theories and practices was built on the cultural basis that work was to be organised around monetary rewards in return for obedience and compliance. From this comes the American term 'compensation', which suggests that work is not to be enjoyed and so needs to be compensated.

Culture building

The aim of a successful culture or social group is to send its members out into the world as self-regulating mechanisms (Goffman 1969). They will operate consistently within the culture rules even when they are far away from familiar contexts. At work the same could be said in earlier times. The Taylorist methods fulfilled the requirements of a culture. There were readily observable values. Behaviour patterns were laid down. Rules were explicit. They were also inhuman. An argument is that there will always be a shadow culture underlying such an inhuman culture, built by workers themselves. Here, social allegiances, loyalties, hierarchies, rules and behaviours will be built in to the work system to allow the human values, beliefs and actions to be rewarded. We could say this is the natural culture and it will find its way into the workplace. Workers, as well as managers, can demonstrate successful culture building. These worker-designed cultures are all too often anticultures to the desired organisational culture. When informal (and often subconscious) culture building is in process, a whole gamut of activities takes place. Values are articulated. Beliefs about fairness and output are developed. Strategies are chosen. Norms and sanctions provide the behaviour rules and expectations for those who break them. Rituals are installed, myths evolve. Heroes are recognised for upholding the culture, no matter what. Symbols of group identity, solidarity and vision are produced and reinforced. When two cultures, organisational and work group, are in opposition it is called 'culture clash'. It doesn't need a genius to figure out what that does to an organisation's competitive edge. So during almost a century of scientific management cultures many human resources were wasted.

Modern work culture was unknowingly aided by other strong cultural institutions, home and school. It is not too difficult to see that there is a determined socialisation process in operation at home and particularly at school. School values are expressed in a wide variety of ways. The curricula tell you what is valued knowledge and ability. The phrase 'he is good with his hands' is still sometimes a euphemism for not being good at valued academic subjects. For parents, this admission can be a wry apology, and for teachers it might mean recognition of pupils who don't quite make the valued cultural norms. Teachers' choice of language and ways of speaking set a value on pupils' verbal skills. Measures of success are firmly rooted in 'approved' subjects. This has the effect of the self-fulfilling prophecy. Pupils who feel valued, flourish. Those who don't very often follow the Hawthorne group and fashion their own culture and norms. These are often expressed as negative expressions of the school values; for example, failure is success (Whiteley 1987).

At home, the same process is visible. Walk into a German, Lebanese, Indian or English home and you will see very different rules for what is acceptable or unacceptable behaviour. Home is where you learn right from wrong, and you learn this in as many varied instances and settings as it is possible to provide. Concrete examples, in the form of relatives and friends, are produced as outside evidence that the rules are shared by others. We can see that every single facet of culture building including symbols, rituals and ceremonies, heroes, jokes and stories are present in the management of pupils at school and children at home and school as culture receivers.

Much can be gathered about the time, effort and sheer doggedness necessary to build a culture by looking at school and home life. School and home life are both designed so that members will acquire patterns of behaviour which reflect the values of the two respective cultures. Behaviour rules, sometimes implicit, have to be learned incredibly quickly by a sort of osmosis. They are laid down implicitly and explicitly. To help the game along, concrete examples are given of many kinds of desired and valued behaviours. Rewards, which do not centre as much around cash as approval and acceptance, are given liberally for achievements and initiatives. (It is amazing that Taylor did not see the importance of these in the work institutions, given that *the need to belong to a family* was so strong a feature of life at that time.) Negative reinforcement or punishment, usually social in nature, is equally accessible for undesirable behaviours. Boundaries are set and continually challenged because they are living boundaries and are constantly susceptible to external changes.

The management task, if organisations are to optimise their human resources, is to understand the main game, that is to understand culture. It is to recognise that culture building needs to take into account the many work groups operating as small cultures or subcultures, which need to be harmonised when building an overarching organisational culture. And to do this effectively, the manager needs some way of studying what is going on. Otherwise he/she may be treating symptoms not problems or, as managers were in the Hawthorne study, living in a make-believe world. There, the informal life under the surface world was the real one for workers, while the one on the surface was the real one for managers. In the informal system, elected group leaders were, for practical purposes, managers. As this was not studied, it was not recognised. The days will come when the requirements for a manager to study culture will be as mandatory as those to study budget or production procedures. And just in case readers think that Taylorism is not alive and well, let's look at a comment from Konosuke Matsushita, successful Japanese leader looking from the outside in.

> We are going to win and the industrial West is going to lose out and there is nothing you can do about it because the reasons for failure are within yourselves. Your firms are built on the Taylor

> model. Even worse so are your heads. With your bosses doing the thinking while the workers wield the screwdrivers you're convinced that this is the right way to run a business. For you, the essence of management is getting the ideas out of the heads of the bosses and into the hands of labour. We are beyond your mindset.
>
> Matsushita in Pascale 1990:27

And what is such a widespread and deeply held mindset as Taylor's but a mirror of the values, beliefs and symbols which emerge as stable cultural patterns?

2

What is corporate culture?

Corporate culture defined

Culture is, to Schein,

> A pattern of shared assumptions/invented discovered and shared by a given group, as it learns to cope with its problems of external adaptation and internal integration, that has worked well enough to be valid, and, therefore, is to be taught to new members of the group as the correct way to perceive, think and feel in relation to those problems.
>
> Schein 1985b:52, 56

All of us carry within ourselves the essence of our own culture. We know what we value, whether this is independence, fairness, group companionship or, say, professionalism. We know what we believe in. These beliefs are closely related to our values. At work we may believe in fair play, promotion on merit, equality of contribution from colleagues and management alike, and rewards when they are earned. These 'value rules' are best observed when they are infringed. Favouritism, unequal workloads, no recognition where it is due, all infringe the values of fairness, justice and equity. Customs and practices are evidence of culture translated into everyday life. They range from individuals covering a colleague's work to the ritual drink on a Friday evening. Every culture has its moral boundaries where things just aren't done. Any newcomer into a culture usually finds out the hard way about conventions which have been inadvertently contravened. What is being described here is a sort of stretched-out personality, a pattern or template for forming the feelings of shared understanding. This helps people to know how things are done, and how they are supposed to behave.

The culture of an organisation, like that of a society, is a homemade blueprint for seeing the world in a particular way. Societies will organise their key elements, human relationships, resources and social institutions to ensure survival and success (in the unique way that they themselves define them). People decide what they value greatly and they build their beliefs, attitudes and ultimately behaviours accordingly. The blueprint takes the form of behaviour rules which have become solid enough to form everyday, well-accepted patterns of behaviour that everyone knows even if they don't say so. These patterns and rules will be handed down as organisational memory or folklore. In the case of organisations, the values and beliefs will provide the spectacles through which members will interpret organisational life. The patterns and rules develop into agreed solutions to ways of handling threats and opportunities from the inside and outside environment. In many ways folklore is like a psychological codebook for breaking into the language and meanings of those connected to the organisation. Once inside the code, the behaviour rulebook takes over.

The ideal situation in an organisation is that members agree and share one code of behaviour. The code should be dynamic. It should include the behaviour patterns and rules of various groups. Each should be allowed to design a variation on the general cultural theme without contravening the shared values and beliefs of the organisation as a whole. As we saw in the Hawthorne experiments, there are often competing cultural codes of behaviour inside the organisation. The existence of competing codes is not anywhere near as disturbing as the possibility that managers are not aware of the existence of culturally determined codes of behaviour.

Just as individuals have personal identities, so too do organisations. To understand an organisation it is essential to understand as much as is made accessible about its culture and identity. The ultimate 'negotiated reality' is an organisation's culture where cultural rules and behaviours allow shared sense making among many different types of people. This book is mainly designed around the more visible conceptualisation of culture as sense making in organisations, although we acknowledge and embrace the problematic invisibility and unconsciousness of culture (Douglas 1986; Pondy et al. 1983; Lundberg 1991). Like Deal and Kennedy (1982), we are suggesting to the manager that important elements of culture are visible and accessible. The codes of culture making are symbolic. Bolman and Deal (1991) suggest that the symbolic frame of reference (or code) is an important one for managers to use. Clues as to how to do this lie in such activities as the articulation of values through symbolic messages. Telling the organisational story, and therefore reinforcing its lore through stories (tall but somehow always believable), are part of workers' everyday dialogue. But how often are the stories shared around the camp fire with management and workers sharing reminiscences about the good times and the bad? Rites and rituals such as the metaphoric camp fire act as a conduit to deliver social messages and send a visible sign that everyone is important and celebrated. Because culture is not something which can be imparted easily, looking at what theorists and practitioners have to say will expand the idea and feel of culture, what it is and how it can be used to breathe life or death into an organisation.

It is important to note that writers all seem to agree on one thing. This is the existence of a link between the way people are organised to work and high company performance (Frost et al. 1991:1). Kotter and Heskett (1992:11) link this to culture by saying:

> Corporate culture can have a significant impact on a firm's long-term economic performance. Corporate culture will probably be an even more important factor in determining the success or failure of firms in the next decade . . .

Unquestionably culture within an organisation is difficult to pin down, nearly impossible to quantify or measure, and remarkably resistant to change. Given the heritage of traditional management principles and the unsuitability of them to the challenges ahead, change, often deep cultural change, will be the task facing many managers, work groups and individuals. However, culture can be identified and positively influenced by consistent, thoughtful managerial action. Clearly, no cookbook recipes for change are possible. Each organisation's culture, like each individual's identity, is made up of elements unique to itself and rests upon its particular interpretation of what is needed to organise itself for survival and success. But certain idea and concepts should apply across organisations. The most basic concept is that managing change is a three-step process as Schein (1985a:249) explains below.

1 *Understanding culture*
   Management must understand the meaning and impact of corporate culture and must ascertain, mainly through empirical methods, the elements of its own culture.

2 *Designing for the future*
The 'cultural wheat' must be separated from the 'cultural chaff'. Decisions must be made about which elements support future goals and strategies and must be retained, and which elements are no longer appropriate and must be changed.
3 *Action for change: preserve desirable elements*
Appropriate actions must be taken to effect the required changes in a way that leaves the desirable elements unaffected.

In a 'use on Monday' or practical sense, managers need to know what the elements are around which groups and individuals design their behaviour patterns and rules. Guided by Schein (1985b) the following internal tasks would be necessary:

- developing consensus on a common language and conceptual system to be used (it is through this medium of spoken and unspoken language and a 'making-sense-of' framework that meaning is shared);
- developing group behaviour boundaries and criteria for qualifying for inclusion as a group member;
- developing the criteria for allocating status, power and authority to group members;
- developing the criteria for social belonging and relationships;
- developing the criteria for the allocation of rewards and sanctions;
- developing conventions for dealing with differences, such as religion and values.

The thing to remember is that it is the (sometimes invisible) code of practice, the rulebook of behaviours, which has been designed and modified so that eventually the prescribed behaviours reflect the values to the members' satisfaction. The organisation has to go through a similar process with its external publics articulating values and beliefs, and reinforcing them through collaborative practices.

More and more the distinction between an organisation and the groups with which it is interdependent is becoming blurred. As one CEO said, 'things are too important to let loose guns out into the marketplace'. Customers, suppliers and partners are taking a more interventionist role in those organisations which serve them. The notion that an organisation can make its product or service decisions and then persuade the customers to buy-in to these decisions is outmoded. Customers want to be at least compatible and at most an integral part of an organisation's wider culture. Ideally, they will feel an integral part of the culture. This calls for some adaptation from the organisation:

- It needs to test out and arrive at a shared understanding about the vision and mission which will harmonise with its associated organisations/groups (before the vision and mission are solidified).
- It needs to develop shared major goals in keeping with shared values.
- It needs to make sure that 'how' goals which are pursued are in keeping with valued behaviours.
- It needs to define and gain agreement with its internal as well as external groups on much of the above and in particular on how to measure and respond to success or failure.

It may be true, as Schein (1985b) says, that founders and leaders of organisations have a tremendous impact upon the organisation's culture. However, it is the responsibility of supervisors and managers to lead the way in making sure that employees can have as strong an impact. Shared vision will lead to shared culture. Knowledge about the more visible aspects of culture can help organisations produce adaptive cultures. Such cultures harmonise multiple sets of assumptions according to the needs of the total environment. Culture building can be a powerful asset to the organisation, but only if workers (and significant others) are let in to the secret: if they are given real and accountable inputs into the key organising elements of the organisation's culture. After all, not only is everyone in the organisation a stakeholder, but everyone without exception has been intuitively skilled in learning highly complex cultural behaviours since childhood. Literacy and formal intelligence are not prerequisites for this sort of learning. It is so skilfully and intuitively done that following the rules is as natural as breathing.

Culture as negotiated reality

> Perception: Individuals behave in a given manner based not on the way their external environment actually is but, rather, on what they see or believe it to be. Because individuals act on their interpretations of reality rather than on reality itself, it is clear that reality must be a critical determinant of our dependent variables. . . . It is the employee's perception of a situation which becomes the basis on which he or she behaves.
>
> Robbins 1993:158

We would like to share with you a central, yet not original, idea. It is simple and yet profound. Culture is person-made. In its making, a perceived reality is constructed and negotiated. Culture is a specific reality (of values, beliefs and ways of understanding events) as it is constructed by a social group of people as its preferred ways of operating.

It seems almost commonsense to suggest that individuals construct their own reality; that is, they ascribe their own meaning to events, actions and, at work, such things as policies and management decisions. Yet managers are often observed reacting to the problems and communications of their employees from the management or organisational perspective as though it is the only reality that exists. The important thing to be confident of here is that, just as surely as managers are busy constructing a reality, others in the workplace are busy constructing their own reality. It is unlikely that one can take for granted that without special effort the two realities will be congruent. Why is this so? Individuals see the world through the lens of their own experiences, values/beliefs and personal approach to life. This view of life, work and workers can be called the 'individual world view'. Rather than deny this view, managers and organisations need to explore it, and to see what it has to offer in terms of achieving organisational goals. In the past and particularly in the modern era this has been difficult to diffuse into working life.

One particular aspect of modernism, Fordism and scientific management (discussed in chapter 1) had a significant impact on the ability or willingness of organisations to develop systems of shared understanding with employees. This was the prevailing perspective of 'objectivism' (Bergquist 1993:18). Simplistically stated, objectivists hold that there is one true version of reality that can be construed, given enough facts and evidence. This has led to such things as one best way of doing things, the 'correct' roles of workers and managers, and the development of closed systems and of universal rules and laws such as those described by Clegg (1992).

An aspect of postmodernism by contrast is that of 'constructivism', described by Bergquist (1993:18) as a situation where '. . . we construct our own social realities, based in large part on the traditions and needs of our culture and socioeconomic context in which we find ourselves'. The difference between the two lies at the deepest philosophical level. Either the true nature of things is that there is a reality out there which can be captured through scientific and logical investigation, and catered for, or there is not. If there is not, then this means that reality must be constructed in the minds and imagination of people. Reality can take meaning only when the individual interprets it and endows the reality with a particular meaning, one which may not be logically evident. According to constructivist philosophy, F. W. Taylor, the workers in the Hawthorne experiments and every single worker and manager in Australia share one thing in common: a reality constructed by themselves for themselves.

The next section further develops two aspects of constructivism. The first is that reality is constructed by people according to their societal values, beliefs and the norms of their referent groups. The second is that where it is necessary and desirable for two or more realities to come to a shared, workable reality, then the new reality will need to be negotiated to very special rules.

Construction of reality according to values, beliefs and norms

It is an amazing characteristic of humans that they can gather and extract various aspects of experience and use internal rules to fashion the experience into a version of reality. Senge (1992:5) explains these realities as mental models which '. . . can be simple generalisations such as "people are untrustworthy" or they can be complex theories. But what is important to grasp is that the mental models shape how we act. If we believe people are untrustworthy, we act differently from the way we would if we believed they were trustworthy'. We can think of these mental models as blueprints — special blueprints containing sets of rules for interpreting events into meaning and the meaning into a self-designed reality. It is these rules which are of importance to managers whose sole purpose is to achieve results through people.

Examples abound where the same event is construed differently by people who are working by different rules. We can imagine that the work group in the Hawthorne experiments (Mayo 1945) gave the official productivity worksheets a different meaning from the management group. One can imagine rules about fairness, solidarity and protecting the underdog impacting on the validity of the worksheets from the work-group side. The management side would apply rules of the labour bargain, with compliance and obedience giving the record sheets a logical, rational validity. Thinking about how these rules are given the status of work-group ready-made decisions, the rules in this case (involving as they did money and recognition) would not have been made lightly. The actions assumed values and beliefs about work and management which dictated codes of practice and behaviour. If such values, beliefs and practices become stable, then they will probably become cultural for that particular group. The manager does not have only the work group to consider. Each individual worker is a member of his/her societal culture. Each organisational member has the organisation's values, beliefs and codes of behaviour to follow. Figure 2.1 shows that the organisational member achieves a sense of identity through three sets of values, beliefs and codes of behaviour. The deeper home values, the more immediate work-group values and

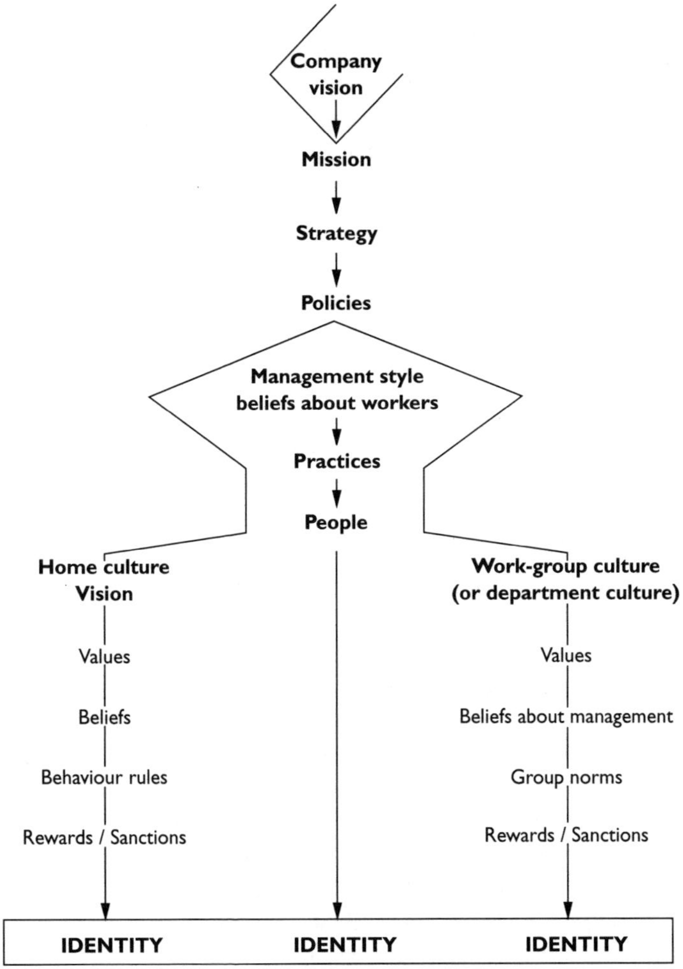

Figure 2.1 *An employee's membership of three cultures*

the (perhaps more distant) organisational values will fuse into a way of looking at working life within the bigger picture of life.

The way managers perceive work, the role of workers and such things as authority, leadership and control is crucial in understanding how they would relate to, and appear to, employees. Employees do construct their own world of meaning. Managers need the help of their employees as interpreters of their (employees') own reality. After all, it is a manager's job to work through people, to go where they are and understand the signals they send. It is a manager's job to try to negotiate a shared world of meaning where the organisation's and worker's needs can come together. Take the signals sent by lateness and absenteeism for example. Any experienced human resource manager knows that these are more than likely to be symptoms of an underlying problem. The behaviour, lateness or not coming in altogether is a symbol of disassociation. The objectivist manager would say that the reality was that person X was late or absent. Such things as number of times and severity of the lateness, or length of absence, would be quantified, set against rules of discipline and appropriate sanctions imposed. Docking pay (dollars for minutes) used to be a popular sanction. The constructivist manager would be asking what the reality of this lateness and absenteeism meant. Why had work become unbearable? Was it the task? Was it the manager himself/herself? Was there a domestic problem and the worker felt the employment contract stopped at the workplace door? Most importantly, as every employee represents a large investment of recruitment and training, the question would be 'how can a new reality about work be created for mutual benefit?' It is clear that if a manager was fixated on one, observable reality there would be no opportunity or need to think about how others see the world.

A shared workable reality

The quality of a manager's own ability to embrace others' realities is, to Lessem (1990), essential to create shared meaning and renewal within the organisational environment. Figure 2.2 shows how the joining of perceptions can be an embedded way of constructing reality with a person or a group of people. This, with self-awareness and self-acceptance that together produce goal-directing ability or competence, allows managers to invest in, embrace and synthesise the incoming realities of other individuals and groups.

Arriving at this level of shared understanding will not be easy to many managers because of the underlying assumptions about *one reality*,

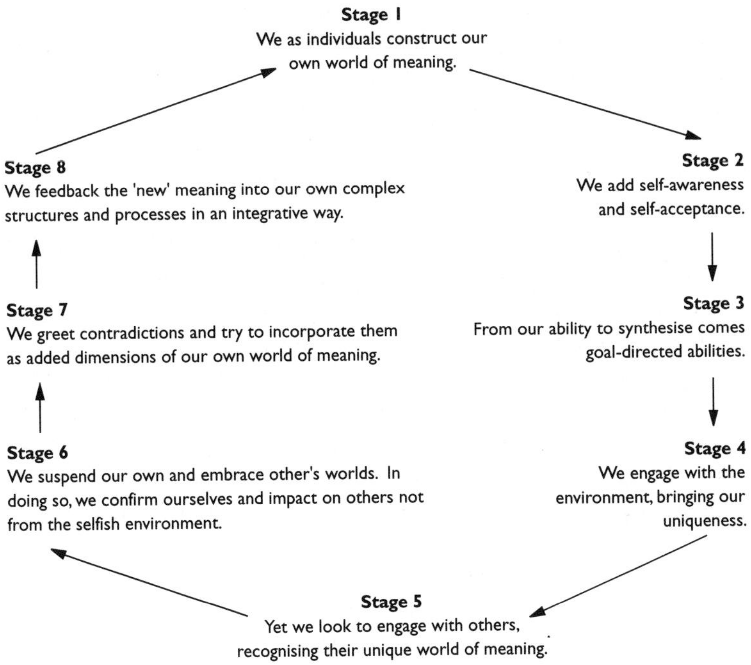

Figure 2.2 *Developing shared worlds of meaning* (adapted from Lessem (1990) and Hampden-Turner (1990)

which have been built into management communication systems for as long as they can remember. Also, the following step-by-step approach will require some new thinking and some commitment to management and employee development. We can use the model in Figure 2.2, based on an idea by Lessem, as a worked example of what the manager may have to do or think in order to intentionally create a world of shared meaning.

Stage 1 is the most important stage. It is a philosophical statement of truth which says that there is no one logical and rational reality out there. It pursues the idea of multiple realities in which individuals construct their own 'true' version of events and experiences. This statement or particular world view leads on naturally to the next stage.

Stage 2 requires that all parties who are creating meaning together need to have self-awareness and self-acceptance. More than this, both managers and workers need to know things such as what they value in human relationships. They need to know how they themselves learn, how they communicate knowledge, what their preferred team roles are and how they would be likely to react in conflict situations. Although there may be some surprises, and some resolve to change some of the self characteristics, there needs to be a strong acceptance of the self as OK. Extracting from the self-development needs comes stage 3. We will follow the model using the manager as an example while pointing out that exactly the same process, training and development needs to be followed for the worker.

Stage 3 requires the manager to develop goal-directed abilities so that his/her self-awareness translates into desirable goals, particularly those concerning relationships. Now the manager has an idea of the unique self that he/she is bringing to the work environment.

Stage 4 is a recognition and continuous assessment and review of the nature of that unique self. Are you changing? Have your values changed? Have you had some experiences and/or training and development which brings something different to your unique self?

Stage 5 is the other side of the coin. It is a recognition that we will be engaging with one or more persons' unique worlds of meaning. What might we want to know about these worlds of meaning? Going back to stage 1 there are things we know about ourselves which might be important to know about the other person. This is nothing new, you may say. Finding out how someone ticks is as old as management itself. Let's look at this. Finding out in the modernist tradition is usually done in the objectivist way, using one's own frame of reference to make sense of what someone else is doing and judging their actions in the same way. Managing shared meaning does not mean 'let me show you how to share my meaning (and let me show you that you're wrong when you don't)'. It means 'let me find out as much as I can about this other self with whom I am dealing so that we can make commonsense'. Finding out becomes an essential management activity. Being an Action Researcher becomes an essential management role. Stage 6 shows another activity to be done which is one of the most difficult parts of the process yet.

Stage 6 requires the manager to suspend his/her own world of meaning and embrace the other's. This 'self as other' activity does not mean looking from someone else's point of view but using one's own psychological and philosophical framework to judge or evaluate it. The manager's own self remains intact but is not used to construct meaning on behalf of the other person. This way both selves are confirmed. However, the manager's own way of looking at things is also required before meaning can be shared. The way the two worlds are blended is the key to success. Stage 7 illustrates this.

Stage 7 predicts that there will be contradictions and disagreements on many levels. These contradictions can be treated in one of two ways. Either they can be the material for consolidating disagreement or even what Chris Argyris (1992) calls defensive routines ('any action or policy that prevents human beings from experiencing negative surprises, embarrassment, or threat, and simultaneously prevents the organisation from reducing or eliminating the causes of these surprises, embarrassment and threat'). Or they can be incorporated into the manager's own world view as added dimensions of his/her own world of meaning. There is a direct impact on the manager's unique world of meaning, which comes as a direct result of owning the other person's meaning.

Stage 8 is the enriching step in the whole procedure. This is where the other's meaning is actually integrated into our own mindset — what Lessem calls our complex structures and processes for seeing the world in the way we do. It also leads to synergy in the sense of making a third and richer reality out of two different and maybe somewhat contradictory ones. This leads us back, of course, to an amplified construct of meaning, which is stage 1 in the model.

Building on this model and acknowledging the idea of constructed reality, we can consider the very familiar situation of when two worlds of meaning collide. Often we have seen each recoil, and return to a comfortable, contradiction-free, familiar mindset. This does not have to be so. Each person can seek genuine dialectic, agreeing through the process of disagreeing until each has confirmed or transcended an individual view, giving to and taking from each other. From the original two worlds of meaning comes a third world: a synergy. From this synergy can come new ideas, structures, processes or even philosophy.

Before looking at how this model and the idea of constructivism can help produce an effective communication system, we need to look at the key quality a manager needs to be able to cross over into creating shared worlds of meaning.

This key quality is 'criticality' (McKenzie 1992:2). This is '. . . a strenuous criticism of oppressive established values and institutions. In a more moderate form, critical theory maintains the necessity of examining the hidden assumptions that undergird thinking'. The criticality takes the form of critical thinking about what Senge (1992:6) calls deeply embedded mental models or internal images of reality. However, the very nature of deeply embedded and internalised mental models of how the world operates means that they are all but invisible to the manager and almost inevitably so to the worker also. There is a rightness about traditions which makes them produce their own inertia and thus makes them extremely vulnerable to change. 'The inertia of deeply entrenched models can overwhelm even the best systemic insights. This has been a bitter lesson for many a purveyor of management tools, as well as for thinking advocates' (Senge 1992:6). Senge makes a powerful argument, which echoes the theme of this book, when he asks why can't mental models be used to accelerate learning if they can impede new learning thereby 'freezing companies and industries into outmoded practices'. The answer is, of course, that new mental models can accelerate learning but first the old models need to be:

- acknowledged; and
- critically appraised for underlying assumptions and theories.

A human resource management system that is of vital importance in negotiating shared realities is the communication system. Communication is basically about transmitting and receiving pieces of meaning. Figure 2.3 shows that all messages communicated from one person (the sender) to another (the receiver) will be subject to selective perception. Perception is the process by which the mass of stimuli which simultaneously bombards our senses is sifted. That which is of

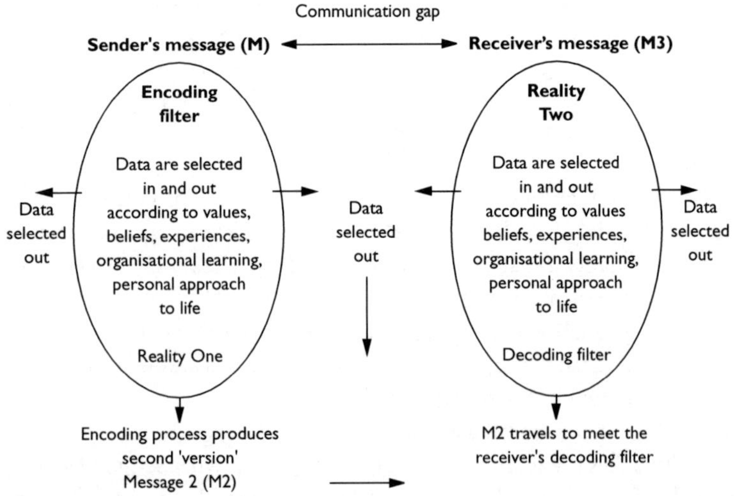

Figure 2.3 *Selective perception of communicated message*

immediate interest or importance, that meets our values and beliefs, and that grabs our attention (positively and/or negatively) will be allowed through the attention filters. We will select out data which are not valued in some way. Then we will further organise and select the pieces of information that stay in. We will give them a unique meaning according to things such as our values and beliefs, experiences, organisational learning and personal approach to life. The message has been encoded. A piece of meaning has been constructed. It will be different from that originally thought or sent because it has gone through the filter of a personality.

A message will suffer the selective perception or coding system of both the sender and the receiver (and the method of communicating, the channel) as Figure 2.3 shows. Inside the lens or coding filters is the sender's and receiver's tools for constructing their own reality about a message. It is clear to see what would happen if the sender and receiver chose not to be aware or embrace each other's reality. That is to say, if the sender ignored the receiver's decoding system and the receiver in turn ignored the sender's coding system. The result would be the charade which is common in organisational life. Figure 2.4 shows this as parallel line communication.

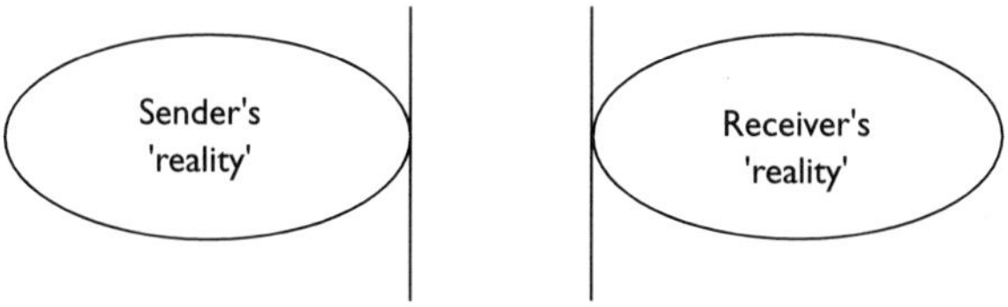

Figure 2.4 *Selective perception acting as a communicated message*

In the model in Figure 2.4, we can see that although plenty of words may be being shared, not so much meaning is being transmitted. At worst, one person will wait until the other finishes speaking to carry on his/her story. The partner will be doing the same. Almost all data will be selected out and the two realities will be preserved almost intact.

Let's look at Figure 2.5 which tells a different story. Here, each communicator has contributed to the construction of a new reality. For this to happen, each will have had to suspend his/her personally constructed version of the message to find out about how the other person codes information, and what is in the lens to be selected in or

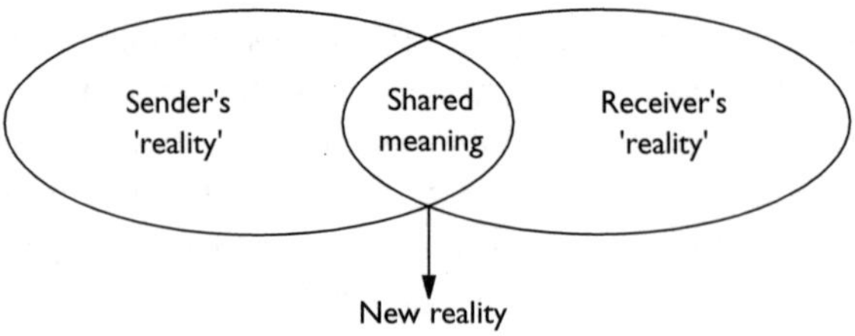

Figure 2.5 *One plus one equals three*

selected out. There is an intersection of two realities and the communicators can be said to be sharing meaning.

Culture is negotiated reality at its most powerful, and mental models of culture are embedded at the deepest and least visible levels. Having studied culture as an identity-forming activity, we need to grasp the nettle of history and consider some realities which may have been constructed — ones in which there would be one dominant reality, that is, management's. Within the management reality or culture, an employee would be either a conformist or a deviant according to how well she/he fitted. The deviant idea is supported by Van den Berghe (1963) who criticised structural-functional theory for its reliance on a biological metaphor, for its positivist [objectivist] stance, for its insistence that social order is created and maintained through individuals internalising dominant social norms and values, and for its treatment of people holding alternative norms and values as being socially deviant. There are organisational writers who suggest that the dominant order is so pervasive that often studies about culture 'promulgate the idea that culture is the collective consciousness of the organisation, "owned" by management and available to management for manipulation' (Meek 1988:453–73).

Meek, in the same article, describes writers who define culture in such a way as to link it firmly with the interests of management. One writer is reported as taking culture to mean the beliefs top managers in a company share about how they should manage themselves and employees, almost as a definition. Another writer studies an upper level group because of a belief that the corporate values held by management will be the ones reflected in behaviour throughout an organisation. The beliefs by researchers and writers on the legitimacy of management values in shaping corporate culture would, no doubt, be supported by managers. These beliefs may explain why a model such as the core values model (described in chapter 4), which is expressly built to include *employees* values into the social structure and fabric, was not adopted at least fifty years ago.

One concept which is universally accepted by organisational researchers and managers is the central role that values play in the development of organisational culture. Chapter 3 explores the notion of values in the context of change.

3
Changing corporate values

> There is much still to learn about the anxiety and stress during change. Clearly, our culture triggers not only power struggles but also nine key questions on everybody's mind. The first three are — me, me, me, what's going to happen to me? The next three are when, when, when and the final three are why, why why? The journey must therefore start with full enterprise-wide understanding of the need for improvement in quality and its leadership by top management.
>
> David Stringfellow, Fuji Xerox Australia

Change

Change can be expressed as the negotiation or the renegotiation of shared meaning about what is to be valued, believed in and aimed for. Organisational change constitutes a *renewal* of parts or even the whole of organisational culture, structures, processes and relationships with the outside environment. The whole notion of culture is that it is designed to be stable and enduring even, as with religious cultures, across national boundaries:

> . . . . rational suggestions for implementing change are most useful when they are addressed to the entire range of people involved in the change process.
>
> Kanter, Stein and Jick 1992:375

Telling someone that they're valued for being, say, efficient, compliant to regulations, or impersonal for a whole working life is bound to secure his/her belief that this is so. Try telling the person that he/she is no longer valued for being efficient and good at following instructions impartially, because what is valued is creativity, innovation/risk taking and interpersonal relationships. In situations of culture change such as that from autocratic to participative values, there is a threat to the fundamental work identity. This is so even when it seems obvious to the outside onlooker that the new values are more enabling and should logically be less threatening.

As managers find, employees meet change with a series of questions, fears, anxieties and a sense of uncertainty about what the future will hold. Organisational writers on change say that those receiving the change feel concerned and worried about what the future will bring. A sense of loss of control, a fear of the unknown, a sense of being rejected (sold out) for traits which previously made people valued, as well as worry about living up (or down) to new demands, are felt. Often, also, a sense of bereavement, of loss, are well-documented responses. Mourning the old self, the old and valued ways, and the old (and comfortable) methods is understandable. Coping with incompetence as a learner and the relative loss of confidence this brings is not an attractive proposition for a person who has enjoyed being swift, able and highly skilled and who has perhaps enjoyed a reputation as an expert.

It is all the more understandable when those fairly removed from the decision to change the culture and values are not involved in the core decisions about the sort of new being the organisation should be and the ends it should pursue. Therefore, Kanter, Stein and Jick (1992) suggest that the 'Change Strategists' (senior management) are concerned with the ends — setting corporate values; 'Change Implementers' are concerned with the means — overcoming resistance and projecting the image and 'Change Recipients' are concerned with making the means fit the end while working out some personal benefits. This view still gives a sense of the status quo and almost excludes the Recipients from important organisational design activities. Richard Semler (1993) has put in practice a model where *all* organisational members fulfil the three roles of Change Strategists, Implementers and Recipients to some degree. Semco's employees are not too distant from decisions about the sort of being the organisation should be. They help determine what it should continue to value, and what should be the deeply enduring identity characteristics which could help the organisation endure the vagaries of business. The question is, does managing an organisation the way Semler does have to be so rare as to be 'the world's most unusual workplace?'

Burns (1993:36) suggests some optimal conditions for change. For example, when change is voluntary and predicted and other changes are kept to a minimum, supportive relationships can be built so that self-esteem and confidence are high and an environment is designed where alternatives and opportunities are open.

Kanter, Stein and Jick's (1992:383) 'Ten Commandments for Executing' would help with change management. (These include analysing the organisation and the need for change, creating a shared vision and common direction, crafting an implementation plan, developing enabling structures, communicating and involving people, [being] honest and reinforcing and institutionalising change.)

However, the Semler method of recognising employees as well as managers as *the* organisation, its heartbeat, recognises that employees too can be philosophical and can contribute to an organisation's vision. This approach moves a lot of the responsibility for change to the workforce, and employees as well as managers can 'see' themselves as negotiators of shared meaning. Quite apart from the 'soft' and enabling side of Semler's management approach, he incorporates a strong and almost ruthless determination that everyone in the organisation will have a business focus. Viability and success are everyone's business, not just management's. It has become accepted that decisions, including human decisions, must make good business sense: '. . . many corporations believe — no proclaim — that it is their duty to employees struggling with drugs, booze or personal problems. They mean well, I'm sure. But we don't want to turn our managers into Father Figures, even if it makes them feel warm and cuddly inside. We don't want to be a big, happy family. We want to be a business' (Semler 1993:131).

The message which is reinforced by organisations (such as the ones in this book) and writers is that human and humane methods of organising, rather than being philanthropic, make good business sense.

The role of values

Understanding values

Understanding values is crucial to the understanding of organisational culture and the negotiating of shared meaning. Values are philosophical. They are an expression of 'truth' as the person sees it. Of course, in ordinary life values are reinforced by the strength of generations as each generation takes an implicit responsibility for handing down values to the next. In this sense, we are a product of history, and bound up with values that did not encourage the majority of workers to pour their creative and reflective energies into the work endeavour. The sheer strength of power behind the early organisational value making has become recognised as we move to a more liberated organisational society of managers.

Bureaucracy, Taylorism and Fordism all displayed values which reinforced each other. Clegg (1992) suggests that bureaucratic values of *control and impersonality*, Taylorist values of *mechanising, controlling and 'scientific' organising* of humans, and Fordism values of *hierarchical authority* were also supported by the *control* value. Here we see an overarching value of CONTROL, which was well supported by the societal values of objectivity (workers as objects), positivism (one 'correct, factual and visible' reality) and intellectual elitism (managers think and workers do).

Do workers actually value control? Do they value mechanising all aspects of their jobs? Do workers value dependency as managers think for them? In many 'core-value' workshops (described in chapter 5), not once have these values been given. Examples of values which are generated unfailingly are honesty and honest feedback, integrity, loyalty, commitment, mutual respect, customer focus, creativity and autonomy/'giving me the freedom to do things my way'. Looking at the following quote, if there is a values gap between what workers value and what managers think workers value, then this is an important discrepancy in terms of mutual expectations and psychological contract.

> Values are among the most stable and enduring characteristics of individuals. They are the basis upon which attitudes and personal preferences are formed. They are the basis for crucial decisions, life directions and personal tastes; much of what we are is a product of the basic values we have developed through our lives. An organisation too has a value system, usually referred to as its organisational culture. Research has shown that employees who hold values that are congruent with their organisation's values are more productive and satisfied. Holding values that are inconsistent with company values, on the other hand, is a major source of frustration, conflict and nonproductivity.
>
> Whetton and Cameron (1991:57)

Examples of values

Examples of values which can become installed in a whole industry are evident in the pre-1990's Australian public sector. Like all 'ideal' bureaucracies, the Australian public sector would value hierarchies of control, impersonality of work roles (it's the position that is important and not the person), conformity rather than creativity, and authority through position rather than personal leadership and, above all, it would value administrative efficiency. Values may be an abstract concept but they have a very practical day-to-day impact on working life, beginning with strategy. A human resource strategy of empowering employees by developing creativity, challenge and critical questioning would not fit the old or traditional bureaucratic value system. In order for a person to perform well at the strategy, he/she would have to perform badly at the values. It is this feeling of inner conflict which can add stress to a job, particularly if the manager espouses the empowering values, but does not follow them in practice.

In a practical sense the policies, procedures and practices to operationalise the empowerment/creative strategy would be in daily contravention of what the bureaucratic organisation valued and psychologically rewarded (which would be conformity and compliance). Creative interpretation of coded instructions and standing orders would upset standardisation. It would also bring the personal idea to the fore instead of the impersonal instruction. It would introduce ambiguity where there should be certainty. Autonomy would replace compliance. And so on . . .

Values are the vital essence of a work group, company or department. This makes it surprising that much of the training and development we see centres around tasks, procedures and problems and not the assumptions and values which underlie them. A recent case was a training organisation which wanted problem solving on how to evaluate its services and retain/gain new customers. After some time, it became clear that there were two conflicting sets of values impacting upon the problem. The trainers and consultants valued educating and developing their clients in the workplace. The management were designing systems and rules which made it evident that they valued making the training a profitable venture first and foremost. Thus billing time became an approved activity and a performance indicator. This worked against the needs of skills mastery where some groups learn more quickly than others. The knowledge of the importance values can place on motivation and commitment influenced the training group to redefine the problem. Before investing in an evaluation or continuous improvement system, some value assumptions had to be taken to the negotiating table. In this particular case, management reaffirmed its values and a framework for continuously reaffirming the organisation's values was put in place. The endeavour to win and keep customers was placed on the sure footing that customers were prized for more than their money. Some of the solutions which were generated were not only customer-focused but customer-enabling.

Explaining countries by their values

Whole countries can be explained by their values. Singapore, for example, was faced with building a culture when it became independent from the influences of strongly embedded cultures in the 1960s. What did it value? Even though Chinese, Malay, Indian groups and many others all possessed their own inviolable cultural values, they all recognised the need for a common, encompassing set of values. The Three S's — Security, Success, Survival — became the common values and that is what Singapore built itself upon. Where needed, Singaporeans are called upon to perform to excellence, even in areas that might be out of the comfort zone for them. Encircling the organisations which make up Singapore are regular culture-binding activities using heroes, stories, symbolic events and rituals. Organisations coming to Singapore would be advised to learn Singaporean values of family, paternalism, belonging and feeling secure. Most importantly, Singaporeans value harmony at work and 'face' as the way of expressing pride and honour.

Australia is not so specific and articulate in its values as Singapore. However, the values of fairness, justice and equity are visible in almost every walk of life. 'Give it a fair go' is the motto. 'She'll be "right"' expresses things like 'we're so good you don't need to worry' (or 'don't worry, it'll all turn out OK'). This last Australian value captures the optimism, compassion and confidence in good workmanship, but also, at times, 'if it doesn't fall down it's good enough'. Culture, like human beings, is sometimes contradictory and it certainly isn't simple.

The nature of values

Values are so soft as to be invisible in terms of rational explanation. You can observe behaviours but it is necessary to look underneath for the values which are driving the behaviours.

We can take values as the very deepest level of thinking and feeling about an issue. Values dictate standards: moral, thinking and judging. For example, judging what might constitute corruption will always be relative to particular values of honesty. Next comes beliefs. These express what people 'know' and are based on information. This information is often acquired over a long period of socialisation. Information is the key to changing beliefs. Attitudes are the predispositions to think and behave in a certain way, being close to values. They are based on the ways individuals 'see' things, or perceive them in their own way. If an attitude is important and closely related to a value, it will be difficult to change.

Actions	always under review
Perceptions	what we *select* in to 'see'
Attitudes	may be superficial, easily changeable or close to a value and difficult to change
Beliefs	based on information and closer to values
Values	absorbed through socialisation and deeply embedded into the consciousness

Companies and values

Some Australian companies recognise the importance of values and the quotations listed below are from the organisational cases in this book:

> Management is committed to change (BHP Iron Ore)
>
> A passion to achieve a highly professional customer focused human resource function (new regional bank)
>
> Communication to encircle the organisation [Kellogg (Aust)]
>
> Our approach will be one of continuous improvement (Gas Cylinders)
>
> We encourage teamwork and delegate responsibility (DuPont)

However, other organisations may not recognise the importance of values. They may leave values to sink down to the organisational seabed, letting them rust and become half-buried under the silt of administrivia.

You can see in the values described above that there can be no one right value. Just as individual characters vary, so do corporate characters. Circumstances, company size and wealth will shape values. The meaning that the marketplace impresses on organisations (private and public) will stimulate the choices of those valued and valuable customs and practices.

Values do not only have a role in culture though. They can and should drive a company's business goals (hard and soft), strategies and policies. In today's global marketplace it is no longer enough to capture the minds of managers, employees and customers. The heart needs to be captured too.

> As the essence of a company's philosophy for achieving success, values provide a sense of common direction for all employees and guidelines for their day-to-day behaviour. These formulas for success determine (and occasionally rise from) the types of corporate heroes and the myths, rituals and ceremonies of the culture. In fact we think that often companies succeed because their employees can identify, embrace and act on the values of the organisation. These values may be grand in scope ('Progress is our most important product'), or narrowly focussed ('Underwriting excellence').
>
> Deal and Kennedy (1982:21)

Whether broad or narrow, it is evident that clarifying, adopting and sharing values needs to become a key part of the manager's job. The idea of Management-by-Values-Objectives (MVO) needs to accompany Management by Objectives (MBO). The scientific, impersonal objectives can be pursued in appropriate, technical situations. The interpretive, qualitative approach can be pursued in the social and psychological aspects of working life. In the following pages, we will see how to use values as part of the manager's skill repertoire. Introducing values skills to employees and their management is like switching on a brilliant light in a pitch-black tunnel. It's magic. When those values are worked into agreed behaviours, a blueprint as valuable as any architect's or engineer's drawing emerges. As Robbins (1988:65) points out, patterns of values affect the way we approach work tasks and processes. The importance of values cannot be overstated.

Chapter 4 suggests a practical way to start or reinforce culture building or reinforcing. In particular, it shows how to generate a truly shared vision so that shared values become the bedrock of strategic planning and implementation.

4
The core values model

The core values model is a practical model for building or renewing culture in an organisation. It is built on the philosophy that every person, every human resource in an organisation, is able to construct a personal reality of the organisation to whose success he/she contributes. The model seeks to bring together sets of reality so that a holistic identity can be formed.

Core values

There are some values which rest at the very core of the organisation's being. These can be called the *core values*. There are some values within the core value framework which are *key values* in the sense that they are owned by a collection of individuals. Key values are those that each person contributes to a core values workshop. Core values are an expression, gained from the key values list, of the values that lie at the core of the group value system. Both sets of values need to be taken into account when negotiating a shared reality of what the organisation should be doing, why it should be doing it and how it should be doing it. The core values model in Figure 4.1 provides a framework for building culture so that all key stakeholding groups are represented. The model first rests on the assumption that, internally, two important groups in an organisation need to contribute something of themselves to form a common identity. The two groups are management and employees. The contribution from each is a statement of the core-values behaviours each expects of the other. These can be translated into sets of 'value rules', which are negotiated and shared rather than imposed and followed.

Negotiating the internal core values is not enough in an organisation though. Each organisation does not exist in a vacuum. At the end

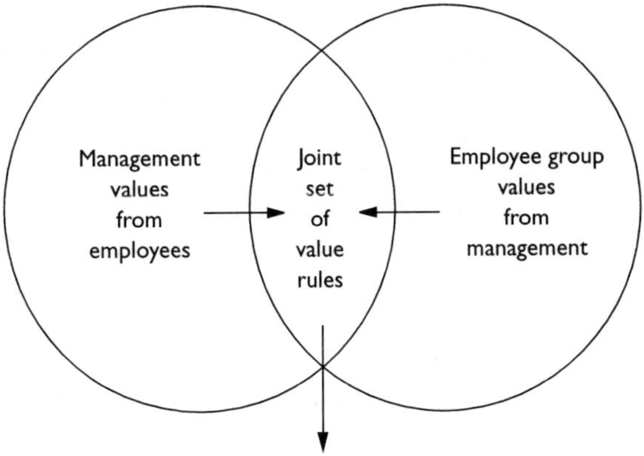

Figure 4.1 *Internal core values (the way 'we' do things here)*

of the day, there are markets, customers and consumers to serve. This goes for public and private sector organisations alike. There is usually one predominant characteristic that the market values from the organisation. This can be taken as the market core value and is an essential part of culture building.

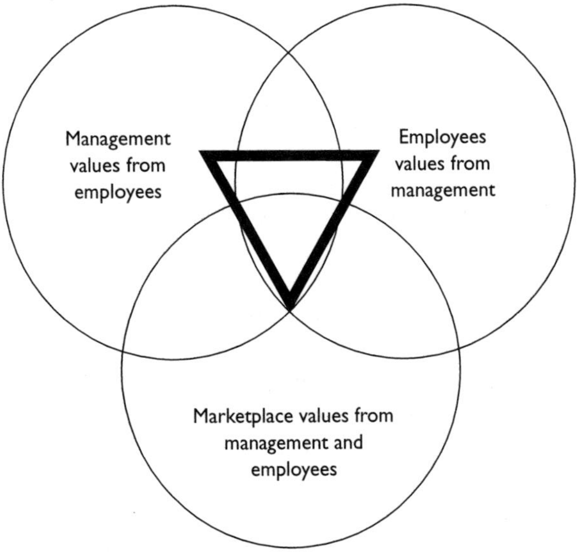

Figure 4.2 *The three core values players*

The business of aligning the three sets of core values shown in Figure 4.2 (on page 44) becomes the manager's major preoccupation in the task of culture building and the aligning of human resources. These three sets of values form the basis for developing a shared *vision* — an imagined future based on valued behaviours. Flowing on from this are the major activities of the organisation as it cascades its *mission*, *strategy* and *policies* into everyday work practices. The core values schema or model is a framework for visualising the organisational process from a culture-building point of view and it is important to remember that the individual will already hold strong values from his/her home culture. Figure 4.3 shows the underlying cultures which interplay as organisational life is acted out.

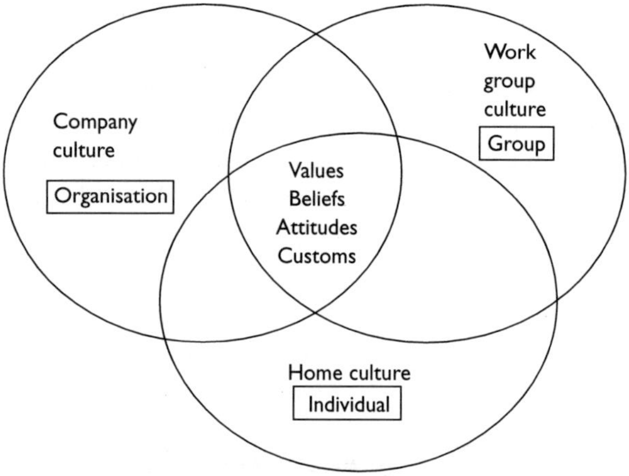

Figure 4.3 *Three intersecting sets of core values underlying corporate culture*

Vision

Taking the culture-building framework step by step, an organisation is its vision. The values expressed in the vision form the mental model or paradigm of 'the things it is legitimate to do around here'. Vision represents a stable, future-looking value system, which dictates appropriate and approved behaviours. The vision governs methods of doing business, methods of interacting in the workplace and methods of relating to outside forces. The expectations are that the negotiated values will be upheld in daily transactional business.

The role and function of vision statements are to make the organisation's values publicly accessible. The chance of their being acceptable relies, among other things, on whether the statements are espoused

(Argyris 1993) or are genuinely practised. As can be seen in the two contrasting examples of vision statements from Stephen Covey (1989), visions are about values:

> To enhance the asset base of the owners

> To improve the economic well-being and quality of life of all stakeholders

It is easy to infer from a vision statement what the organisation values are and whom it considers as 'we'. In the former example, assets and profit are valued and the 'we' seems to be managers and owners. In the second example, well-being and quality of life are valued. There is a more encompassing 'we' to take in not only the employees but also other stakeholding groups.

A second desired characteristic of a vision statement is that values should be definable in such a way as to give meaning, direction and internal logic to the organisation's strategic decisions. Take Covey's vision of 'economic well-being'. What is economic well-being? Covey goes on to define his vision in philosophical terms. He does the same with his vision of quality of life, giving five dimensions which include acceptance and love, challenge and growth, purpose and meaning. Covey also defines 'all stakeholders'. The point about this and other successful vision statements is that they express values in such a way that they can be translated into goal-directed activities.

Mission

The mission statement defines 'the business we are in'. In doing this, it also defines 'the business we are not in at this time'. Mission is inextricably linked to the strategic view. This means that it also concerns 'the business we will be in five to ten years from now'. The mission is linked to the vision and values.

Take an organisation in rail transport. It has negotiated a vision where 'growth, innovation and expansion will be achieved through increased employee involvement in work redesign'. That job is done. It then goes on to the next job which is to define the mission of the business. An organisation which thinks that vision is only about inspiring and not connected to business reality as expressed in the mission may define its mission as 'maintaining an efficient, timely and accurate passenger service'. Although timeliness and accuracy may be valuable aspects of travel in themselves, the question is 'how would such a definition of the business help achieve the values of innovation and growth expressed in the vision?' Would efficiency-oriented strategies allow for the more time-consuming inclusion of employee participation? Time lost in negotiating and consulting with employees will often make for effectiveness but not always efficiency. An organisation's values must be expressed in the definition of its business. The effect of not doing so, in the rail case, would be that strategies necessary to achieve efficiency and accuracy may actually work against the values of innovation and employee involvement.

One of the chronic problems Covey (1989:145) sees in organisations is 'No shared vision and values: either the organisation has no mission statement or there is no deep understanding of and commitment to the mission at all levels of the organisation'. Let's pursue this a little further. We could say that even where there is a shared vision and even if there is a very clear understanding of the mission, employees will feel cheated if the expectations raised by the vision and the values are not met in the mission statement, no matter how clear that is. If, alternatively, the rail organisation had defined its mission as 'providing land transport to international best practices standards through an educated and motivated workface', there would be a good fit of mental models or paradigms between the vision and mission. Employees could see consistent performance indicators implied by both and there would be a sense of internal coherence and harmony. The vision and mission cannot be considered independently of each other because the vision provides the values parameters of the mission.

Strategy

Strategy is the mediator through which the vision and mission flow. It is about choices, priorities and resource allocation. In today's world, it is about developing a competitive advantage for benchmarking purposes. Examples of strategies would be:

- cost control and conservation;
- growth and innovation;
- quality through teams;
- increasing market share;
- internationalisation.

Essentially, strategy becomes a shared understanding of what the organisation should be doing in an imagined future. Because organisations do not have unlimited resources, strategy also articulates the most important things an organisation needs to be doing to achieve business success as defined in the mission. To employees, of course, strategic choices tell another story. The choices either confirm or deny whether the values are being taken seriously by management. The way that strategy is formulated also tells a story to employees. Have employee groups been involved in the strategy-formulation process? Have they been entrusted with strategic input? Have they been trained and educated to understand strategic issues? If the answer is 'yes' then the chances are that employees will own and commit to the strategic choices made, even if they are unpalatable. If they have not, then the strategies will take on an 'ivory tower' quality and seem to be removed from the immediate understanding of employees.

Policies

A policy statement is a statement of intent. It translates strategies into procedures and standing orders. Typically, policies designate people, resources and time frames for things to happen. Policies also set boundaries and reporting systems for monitoring progress. Policies are 'how to'. Often norms or expected behaviours are included as guiding principles. Examples of policy would be:

- Pilots will have medical/fitness tests at six-monthly intervals.
- Addresses of staff will not be disclosed.
- Files which have not been used for three years will be archived.
- Internal recruitment will be at 3 per cent for the next three years.

Alongside the policy will be operational systems. Monitoring, accountability checks, communication and reporting systems, and remedial systems are all aspects of policy design. Here too, it is very possible to see a match or a mismatch with espoused values and those expressed through structures and processes.

Values, strategy, structure and systems

In brief, vision, mission, strategy and policy are as follows:

- *Vision* is about *desired ends*. It is imaginal, a projected future where valued principles are preserved.
- *Mission* is also about *ends*. It is definitive. The business is defined in behavioural terms. It must reflect the values stated in the vision.
- *Strategy* is about *choices between desired ends*. In this sense, strategy trans-

lates *ends* into *means*. It describes the priorities needed to achieve the mission while also being true to the stated values.

- *Policy* is about *operational means of achieving the desired ends* specified by the vision, mission and strategy. (Because policy is derived and interpreted from strategy, through the medium of various management styles, it is particularly vulnerable to misinterpretation and mismatching of values and practices.)

It is important to note here that *vision* is a *mental model* of the way the organisation will organise for survival and success. It is a *mindset* constructed by the people who play key roles in organisational life. It has become increasingly recognised that employees can be profitably included in these key roles. The mindset is really a philosophical statement about the 'true' nature of the marketplace, management and employees, and of the contribution each makes to organisational success. The assumptions upon which the right way to do things are based are powerful determinants of how organisations are structured. How systems are designed are also a function of the assumptions upon which the organisation is built. These include communication, performance management and appraisal systems. Formulating new strategies without critically reviewing the prevailing philosophy and assumptions may produce mixed messages and even an increasing sense of unreality. In times of change, a strongly held mental model

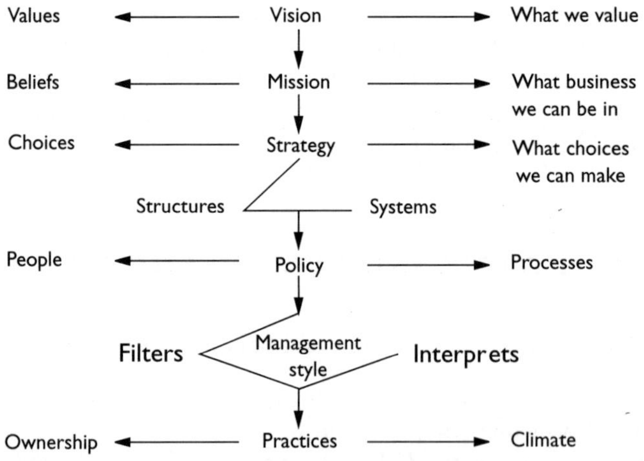

Figure 4.4 *Values strategy structures and systems mediated through policy and management style*

which has not been internally challenged can have a dinosaur effect, holding back new ideas and strategies.

As Senge (1992:5) says:

> Experienced managers know that many of the best ideas never get put into practice. Brilliant strategies fail to get translated into action. This lack of implementation is not the result of poor management [but] because they conflict with deeply held internal images of how the world works, images that limit us to familiar ways of thinking and acting.

The culture-building process is dependent upon a critical re-examination of underlying assumptions about the true nature of work and of workers in relation to management and customers. Figure 4.4 places vision, mission, strategy and policy into an organisational and managerial framework.

Traditional mindsets

Often organisations *with a traditional mindset* do not understand the importance and role of vision and mission in the flow of events that results in the strategic planning process. They begin to manage change at the strategic planning stage (which is two stages too late). Often there will be a top-down approach. Strategic planning is typically carried out by a senior management group and possibly some outside experts. Heads of business units or departments, together with customers/suppliers and financial or marketing consultants, will be represented. A strategic planning model will be selected. Included in the process will be a reference to the historical culture of the organisation, although there will often not be a serious effort to challenge prevailing values. Predictions about which activities will give the organisation its future competitive edge will be chosen over others by this senior group. The result will be a set of strategic options.

Looking ahead to the communication of the strategy, senior management may reason that now is a good time to formulate a mission statement. This will make it clear to those involved what the future business is all about. It is only one step from there to do the same with a vision statement. In this case (Figure 4.5) the vision and values will be generated from the strategy and not the other way round. Instead of

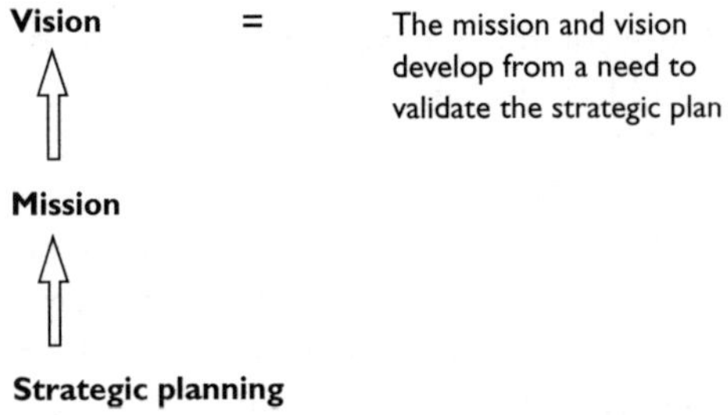

Figure 4.5 *From strategy to vision*

providing a deeply valued foundation for the mission and strategy, the role of the vision now becomes an activity to validate them.

During the strategic planning process, the major groups involved — *management and customers* — will probably emerge with a good idea of what each values from the other. Not only that but the core values, those most deeply held, will also have emerged. The areas of agreement will produce a common core of ownership and commitment between the individuals representing management and the marketplace. There will be a shared understanding between these stakeholding groups about the ideals to be pursued and the agreed means of pursuing them. See Figure 4.6.

While all this is going on, what might be happening to the other key groups — the employee groups? These groups are also busy — they are constructing or reaffirming their mental models of the strategic planning process (which they have heard about from a variety of sources, formal and informal, with varying degrees of accuracy).

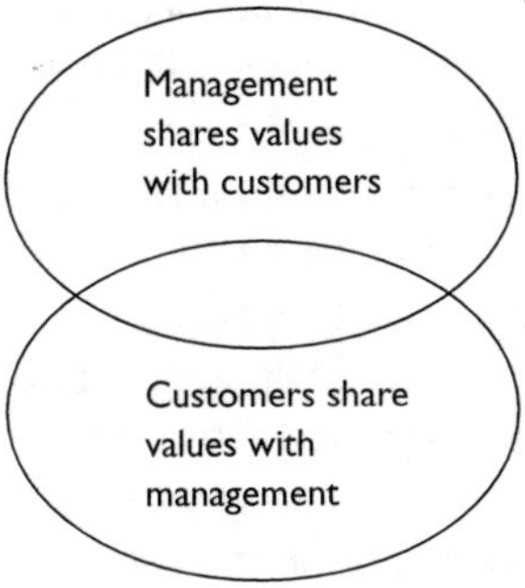

Figure 4.6 *Shared values of management and the marketplace*

At this point, the opportunity of securing ownership of the vision and the process of culture building, and strategy formulation can be realised only in the abstract. The strategies will be theoretical to employees, in the sense that they are someone else's ideas and hypotheses. Does this matter too much? It matters on two scores. Firstly, values are reflected in the strategy, which the employee group have not helped to negotiate. Secondly, the employees will be a key group in implementing the strategy. If employees need to fashion an identity at work as well as at home, then it does matter. If the 'we' of the vision and mission does not include the employee group, then the employee group is likely to form one of its own. Furthermore, without an overarching vision, there are likely to be as many visions and interpretations of what the business is about as there are departments in the organisation. Each department will produce its own subculture, complete with values, goals, strategies and operating procedures, just as we saw in the Hawthorne experiments. Suboptimisation, where the department's or group's goals will be more important than those of the organisation's, is a likely outcome as is interdepartmental conflict, which sets departments or groups to guarding their boundaries and their information flows.

The situation is nearly as bad when management does make an effort to include the employee group by inferring what it thinks employees value. Only too often the inference is a reflection of management's mental model of what employees *should* value. We can imagine that F. W. Taylor as a human resource manager would think that employees would value money rather than a say in strategic decision making. Because he had a mental model of employees as doers, rather than thinkers, it would not be conceivable for him to infer that employees may value being included in strategic activities. Figure 4.7 shows value building where the employee values have been imposed by management as a result of management's own mental model. These are the values management perceives are held by employees. They are often a reflection of the mental image of what managers think employees *should* value. And, as Pascale says, the managerial mindset is not always readily discernible.

> Most people think that a managerial mindset is easy to spot. But mindsets are more perceptual than tangible. The filters through which we perceive are seldom, if ever, explicit. Our mindset is composed of unquestioned, tacit understandings, transmitted

through 'folklore' and 'war stories' — and internalised through the behaviours that surround us day to day.

Pascale 1990:28

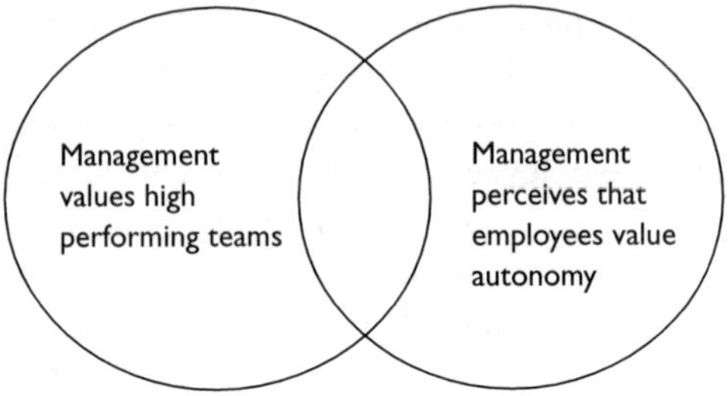

Figure 4.7 *Management thinks it knows what workers value*

When the customers' core values are added to the perceived values of management and employees, it would seem as though the basis for a comprehensive vision statement is present. However, it is likely that only two-thirds of the input for shared vision is present, the missing sector being the employee group. See Figure 4.8.

This is probably the current situation in many organisations. Management becomes increasingly aware of the importance of the human resource. Within the scope of their own mental models, managers will assess employees' ability to look into the future, to understand the

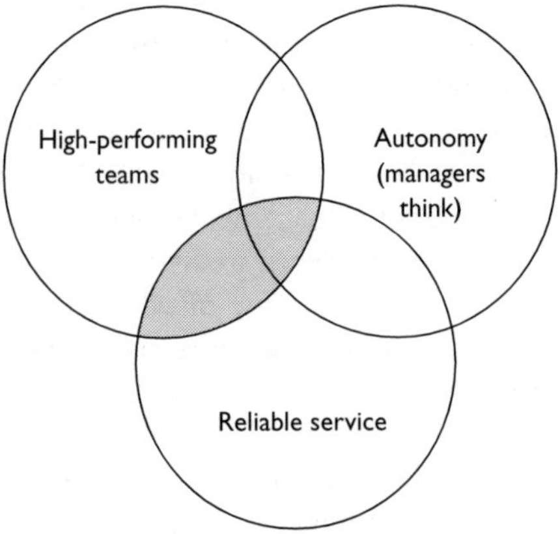

Figure 4.8 *A two-sided set of core values*

concepts and issues in marketing, and to make comparisons about competitors' performance. If the assessment is positive, managers may seek the input of employees' values. This can take several forms. Managers can construct questionnaires based on their ideas of the things which interest employees. Few would argue the appeal of Hackman and Oldham (1980) when they say that task significance, task identity, variety, feedback and autonomy are very important in a job. However, this is still within the confines of employees' world of prescribed tasks. Considering that we don't know what we don't know until someone enlightens us, how can we tell whether employees value being involved in strategy until they are trained in what strategy involves, and trained in ways compatible with the language of work?

The omission of management in not including values at the strategic level in employee surveys is more to do with the management mental model than the inability of employees to understand strategic issues or on evidence that employees can't take it in. Those managers who have operated profit centres which buy in managerial expertise will agree that the most sophisticated and global understanding of strategy will often be forthcoming from shop-floor operatives. And what about the human values which seem to be the dominant ones in any work group? No one in an organisation will be able to give the answer until a very special sort of action research is undertaken by management. The research begins with reflection about senior man-

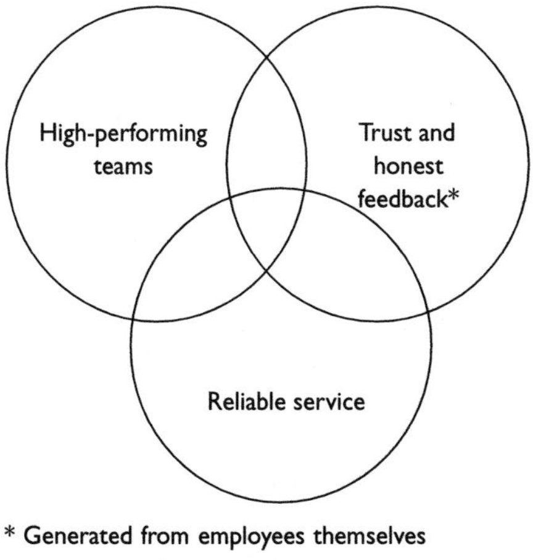

Figure 4.9 *Three researched sets of core values*

agement mindsets or mental models. The desired outcome is to achieve three *actual* intersecting sets of values as they are perceived by *each* key stakeholding group in an organisation. See Figure 4.9.

If vision is really shared with key stakeholding groups, employees become placed in the forefront of the important issues. They are listened to, and are informed of managers' expectations of themselves, in concrete behavioural terms. In other words psychological contracts are brought out into the open and the implicit becomes explicit and part of the partnership or performance contract. Research, which is richer than that offered by an impersonal survey, is conducted to find out what customers really value. This applies to internal as well as external customers, to suppliers and to partners. The result is robust data upon which to plan strategies. These strategies stand a high chance of being owned and committed to because of the involvement and participation of those charged with making the strategies happen. The strategies must pay allegiance to the values expressed in the vision and mission. Strategies depend upon compatible structures and systems to facilitate the day-to-day activities of working life.

Within the overarching organisational culture, various departments will forge their unique but interrelated cultures. The same core values methodology can be used at each level of the organisation. Executives and heads of functional areas can work out senior managements' core and key values. They can, with suitable research data, work out the major marketplace group's values. They can research the values of their employee group of regional, district or departmental managers (or even supervisors/team leaders if the organisation has a flat structure). In turn, each of those managers/supervisors/team leaders can replicate the process to produce a work-group subculture, which is in harmony with the overarching values of the organisation but modified to suit particular needs. Sitting on a bedrock culture should be several subcultures, each with its own set of internal and external customers. The one thing to be held in common is the philosophy, the vision and the mission of the organisation. At each level the manager will be a facilitator, an action researcher and a co-ordinator across departments. It will help if there is an organisation-wide encircling information and communication system. Using the core values model, the whole organisational undertaking is dynamic and continuous, and revolves around values and vision. While it *revolves* around these two it *depends* heavily on the mindsets and assumptions of those involved, particularly managers.

Changing mindsets

Successful culture building needs senior management resolve to bring employees into the self-management game. This entails recognising employees as decision makers, especially about the decisions regarding

Table 4.1 *Traditional (comfortable?) mindsets*

	Managers	Employees
Task	• Receive strategic information • Plan and set goals • Brief supervisors • Monitor performance • Troubleshoot • Provide outcome rather than process feedback	• Receive interpreted filtered information/ managers' version of organisational goals • Negotiate goals within given plans • Perform as requested (could range from being supervisor's extra arms and legs to autonomy/ freedom) • Are monitored • Report problems — may help solve them if requested • Receive feedback and/or solutions
Social	• Are part of a management team • Act as interface between markets and employees • Express values through organisational self-talk and humour, which tends to be management oriented	• Are part of work groups within a department • Relate to supervisors • Express values through organisational self-talk and humour, which tends to be employee oriented
Cultural	• Value managerial prerogatives • Receive rewards that come from differentiated status and personal achievements	• Value customs, worker prerogatives, work-group norms, group goals • Receive rewards that come from within the group as well as from outside

what they really value from management. There are two sets of assumptions or mindsets to be challenged here. If the organisation rejects the traditional mindset where managers think and workers do, then senior management and managers will need to leave the control/competitive mindset concerning employees behind. At the same time, if employees relinquish these values in favour of being enabled to think and choose, they will need to leave behind the 'iron rice bowl' of dependency and restricted accountability. For some employee groups, the change may bring several new types of unfamiliar activity, at least in the formal sense. The process of negotiating shared meaning about what sort of management behaviours are most valued means that employees will need to critically compare their own assumptions with organisational values. For both groups, it means being prepared to reward and reinforce the new or revitalised behaviours. It means, for both parties, coming out from behind the screens of worker prerogatives and management prerogatives respectively and into the area of shared prerogatives.

At the very outset, the resources needed to effectively build or change a culture are evident. Changing mindsets is easier said than done. The task involves relinquishing some of the very things that have made both managers and employees successful — that is, knowing and operating within their own milieu. The traditional mindset of management versus employees may result in clearly defined activities such as those in Table 4.1 (on page 55), which are task, social and cultural.

Task

The managerial assumptions about how tasks should be undertaken within the mindset in Table 4.1 are transparent. Managers are the possessors of strategic information — a prized resource. There is a peer group of managers. There is a level, the managerial level, at which traditionally planning is undertaken. The result must be a framework where *taught solutions are expected* by employees. Whether or not they are accepted is another matter. The intention is to ask employees to implement instructions rather than formulate the plans that led to them. The assumptions here might be that managers will lead and employees will follow.

From the employee perspective, the assumption is that employees must work on a need-to-know basis. Information will be filtered and converted into task instructions. The manager will define the boundaries of performance. These could be either constraining or liberating. Even where they are liberating, they are that way because the manager has defined them as such. Each method, constraining or liberating, rests upon the managerial control and accountability mindset.

More pervasive and not so easily discernible is the assumption that employees do not need to operate in the emotional and imaginal modes (Heron 1989), but mainly in the practical and conceptual modes. Yet activities such as vision making and strategic planning, which call for the search for future scenarios, require strong use of the imaginal abilities. This means that changing the mindset alone will not necessarily result in immediate acceptance of change by employees. It needs to be accompanied by employee education in areas which were previously excluded because of managerial and employee assumptions.

Social

Social systems and symbols have long been recognised as strong indicators of organisational values. The director's dining room, the executive rest room and the manager's car park are the more ostentatious and socially differentiating symbols of the traditional mindset. The implication is that managers are a more valued resource than employees. Such differentiating symbols are not necessarily the more divisive ones, although they are often the most quoted. Being part of a team, sharing the same level of information, and receiving the same sort of development and rewards sets one group apart from the other. This can have a tremendous impact on the way the organisational history is developed. Instructions through memos, plans, policies and other official sources do not represent the heartbeat of an organisation. Social relationships are extremely important to employees even when the task areas are machine-oriented (Whiteley and Jordan 1990). Internally, within the organisation, values are expressed through organisational self-talk conducted in formal and informal settings. Almost exclusively, managers and employees will describe their workplace by using social and symbolic frames of reference (Bolman and Deal 1991). In the case of differentiated social systems such as the ones in Table 4.1, there may be two versions of life perceived within the organisation: the haves and the have nots.

Sometimes each group will be aware of the other's organisational self-talk, sometimes not. Sometimes organisational humour is semiaffectionate, sometimes not. The important thing is that social roots often go deep. The branches of managers' and workers' talk become entwined. Asking each group to disentangle and reconvene as one effective workface is asking a lot. There has to be a good reason for change, a good cause. This cause has to be explained, supported and

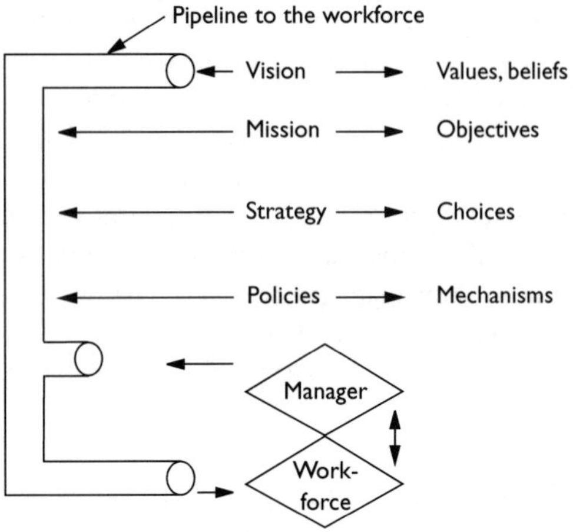

Source: Whiteley 1991:180

Figure 4.10 *The need to develop a pipeline of communication down the workface*

resourced at the highest level, continuously, consistently and passionately.

Cultural

Culture is expressed in the way both social and task arrangements are made in an organisation. Close supervision with a narrow span of control expresses a value which has been converted into a theory of organisational behaviour. Values expressed by such an organisation would be that employees can't be trusted too much, are not able to make decisions, are not self-directing and are willing to obey orders. Problems arise when desired values are espoused, but behaviours demonstrate the values are not rewarded (Argyris 1993).

The area of communicating values is very tricky indeed. It is so easy for ambiguity and uncertainty to occur when the communication system is not geared to exhaustively clarifying and reinforcing organisational values. As Figure 4.10 demonstrates, it is necessary to have a pipeline to the workface which acts as a conduit, carrying cultural information from the workface to management and on to senior management. Senior management, management and those responsible for training and development would have particular roles to play here.

Prescribed and negotiated realities

At the highest level, there has to be some method of communicating continuously up and down the workface hierarchy. Eventually, this would become around instead of up and down. The pipeline would act as an encircling system of mutual communication. Reinforcement of the organisational values is vital to strengthening the position they have in employees' and managers' minds. There needs to be a pipeline of communication so that this can happen. Continuous information needs to flow through about how the organisation is achieving its objectives — its business mission. The same goes for strategy. Were the choices the correct ones? Is the employees' investment of energy and commitment showing a good strategic return? The important thing about the structures and social/technical systems needed to realise the strategies is that they must be in harmony with the organisational values. It is little use valuing an autonomous workplace if there are heavy control systems in place. The same goes if there is autonomy over the less important aspects of the job, but not over aspects such as scheduling, holiday arrangements, and decisions concerning aspects of performance appraisal and reward. Similarly, policies need to reflect the intended strategies. This is where the mental model or mindset of the interface person, whether this is a supervisor or a manager, is of vital importance. Say, for example, the person had a model of the employee as depicted by McGregor's (1960) Theory X.

> The average man is by nature indolent — he works as little as possible. He lacks ambition, dislikes responsibility and prefers to be led. He is inherently self-centred, indifferent to organisational needs and is by nature resistant to change. He is gullible, not very bright, the ready dupe of the charlatan and the demagogue.

And say that the vision of the organisation was an enabling vision. Here the CEO or management might say, 'This organisation values its employees as empowered and accountable individuals and teams. Through participative management we will deliver high-quality products and excellent service to all our customer groups.'

The interface supervisor or manager would translate the vision and the strategy into *real* language. He/she would be an interpreter, defining what management *really* means. This will surface as management style as shown in Figure 4.11. This *real* meaning (*reality* as interpreted by the interface person) will be expressed through policy documents, procedures, instructions and meetings with employee groups. It is as though the interface person were a filter, filtering meaning through his/her own internal image or theory of management. The activity of investigating management, not at the practical or even the theoretical level but at the philosophical level, shows that for many years it was considered to be both natural and acceptable to prescribe a real and substantive belief system about work. How work should be organised and conducted, who should wield power, and who should accept authority were determined by management. That there was one best way to design work and workers' lives held sway, at least on the face of

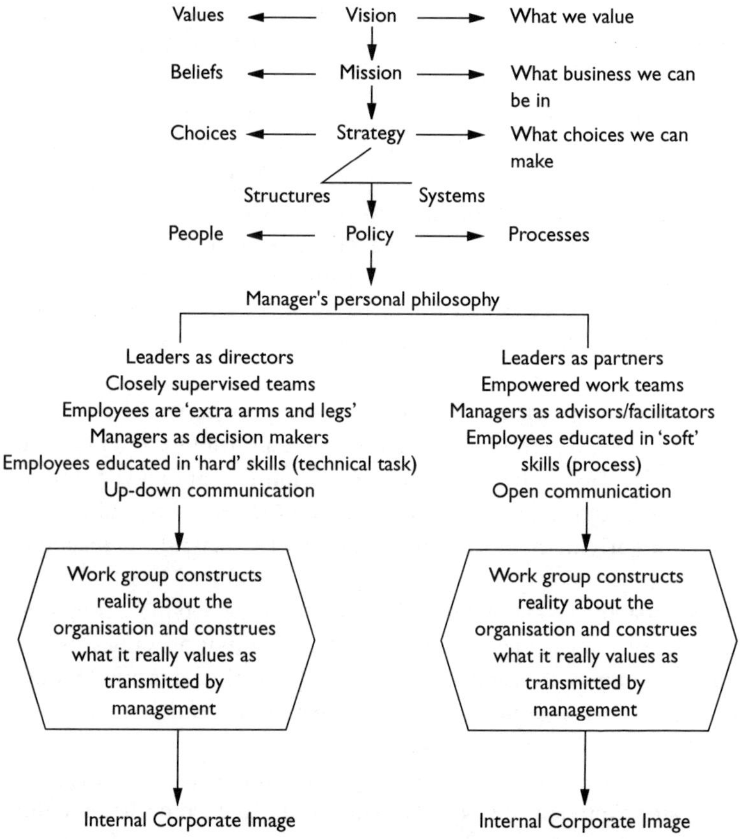

Figure 4.11 *Core values translated through management style*

things. The seductiveness of the prevailing status quo was evident even when more liberating ways to manage and control workers were suggested by motivation theorists. It is only now, when there is a ground swell of approval for the liberation of workers from controls,

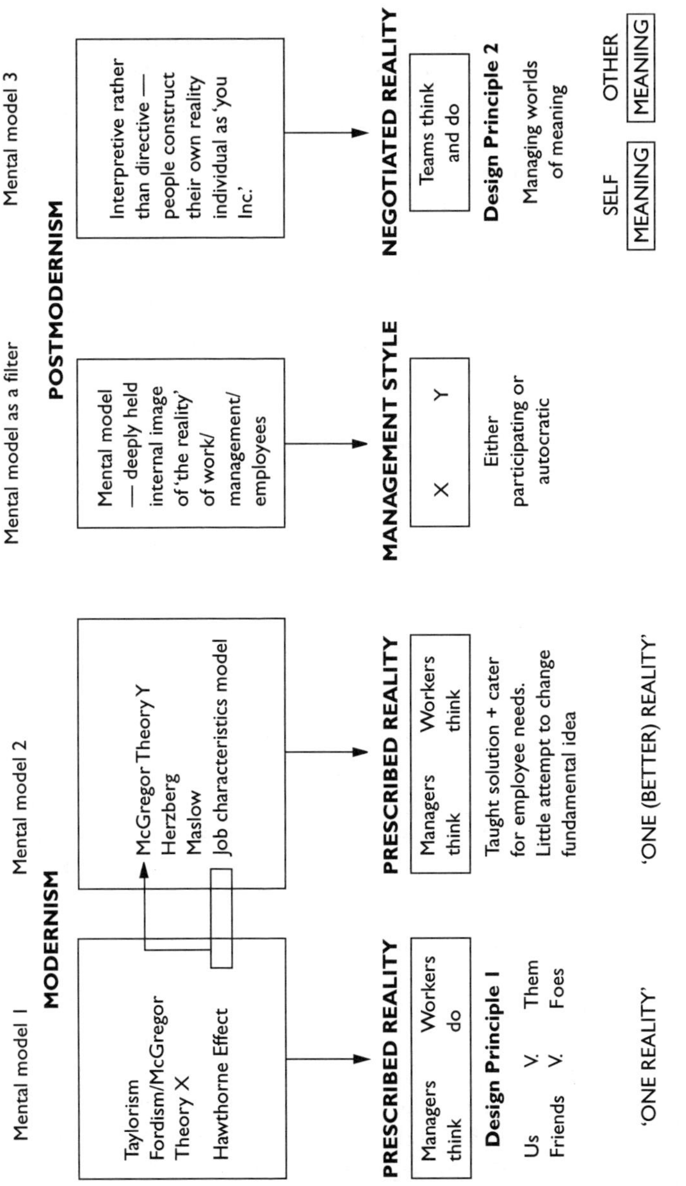

Figure 4.12 *Towards a negotiated reality. 'You inc.' concept from Limerick and Cunnington (1993)* Managing the New Organisation: a Blueprint for Networks and Strategic Alliances, *Chatswood, NSW: Business Publishing*

that the mindset of prescribed reality has hit hard times. However, the demise of *prescribed reality* will succeed only when the mindset of how others should be managed is changed. Figure 4.12 shows three models of organising. Mental models 1 and 2 are models of prescribed reality: one controlling and one more benign. Mental model 3 is a model of negotiated reality. Always within the organisational mental model or mindset will be the personal mindset of the manager, expressed as management style, and acting as a filter (see Figure 4.11). Theory X and Theory Y (McGregor 1960) are examples of two such mindset filters.

A key feature of the prescribed reality mindset was that it encouraged the institutionalising of structures, systems and processes. Under mental model 3 in Figure 4.12, leaders and senior managers need to contribute to the management team the special information about impending crises, the need for change and future directions. Rather than communicating a new vision and then persuading or motivating employees to accept it, senior managers need to design an organisation where the vision is created collectively and collaboratively. (This may not be possible in the first formative stages of culture building, but as the workface becomes more versed and educated in the issues, individuals and groups can input their values.) Leaders need to supervise the demolition of dysfunctional structures, systems and processes, and they should support their managers while this is happening. They also need to help redefine roles in management and supervision. In addition, they should combat the freezing of values and behaviours where these have a dinosaur effect. In fact, they could do worse than rethink the freezing metaphor altogether.

In Figure 4.13a (and acknowledging Lewin's (1947) early work), expectations that there will always be a frozen position may be a latent outcome of how functional management has developed over the years. Having to change current systems used to be seen as disruptive and upsetting to the smooth flow. In human resource terms, people and jobs are often matched on the basis of KAS — Knowledge, Attitudes (interpersonal skills) and Skills (technical skills). Employees and managers alike go for excellence in Knowledge, Attitudes and Skills, and expertise becomes something to be cemented, and celebrated. Ego, status and prestige are attached to this. There is a vested interest in resisting situations where the individual becomes a virtual beginner again, robbed of the accumulated 'specialist' status. In a competitive and fast moving world for both products and services, leaders and managers need to see that the right things are rewarded. Eagerness to

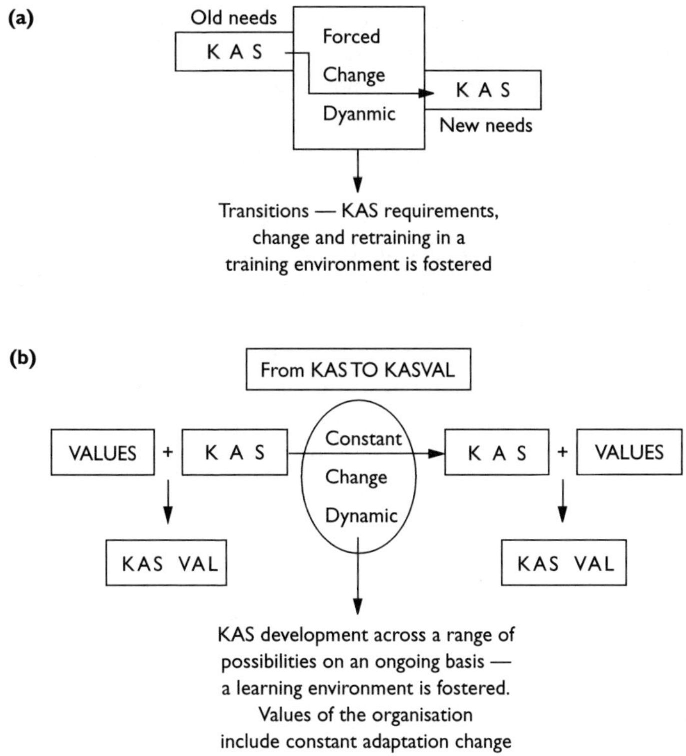

Figure 4.13 *The constant change dynamic: From Knowledge Attitude Skills (KAS) to include Values (KASVAL)*

learn, to adapt and to tackle something new, including a work role, and even perhaps to take risks and make mistakes, would be more appropriate to celebrate than superskills which are safe. The culture to be developed would be one which embraced change as a constant dynamic and values as a central feature, as Figure 4.13b shows.

In particular, the concept of values needs to permeate *all human resource functions*. The most dominant of these are recruitment and selection, socialisation, work redesign and performance partnerships. An example of how values can be incorporated into human resource systems can be seen by taking recruitment and selection as an example.

Say the organisational vision is based on values of *teamwork, mutual respect and a strong focus on customer needs*. Say the organisation was designed around team projects and team accountability. The process of recruitment and selection requires job analysis, job description and employee specification; that is, a pen picture is needed of the ideal candidate. Using these data, advertisements would relay the job (and the corporate image) to the inside and outside world. Values would dictate *who* should draw up the job analysis, description and employee specification. With team and mutual respect values, the work group would naturally do this. In order to do it in keeping with the organisational goals the group would need to have the vision, mission and strategic/human resource plan available. To do it in keeping with group goals the group would need an articulated, transmittable statement of its own group culture as well as group business plans.

Remembering that advertisements are images, perhaps others would need to become involved in translating the group's needs into a public statement. Design teams, joint consultative committees and quality circles would be appropriate devices as sounding boards. At interview, once the base line data about knowledge and skills have been established, value orientations of candidates should be probed rigorously. Questions about past experiences, preferred ways of working, and likely responses to hypothetical situations would be sure to reveal values. If a candidate valued individual achievement, personal recognition and reward, and survival of the fittest, then clearly he/she would have a values clash with this particular organisation. A judgment would need to be made as to whether the knowledge and skills were sufficient to outweigh the problems likely to be caused by a clash in values. This type of recruitment and selection, which is strategic in nature, helps to pave the way for the work of those responsible for socialising the newcomer into the organisational culture, fitting him/her into a work group and being able to match the two sets of expectations embedded in the performance contract. As yet there is little evidence of a holistic and strategic approach to the core activities of human resource management. As long as these remain 'functions' and stay removed from the daily activities of work itself, it will be easy to underestimate their strategic importance. In the competitive world of the future, organisations cannot afford the relative lack of commitment which results from hiring and keeping individuals who do not share the organisation's values.

The use of the core values model depends heavily on the sort of knowledge discussed so far. In particular there is a need, when culture building, to closely examine the historical development of human resource management and identify the value systems which were imposed on management for many years. This leads to an understanding of why managers are only now seeking to engage with employees' intellectual and emotional/imaginal development. Management thinkers in the modern era not only *prescribed* value systems for managing people, they also *prescribed* systems for studying organisational life. Both systems strengthened the paradigm of managing people as rational/economic beings and that of an objective approach to the study of management processes. Thus management dialogue was as removed from the inner language of human life as possible. Breaking out of this mindset frees managers to recognise that there is not one objective and factual reality which captures organisational life. There are many moments of truth where reality has to be negotiated and renegotiated, in every day of working life. A particularly important opportunity which emerges from the negotiated reality perspective is the opportunity to negotiate shared values and shared meaning about what key groups of people value from each other. Central to the idea of shared meaning is the need for managers and workers to become self-aware about the particular lens through which they see the world. The ability to suspend one's own perspective to embrace that of another person or group will result in enriching one's own viewpoint but not at the expense of the other's. The risk of imposing one set of values (probably those of the dominant group in power), or of espousing one set of values while embracing another, will diminish as the willingness and ability to challenge traditional mindsets increases.

The task now is to find practical methods for generating shared values and vision in the workplace. The core values method in chapter 5 has been used with many organisations, slightly refined in each case according to the current stage of development of culture in the organisation.

5
The core values method

The core values method rests on the assumption that the most effective internal vision for an organisation is one which is designed in collaboration with employees and, in particular, with employees as decision makers.

Employee as customer

Traditionally, the role of the employee has been to accept the value system of management. The worker was perceived as a person who valued rational systems of being managed as long as they brought financial reward. There was no notion of the worker as a customer of any sort. The notion of a 'customer' would commonly be connected to purchasers of the company's goods and services out there in the marketplace. Inside the organisation, the main forum for talking about the customer would be in the marketing department. The main forum for talking about personnel would be in the production or personnel department. In keeping with the closed system of functional management, production managers and marketing managers would typically meet only to compete for information and resources (Whiteley 1992b). Yet in order to be a contributor in the negotiation of shared values, the employee needs to be considered as a decision-making customer. Instead of consuming a tangible product, the employee, as internal customer, will consume the range of job experiences and rewards that are presented through the company's human resource and line management systems. Table 5.1 shows a mental model of some of the dimensions of the employment product that an employee makes decisions about 'buying' into or out of.

Table 5.1 *Hard and soft dimensions of the employment 'product'*

Hard dimensions	Soft dimensions
• Jobs and tasks	• Manager's philosophy
• Wages and salaries	• Social/Psychological rewards
• Physical conditions	• Social processes
• Work structures	• Group processes
• Decision-making processes	• Level of participation
• Reporting systems	• Communication

It is the notion of decision making that is so important to the adoption of change and particularly cultural change. We can see from Figure 5.1, the marketing model of consumer buying behaviour, that employees constantly make decisions about the work 'product'. Given that these decisions are being made, it is important for managers to become an intentional and integral part of employees' buying decisions.

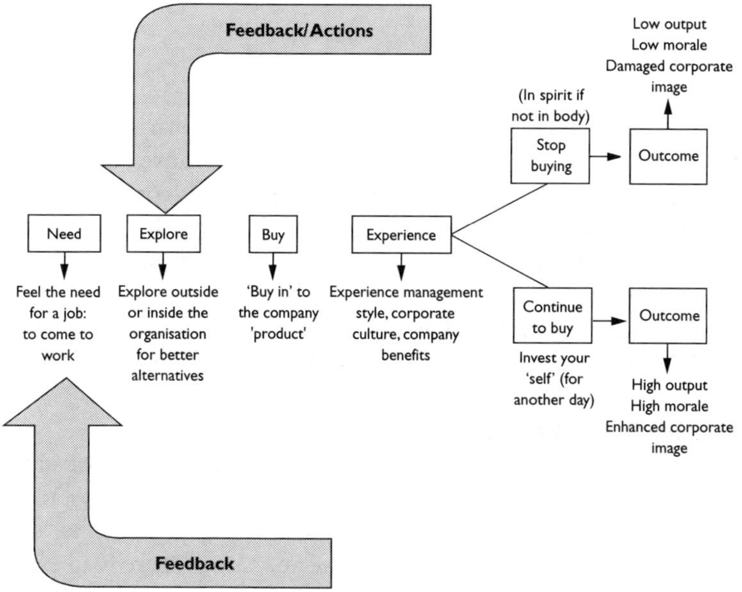

Figure 5.1 *Consumer buying behaviour model* (based on an idea by Wilkie 1990)

Feeling the need

This model (Figure 5.1) shows the employee in a position of power. He/she will feel a need about work in one of two ways. Either the need will be to *have to* have a job to keep the wolf from the door or to *want to* come to work for some sort of personal or social fulfilment. In voluntary organisations, it is clear that the need (or want) is to come to work to contribute, to feel one has made a difference. The important thing about feeling a need or want is that energy must then be released to satisfy it. (See Figure 5.2.)

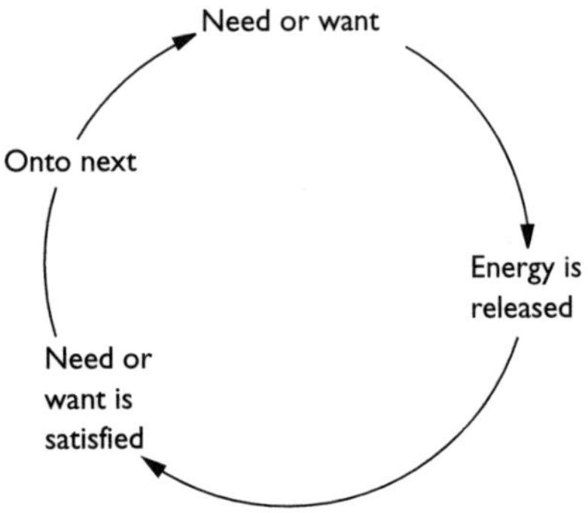

Figure 5.2 *The motivation cycle*

Looking at the arrow in the consumer buying behaviour model in Figure 5.1 which loops back to exploring alternatives rather than feeling a need, it is clear that the motivation cycle is constantly being bypassed. Rather than employees releasing the energy that comes from driving towards an organisational goal (and experiencing the satisfaction which comes from reaching the goal), employees may habitually explore other ways of achieving satisfaction. One such way is to explore alternatives that have worthwhile goals attached to them.

Exploring alternatives

The initial decision does not rest once the need has been satisfied the first time. It seems to be a quirk of human nature always to be exploring alternatives. Even those with fulfilling jobs can be seen scanning the recruitment sections of the newspaper. There is an evaluative element here, and it is relative to the same jobs elsewhere or different jobs with similar skill levels. In a 'buyer' recruitment market, the person may not be able to physically act on a decision that the current job does not hold up well against others. In such a job market there are no other jobs and the person has to stay. The employee may have to stay in body but may well leave in spirit, taking away that valued 'Big E' (energy, enthusiasm and excitement). The same goes for the alternatives inside the organisation, such as working hard or easy.

Buying in

To a greater or lesser degree the employee will buy into the job. He/she will come to work and follow instructions to a greater or lesser extent. This will be the beginning of the experience phase where the job will be set against the expectations raised by market alternatives, by management during recruitment and the ongoing socialisation process, and by the job itself. One important element here is that expectations and perceptions which are set within the work situation are what the employee expects to buy into. If expectations of a challenging and enabling job have been set and the reality is that the employee is powerless to make any decisions that count, important expectations will not have been met, even though wages and environmental conditions may be as expected.

Experience

The complex product that is the employment experience includes hard and soft dimensions. The tasks and rewards, corporate culture and management style all mesh together to form an impression of an experience. It is this which forms the moment of truth for the employee (Carlzon 1987). The experience is interpreted by each employee in a unique way. It becomes a constructed reality, which can be interpreted only through the eyes of the employee and therefore needs to be studied through the employee's lens. The employee's reality forms the basis for a decision. The decision will be either to continue to buy in to the employment product or to stop buying, at least in spirit. Given that this process is continuous and dynamic, it is necessary for the manager to conduct continuous action research. Instead of conducting investigations of expectations in the workplace for a particular purpose, such as deep change, the manager needs to fit into the employee's decision-making cycle to look for continuous feedback about the match between experience and expectations.

Decision impacts

In the case of continuing to buy in, the employee will decide to invest the 'self' — for another day. The need to work as opposed to the need to have a paying job will be reinforced. The buyer cycle of decision making will start all over again. If the reinforcement is positive, it is likely that morale may be higher, output may be better and the corporate image will be maintained intact. The cycle will return to a felt need, energy will be released to satisfy the need, and the decision to explore alternatives may remain only investigative rather than purposeful.

In the case where the employee decides to 'buy out' and to discontinue (whether this is in body or spirit), the organisation will suffer a loss of the employee's personal investment. Over time this may show as low morale, disinterest, low output and a damaged internal corporate image. The buyer cycle in this decision mode will almost bypass the need phase and go straight to the explore phase. 'Felt need' is an important motivator as the feeling of need drives the action to satisfy it. The manager in this case, in failing to secure the right sort of felt need, will fail to achieve the goal of human resource managers, which is to optimise *every* human resource. Intellect, creativity, problem solving and diligence may all be left lying on the workplace floor. The process outlined in Figure 5.1 is the consumer buying behaviour process, and it is evident that it is as equally valid in human resource management (HRM) as it is in marketing, even more so if one considers internal marketing as an added dimension of HRM.

Manager as facilitator

The successful transmission of values rests on a two-way mentoring philosophy. Managers and employees are first assistants to each other. Managers will need to relinquish many of their old functional tasks. Managers will think of themselves as facilitators, helping workers to define and discriminate important problems and issues. They will need to develop and use interpersonal tools to draw out ideas, objectives, problems and solutions. They will be keeping individuals and teams on track, motivated and, above all else, communicated. Initially, the manager will take a scanning role, looking out for opportunities and threats in the environment outside the immediate work area. Eventually, everyone will share the activity of scanning the work environment for opportunities and potential threats.

Most importantly, managers will be keepers of the culture. They will play a key role in building an organisational memory which supports and reinforces the valued rules and behaviours. Above all, the manager will need to feel involved across many levels. For example, following Figure 5.3, the manager will be involved in aligning workers' and management's values, capturing the hearts as well as the minds of employees. To achieve this, a mentoring philosophy and action-research approach are required. The focus of the action research will be to determine those deeply held core values around which culture building revolves.

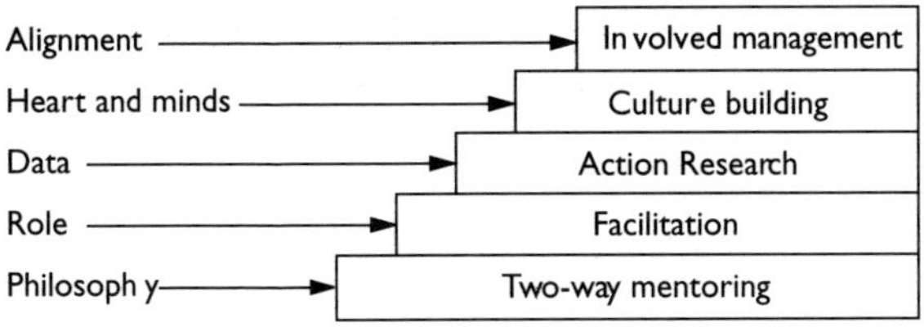

Figure 5.3 *The involved manager hierarchy*

There will be some preparation, perhaps over months, for the sort of change which requires organisational renewal. Information about the organisation's future challenges and its state of readiness to meet them will have been communicated in such a way that the workforce can have the opportunity to ask questions. During this time, there will be a need to send clear signals that the old days that belong to the traditional mindset are gone. It may be a time for tough decisions. Those who cannot commit to the internal model of genuine employee involvement may not feel that there is a role for them in the new organisational arrangements. Managers may not have had to rely on employee input and/or approval of decisions. They may need convincing that the realities employees construct about the organisation will be heavily influenced by their structures, systems and willingness to let employees make decisions. (It is what managers do, rather than what they say, that will influence their employees.)

Employees, especially those who are opinion leaders, whether formal or informal, will need to be prepared for the skills which are required in decision making such as planning, problem solving and communication. Employees will need to be convinced from the highest sources in the organisation that creating a shared vision is not a short-term crisis measure. They will need to have some confidence that the energy they put into championing the new ways of thinking and operating will not be wasted when markets and economies improve. This sort of preparation will take varying amounts of time according to the existing relationships between management and employees. When the climate is right and a reasonable amount of trust in management's and employees' intentions has been achieved, then visioning sessions can be held to determine:

- an overarching vision; and
- internal visions for departments or groups.

The task of leadership is to propose future direction. Given that the senior management group have experience and access to environmental information, this group will need to specify what it values from the workforce.

Using the core values method

Releasing the imaginal

This activity should be done as a senior management group and then replicated in departmental or functional groups as workshops.

Culture building is a long-range business. It is necessary to look ahead and imagine a future where survival and success are assured through methods of relating to others and organising social and technical systems. For this to happen, managers and employees need to draw on the emotional and the imaginal as well as the conceptual and practical (Heron 1989). See Figure 5.4. From these two imagined scenarios, feelings as well as facts can be harnessed to create a vision.

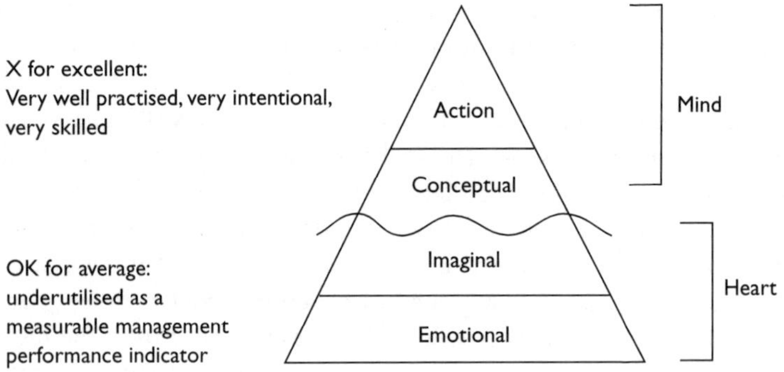

Source: Adapted from a hierarchy in Heron 1989:66

Figure 5.4 *OKX in tapping the emotional and imaginal*

Even though most managers will have experienced the powerful impacts of emotion and imagination on logical decisions, users of the core values method are unanimous in saying that managers usually operate in the conceptual and practical in their daily management lives. Some management development may be required here as the vision and values, once generated, need to be continuously reinforced.

Creating future scenarios

A simple method of releasing the imaginal (and the emotional is usually brought into play as well) is to ask the visioning group members to close their eyes and imagine the organisation as it will be in five/ten years time. The scene they are imagining is bright and light. There is an air of prosperity. There is an aura of success. What sort of buildings do participants see? What sort of physical layouts are in the workshops or other work areas? What can one tell about the human arrangements around the place? Who are the bosses and how can one tell? Are there any signs of the customer? Are there any symbols of how well the organisation is succeeding? How are the employees communicating? What sort of jokes and stories are being told? What values are evident in the scenes which have just been described?

The contributions almost exclusively relate to the co-operative psychological contract concerning things that money can't buy. Typical sets of responses have included 'feeling I make a difference', 'a sense of common purpose', 'a high level of trust and support', 'everybody pulling together and no one pulling rank', 'a strong sense of team' and 'a feeling of professionalism across the board'.

Now the task is to imagine a very different scene. The brightness has faded away. A dullness has taken its place. There is an aura of getting through the day as best as one can. What do the buildings look like here? How are things laid out? How are people relating to each other? How are managers and employees achieving goals together? How are the successes and failures communicated? What sort of stories are being told? What seem to be the things that people here value? Responses have included 'no one knows we're here', 'too many politics and little cliques', 'no overall sense of purpose that we are kept aware of', 'I don't feel I am recognised or that I make a difference', 'boredom', 'a sense of critical parents and naughty children', 'hierarchies and status get in the way or act as a refuge' and 'state of the buildings reflect how little valued we are'.

Creating shared values

It is then time to ask the key question of each participant in the management group.

What do you value most of all from employees?

The question will generate a list of values such as this list which was generated from a private-sector transport organisation.

- Respect us as people
- Be open to new ideas
- Have loyalty
- Integrity
- Team builder
- Be accountable
- Honesty — two way
- Team focused
- Mutual trust
- Open communication
- Have autonomy
- Work hard
- Professionalism
- Willing to learn
- Keep within budget

The objective of the values session is to derive one *core* value that is representative of the individual values and a set of *key* values that can act as parameters for culture building in functional areas or departments. Generating core values is done through the following process. Firstly, the collective group of managers (or employees/customers) brainstorms a set of values by each person contributing his/hers. The result is a list of values. The desired result is to develop a core value in the form of a concept. This concept tells the outside world what the group values, in other words what it sees as its expression of profitability. Synthesising a set of values into one core value is difficult, yet important. There needs to be exhaustive discussion and clarification, usually in small subgroups which each presents its core concept for more discussion until the idea of a holistic concept or statement of values emerges. Following is a real example:

We value building committed teams and high trust environments

The work of the group in generating individual values is not wasted. The list becomes a set of key values for the group, and the values are used as a collective statement of the group (in this case the management group). There is more to be done with the values if they are to be incorporated into the everyday processes of work life. As values are of vital importance, they need to be developed in such a way that they feature in competencies and performance indicators. Therefore, they need to be expressed in terms of behaviours. Because almost every individual will have a different way of expressing a value there is no other option but to take an interpretive approach and subject each value to definition by example. Take the value of 'Committed teams'. The important thing is not what this means in general but what it means to those who are requiring others to be committed teams. What do they have to do and what should they not do? For example, 'What sort of behaviours demonstrate committed teams to a particular group of people?' This question was asked of the transport management group and the answers were as given in Table 5.2.

Table 5.2 *Answers given to question on committed teams*

Positive	Negative
• Teams which run with the organisational goals as theirs • Teams which pull together • Teams which are not afraid to question themselves • Teams which will adapt to our new challenges • Teams which recognise that the chain is as strong as its weakest link and nurture that link	• Teams which argue among themselves • Teams which have superstars • Teams which score in their own goal rather than co-operate • Teams which are committed to the long weekend above our needs • Teams which have no learners

Armed with this information team members know what is valued behaviour and what is not. Particular behaviours can be referred to when having any sort of feedback or appraisal session. Teams or team members who remain conservative and resist change/new developments could expect to have to account for themselves even if they were meticulous in terms of task completion. Teams that celebrated their high achievers and did not recognise more mundane contributions could expect to be set performance targets of seeking out more ordinary people to be stars for their team contribution or effort. Values are excellent vehicles for drawing up 'behaviour specifications' between groups in, and connected to, organisations. These groups could include internal groups, within and across departments, and external groups such as suppliers and partners. Due to the highly task- and technical-centred development of the management discipline, this soft, yet profit-related, area is one which needs to become a competitive edge, particularly where organisations are relying on people as a significant part of the work outcome.

It is essential when dealing with values for organisational design purposes to investigate what values mean in terms of behaviours. A manager or employee can alter behaviour (such as arguing among ourselves) more easily than reacting to a general, and often personal, comment about being a poor team player. Doing this bridges the gap between theory and practice. When developed in this way, the behaviours that are derived from internally generated values become part of the informal appraisal process. Managers are no longer ambiguous about behaviours they value. Employees are the same. Ideally, customer groups should be brought into the process. It becomes possible and acceptable to negotiate social as well as task requirements. It also makes it easier to remember on a day-to-day basis what the organisational values are. Daily reminders make infringements of the values easier to spot and are more specific than a feeling that things aren't right.

The same process is used to generate the core values from the various employee groups within the workforce, although the process takes longer depending on the number of employees. The following sample from the transport organisation is not too different from the managers' list from the same organisation, which was generated quite independently.

- Be supportive
- Share your competence
- Be honest in relationships
- Have integrity
- Show loyalty to the group
- Recognition
- Be a champion
- Open and honest feedback
- Give us freedom
- Trust us
- Give guidance and coaching
- Motivate to excellence through leadership
- Open communication

From these values, a *core* value was generated:

Freedom to excel

The core values method and other such methods of integrating employees into the strategic heart of the business is time-consuming. Such methods require talents that many supervisors don't yet have.

Dealing in the area of feelings has not traditionally been part of management training until relatively recently, and working at the values level is the deepest level at which to work. The decision to do so is itself a declaration of the value placed on employees' requirements by management. As the Xerox case showed when it required every employee to take training, it was prepared to take the employee contribution to quality seriously. In a genuine attempt to create shared vision, workshops need to be held throughout an organisation so that employees can be firstly apprised of management's values and secondly given the opportunity to inform management of theirs. In the case of organisations which have embraced either bureaucratic or authoritarian control values, employees will often choose values such as 'trust and openness', 'honesty and integrity' and 'mutual respect'. The *core* value will often reflect this request for managers to respect employees as human beings. The outcome, whatever the values chosen, is a shared set of core values to translate into assumptions and those patterns of behaviour which make each organisation unique. See Figure 5.5.

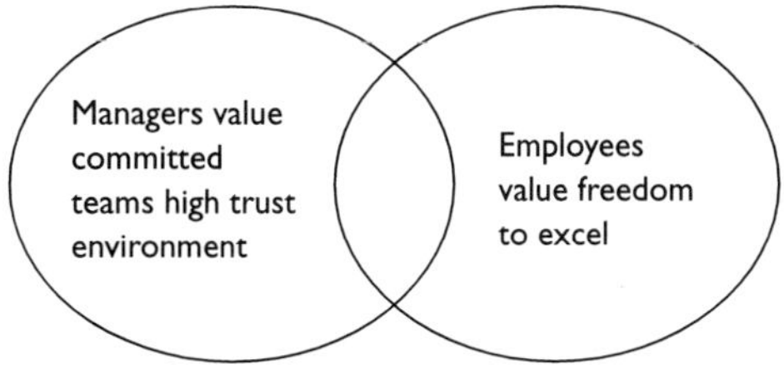

Figure 5.5 *Values of managers and employees*

There is one other key group whose values also need to be gathered but in a particular way: customers. Customer surveys have almost become routine. They are a legitimate way of testing how well products and services are experienced. They are relatively inexpensive to administer and analyse, and the better ones are based on qualitative studies so that the questions are focused on the language of the customer and close to product or service features. However, they run the danger of not being quite in tune with target groups in their choice of language. There are two reasons for this. One is that some groups rely very heavily on body language and a private, as opposed to public, code of language. Rarely will this be accessible to a survey designer who has factual as opposed to experiential knowledge of internal communications within a group. Therefore, answers are to words rather than clearly understood and clarified pieces of meaning. The second reason is that the survey may have pinpointed the important things in the eyes of the survey designers, but there may be important values of respondents which have not been requested. The outcome here is that the survey designer will solicit data to validate his/her reality rather than to probe the reality of others.

Using the core values method allows the participants to generate what is valued and valuable. It also validates the content of organisational surveys to make them meaningful to the respondent. It does the same for customers as it does for internal consumers. It allows them to visualise a future and locate the service or product within that future. It allows customers to play a meaningful role in the life of the organisational vision. Above all, customers have the opportunity to 'come into' the organisation in a human way. Also, there are usually a few surprises when core values workshops are held with customer groups. One of the surprises is that customers can enrich planning with some good ideas. The following list is from the transport organisation customer workshops.

- Give the customer a say
- One-stop shop for information
- Reliability
- Understanding
- A broad view of transport
- Demystifying information
- A human environment
- Give a feeling of being glad to see us
- Reasonable costs
- Creative ways to link with other services
- Safe journeys

The core value from this workshop was:

An informative and reliable service, with the human touch

The three sets of values in Figure 5.6 provide the sort of information upon which it is possible to create a shared vision inside the organisation. A vision statement for the transport organisation would include the values of the three groups:

We will give our employees freedom to excel as committed teams in providing a growing and reliable transport service with a human touch

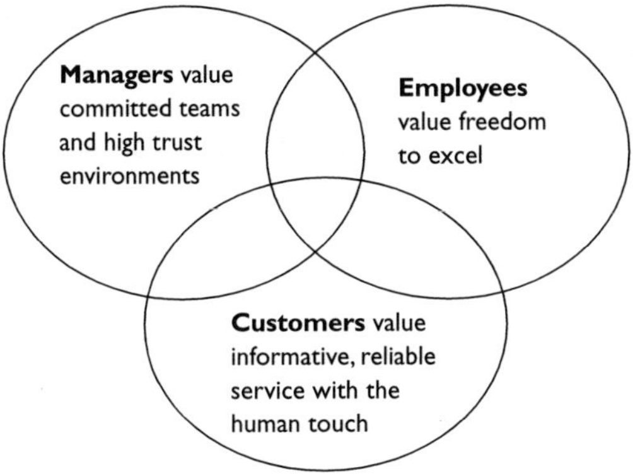

Figure 5.6 *Values of managers, employees and customers*

The set of activities is charted in Figure 5.7 in the order in which they would be undertaken in an organisation. The cycle of activities is dynamic, and there needs to be constant activity to reinforce and feed back information about the values and beliefs in operation, particularly in times of change.

ACTIVITY		OUTCOME
1 Management core values workshops	→	Management core values
2 Employee groups core values workshops	→	Emplo yee core values
3 Marketplace(s) core values workshops + customer surveys	→	Customer core values
↓ VISION	→	Vision (Philosophy) statement
4 Strategic planning workshops + communication/involvement from employee and customer groups	→	Mission strategic choices
5 Review structures and systems (social and technical) to match the vision and mission	→	Work redesign
6 Departmental vision of organisational arrangements	→	Group goals
7 Information and communication system	→	Feedback

Figure 5.7 *Core values model in action*

Creating a vision is only a beginning in the culture-building process. An infrastructure needs to be put into place so that educational strategies, communication strategies and culture-binding strategies can be designed for continuous improvement. Chapter 6 shows a suggested framework.

6
Culture building and binding, and learning concepts

Culture building and culture binding

> The situation [of idealogical doubt] reaches a point characterised by the response 'All this renewal is getting us nowhere; the whole system is losing its meaning for us'. Leaders take up increasingly defensive and retrenched positions in the face of such doubt and tend to revert to highly arbitrary and autocratic management styles. Widespread commitment is lacking throughout the group . . .
>
> Dalmau and Dick 1991

The quotation above serves to remind those concerned with change that there will often be a history preceding change. That history may be one which has included change initiatives that may not have worked, and instead left a legacy of doubt and apprehension. When deciding that there is a need for fundamental change, there should be a commitment to involve organisational members at the values and beliefs level. Then time, energy and resources should be dedicated to rebuilding the world of myth, lore, legend and symbol, which is the emotional core of an organisation.

Once the shared vision and defined mission are generated, the follow-up work of culture building and culture binding begins. A central theme of this book is that culture building is a continuous process. There needs to be a framework to support the initial work on determining (or renewing) the vision and mission. The schema in Figure 6.1 shows the vision and mission, together with those aspects of the shared history which fit the vision and therefore need to be preserved.

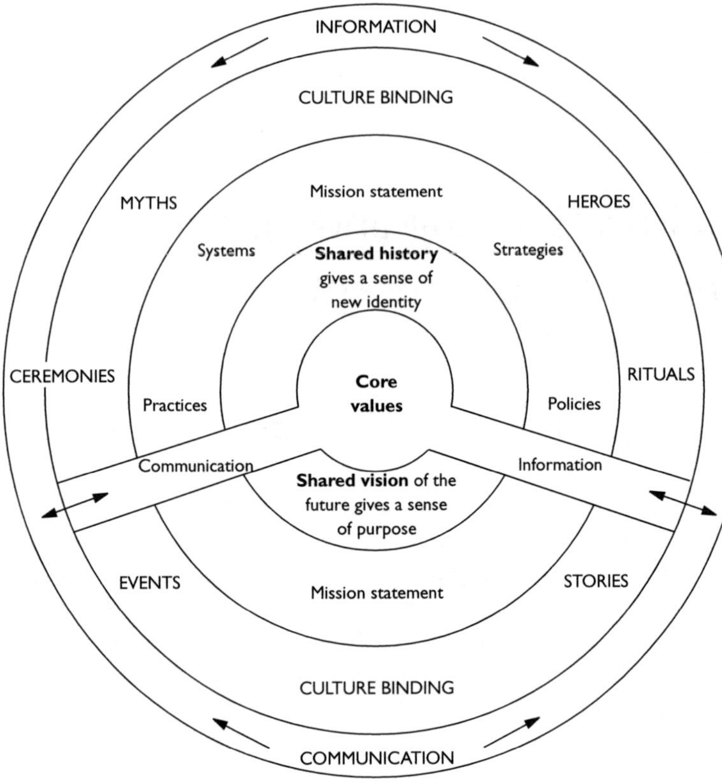

Figure 6.1 *A model for culture building and culture binding*

With the core values at the centre, the history of the organisation gives a sense of identity. Those historical values which harmonise with the vision will become part of the change agenda. It is these core values that drive the organisation. Almost at the time of planning for organisational renewal (Lippitt 1982), structures need to be set in place to facilitate the consolidation of the values and vision. Above all, the organisation will need to be designed in such a way that the social and technical systems and the design principles (Emery 1993) support the chosen values and vision. Values and vision inform mission, that is, the definition of the business. Mission informs strategy. Strategy informs the organisational design, structures and systems.

At the same time, those values from the past which are not in tune with the current, shared vision will need to be addressed and negotiated out of future organisational arrangements. As the cases in this book show, this is not a quick and simple task. To relinquish and help others relinquish past values, managers need to be skilled in critically appraising their own assumptions about why they do things the way they do. Deep internal images, which Senge (1992) calls 'mental models', are the way we picture values in action. They can be changed only by correspondingly deep investigation of the way problems and decisions are approached. Leading into the organisational future should be a shared vision, which is solid as a rock and directional, giving a clarity of purpose to all stakeholding groups.

Keeping the culture alive becomes the responsibility of managers and employees alike. A big danger is when managers and leaders say, 'We've done culture building, why are we going through all that again?' Continuous reinforcement is an essential part of culture building.

Using the mission statement as a working definition of what the business does, and using the strategic plans to show the priority areas to resource, appropriate structures and systems (especially human systems) need to be put in place to make sure that the values can be upheld. Systems of communication and information gathering/dissemination are key systems. Figure 6.2 shows an information system all too familiar to traditional management settings. Both structures and systems are involved here. Structurally we have the vertical, top-down manager/employee-reporting structure as opposed to the horizontal two-way alternative. In terms of systems, we have the filter-type

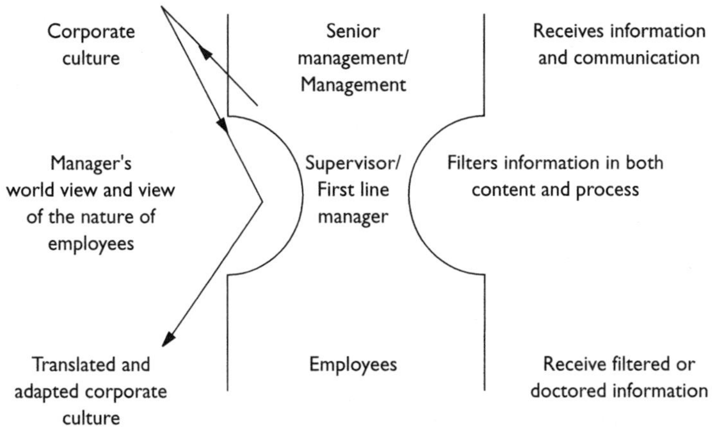

Figure 6.2 *The bottleneck system of communication*

communication system as opposed to the encircling system, depicted in Figure 6.1.

An organisation's structures and systems will either enable or disable its vision, mission and business strategies. It is not so much that managers within their own domains cannot develop lateral and encircling communication structures and systems where these are needed. Rather, the problem will be one of perceived non-legitimacy if they do not. The organisation as a whole is an important reference point for all departmental groups. The organisation will be seen to be serious about its espoused values if these are reflected in its legal structures and systems. The senior management effort needs to become concentrated in these areas to make sure that what is valued can become part of policies, procedures and practices.

The next circle in Figure 6.1 represents the culture-binding area. Some of the soft (that is, human) tools in this zone are currently being given a great deal of attention by certain kinds of organisations. Those organisations are the ones that have decided to bring employees into the organisation at the deep values level. The Best Practices cases described later in this book are characterised by participative management practices. Typically, such organisations will articulate the need for change, usually to meet the challenges of the future. They will negotiate a shared vision with all levels of the hierarchy, not just management. The new vision will help to direct the mission of the organisation for some time to come. Such organisations will set up, as a long-range planning scenario, those structures and systems which will facilitate employee communication, information and, where necessary, education. Once these vehicles are in place, culture-binding activities will become the focus for reinforcing the core values.

Four major tools for culture building are *symbols*, *heroes*, *rituals* and *stories*. Each is explained in turn and you should add as many examples from your own organisation as possible.

Symbols

There are many well-understood symbols in organisational life. Status symbols probably reflect organisational values more than others. These can be visible and unsubtle such as the size of a room, size and quality of carpet, job title, type of dining room, and even toilet facilities. We have all heard of the executive restroom. The major value which seems to be expressed here is that the organisation values some staff more than others. Organisations who want to optimise *every* human resource would have some difficulty in convincing those without such status symbols to give their all in return for being equally valued. Status symbols can also be more subtle. For example, the arrangements for holding employees' performance files and being in a position to set the time, place and agenda of the performance appraisal interview are a symbol of power, authority and control over important elements of the appraisal process. Typically, the supervisor would be responsible for the above: not the employee and not the customer. Therefore, the supervisor is nominally in charge of the employee's performance (even though we know that, ultimately, every person owns his/her own performance decisions). The supervisor is demonstrating control through symbols of ownership such as keeping the files, setting agendas and so on.

Structural symbols are closely related to status symbols. Hierarchical organisations send clear symbolic messages. People talk about pyramids and about those at the top. People informally appraise each other and are recognised by a hierarchical level. An individual in the Australian public sector may describe herself as 'a level two', rather than 'a team leader in the administration section'. Hierarchically designed organisations send stronger symbolic messages than differential pay scales and job titles. 'Being part of a vertical or hierarchical organisation means staffers look up to bosses instead of out to customers. You and your colleagues feel loyalty and commitment to the functional fiefdoms in which you work, not to the overall corporation and its goals' (Byrne 1993:44). Language also plays a key role here. Being an 'internal customer' can cross hierarchical boundaries. The author was often reprimanded for using 'old-style language which signifies hierarchy' when talking about 'employees' (Semler calls them 'associates') by the case organisations with which she was working. A whole outlook is being symbolised here. Hierarchies tend to look up and in. Reporting and control systems tend to perpetuate this outlook. Language is more subtle, but it can be used very effectively to differentiate people. Individuals and groups are perceived in terms of their *relative* value, which in turn is often linked to their *position* in the pecking order of the hierarchy.

Horizontal organisations symbolise something very different.

> In its purest state, the horizontal corporation might boast a skeleton group of senior executives at the top in such traditional support functions as finance and human resources. But virtually everyone else in the organisation would work together in

> multidisciplinary teams that perform core processes, such as product development or sales generation.
>
> Byrne (1993:44)

This sort of structure symbolises a belief in the freedom of the employee to be productive without reporting to several levels of control. It symbolises a move to broad rather than narrow thinking. Recognition and reward systems would reflect the new emphasis. (The two contrasts are captured by Emery (1993) as Design Principle 1 and Design Principle 2, discussed later in this chapter.)

Everything that happens at work is symbolic. From the design of jobs to the ways of rewarding those who perform them. What managers say and how they say it are symbols of respect or otherwise. What managers and employees do and how they relate to each other symbolise the extent to which they feel part of the organisation's goals. Who they recognise as leaders symbolises confidence in the formal system. Who is to be punished, how and for what, also symbolises the organisation's value system. Why organisations structure themselves in the way they do and design systems as they do tells a lot about the underlying values and beliefs actually in operation.

It is possible to analyse any symbolic behaviours once they are recognised as such. Major behaviours in human resource management, for example, are:

- lateness;
- absenteeism;
- sickies and sickness;
- low output.

Each of these can be construed in two ways. One way is to accept the behaviours as statistics, as facts or problems in themselves. This is to take the *objectivist* view. A second way is to treat facts as events which need to be explained and interpreted by those closely connected to them. This is the *interpretive* view.

The lateness, absenteeism, sickness and low output in the example above are verifiable facts. Timekeeping is observable, documentable and recordable. Observation and reasoning are used as a means to understand the late, sick, absent or low-productivity behaviour. This view or construction of reality is objective; it rests on external, objective, physically describable reality. This view is consistent with positivism (Smith 1983) or objectivism (Berquist 1993). With this approach, a person seeking to understand events such as lateness, absenteeism and low output will look for instances of the behaviour from such evidence as timesheets and other records, coupled with instances of responses such as warnings, disciplinary meetings or performance results. Such instances may be used to make inferences about the latecomer, absentee or low-producing person, particularly where there is quantitative evidence to support this. Where there is high incidence of such behaviours, one can find the sort of generalisations such as 'hourly paid workers are not as reliable as salaried staff'. As it is the hourly worker who is being late/absent/lazy, the cause of the behaviour will likely be attributed to the worker.

Principles associated with the positivist or objectivist view are empirical — that which can be observed and counted. There is a sense of determinism — things observed or counted have observable or explainable causes and economy; they reduce things to their most simple. There is a tendency to generalise, given enough facts and evidence. Facts, findings, rules and laws can be transferred with some confidence to other contexts as believable realities.

The second view is using the interpretivist or constructivist perspective (Wilson and Hutchinson 1991:265; Berquist 1993). Here individuals at work create meaningful interpretations of the physical and behavioural objects around them. To the manager who takes a constructivist approach, the lateness, absenteeism, sickness and low output in question are symbols of an unfinished story. The story may be one of laziness, lack of commitment and unreliability. Or it could be there is something so drastically wrong with the work environment that there is a force stronger than the prospects of discipline which is pulling the employee away from the workplace. A person seeking to understand the lateness and absence syndromes would still use the statistics of timesheets. High incidence of the dysfunctional behaviours would probably signal a strength of feeling about work. The immediate questions would be: 'What is the meaning of these behaviours to the employee?', 'What is the late and absent behaviour signifying, within the wider work context', and 'Who are the role partners who contribute to the work climate?'

Principles associated with interpretivism are a belief in the subjective and intuitive consciousness. There is an understanding that this consciousness helps us bestow meaning on things and situations, and affirms the idea that we live in a world of multiple realities. Phenomenologists for the last century have recognised this, and it has become common in the social sciences to look underneath the details of everyday life. We need to look further than the signals that people give and, instead of being caught up in them, release ourselves from them to take a different view (Quinton 1977). To do this we need to look beyond and underneath organisational processes and structures whether they are cultural, symbolic or technical. Interpretivism would hold that there is no world of meaning without investigation. Each person constructs his/her own meaning. To engage in meaningful social interaction, we need to develop ways of negotiating shared meaning.

The important thing about these two approaches — positivism and interpretivism — is that they inform people's and particularly managers' individual world view. The world view, in turn, informs manager's own theories of managing and dealing with people, from the way information is shared to the way interpersonal relationships are structured. In the positivist world, the world is black and white, filled with countable events, behaviours, rules and infringements. In the interpretivist world, the world is no colour at all until someone gives an event colour and interprets what the colour means. Managers will be making dozens if not hundreds of symbolic behaviours, actions and decisions every day. If they are positivists, the risk is that they will be busy constructing others' meaning for them. Sobering, isn't it? The worst thing is when the manager is not aware that symbols represent pieces of meaning, and the meaning given is not necessarily being the one taken. It is easy to see tangible things such as desks or documents or files. Symbols are less tangible but no less meaningful to people in the workplace.

Examples of symbolic behaviour

The following are examples of symbolic behaviour:

- The company has a prize-giving ceremony. Directors and senior managers are on stage, enthusiastically clapping and cheering the winners. Following the ceremony, a private cocktail party is laid on for the director's party back stage. A generous 'bash' is laid on elsewhere for the crowd of the winners' colleagues and their families.
- A mate has an accident and breaks a leg. The supervisor makes a 'this is your life' book by going round to workers and asking them for anecdotes. (Some of them are against himself — they go in too.)
- Enterprise bargaining is on the horizon. The CEO and a team visits each site and explain the proposed arrangements and why they are

necessary. The CEO and the team explain the new culture necessary to make the Enterprise Bargaining Agreement (EBA) happen and give a clear and distilled run-down of current company performance. The CEO's presentation is impeccable. It takes three hours and the company is standing the cost while employees are at the presentation. Immediately after the presentation, the CEO goes back to head office rarely to be seen or heard in person again for the next tricky years of EBA transition.

- A self-reported Theory Y manager engages a consultant to help him facilitate workshops on self-direction and empowerment. They go down really well and several informal self-development groups form. These groups ask to take over some of the 'official' duties such as holiday rosters and time scheduling. The outcome six months later is that the manager continues to do scheduling himself, while still espousing his empowering style.
- A fairly quiet and conservative information-technology manager goes on a management development course. She comes back and spends the next couple of weeks distilling the course notes, especially those on interpersonal/communication skills. From the third week, she begins to 'do' rather than 'tell' the course content to her staff. She demonstrates workshops, simulated situations and, risking looking silly, tries to:
  - pass on the good things learned; and
  - look for constructive criticism for the first time ever.

The fourth example above refers to Theory Y.

Douglas McGregor (1960) suggested that managers view workers in one of two ways, which he called Theory X and Theory Y. Theory X assumes that workers inherently dislike work and will try to avoid it. They must be coerced, controlled or threatened with punishment to achieve goals. They shirk responsibility, seek direction and be motivated by security rather than advancement. In contrast, Theory Y assumes that workers view work as natural and as play. They exercise self-direction and are committed to organisational objectives. They learn to accept responsibility and are as likely as managers to have talents in innovation and decision making.

It is not difficult to interpret various meanings given to the above symbolic behaviours, depending on whether you are a manager or an employee. It is also quite easy to use symbolic behaviour in a strategic way.

Let's say an organisation's strategic directions include:

- accessibility;
- international markets;
- quality accreditation.

Symbolic events, appearances and even policies can be planned to support the strategies as above. An example of the first strategy would be an internal policy of open-door access during certain times. The arrangement would symbolise the new strategy. How can ordinary workers symbolise internationalism, one can ask? Canteen managers can begin including symbolic food events such as dim sum, a Chinese food custom. Work groups can symbolise internationalism by celebrating colleagues' and customers' special national days. They can design symbols such as miniature flags or coffee-time celebrations. A symbolic behaviour to celebrate quality would be to frame and exhibit evidence of the first and subsequent milestones in the quality journey. The attendance of the CEO at the framing session would be a further symbol. Managers often intuitively use symbols to send messages. Rarely will symbols and symbolic behaviour be a conscious and formally planned part of the communication process, and be intentionally linked to strategy. Yet abilities in symbolic communication will be one of the biggest attributes of future leaders because of the need to enable employees to key into strategic thrusts and developments. Once they can key into issues, the question: 'Why are we doing this activity and how does it link to the core goals of the organisation?' can be answered by themselves. As they continuously ask 'why' employees and managers can become experienced in prioritising activities and eliminating all but those that are generic to strategy.

Heroes

Who are the heroes in an organisation? We are somewhat used to a stereotype hero who is usually high profile and often celebrated for having achieved something outstanding either at work or at leisure. While this is acceptable in the general sense, and while those who do something special deserve to be recognised, what is to stop the manager from according hero status to those who contribute in their own way to the work group or organisational strategy and goals? If a core value of a work-group and manager relationship was honesty, the hero of the day may be the person who braves it to tell the manager some 'truth' he/she may not want to hear. If the value was integrity, the hero may be the person who kept a confidence even when there could be some negative comeback. If the organisational goal or strategy was to change from conservative to innovative, the hero could be the storekeeper who finally relinquished much-loved and honed manual stocktaking procedures in favour of a difficult-to-learn electronic system. When identifying and recognising heroes in such a way as to recognise those who support values, strategies and goals, the notion of hero is no longer restricted to 'successes' in general. Those whose contribution may be in support areas, partnership relationships, and even the more mundane aspects of work would qualify for recognition as heroes strive to represent the values of the organisation.

Rituals

Someone, somewhere in every organisation will be busy, intuitively or otherwise, managing rituals. Every facet of organisational life is ritualised at some time or other. Inside the organisation, certain rituals perform the function of constantly reminding employees and management alike about the way we do things around here.

A ritual celebrates some value/belief, person or event in such a way as to give meaning beyond the actual here and now. Of all the culture-binding activities, rituals are the ones that managers and employees alike say can be empty. This could mean that the event has become routinised, and taken for granted as a habit rather than a celebration. Alternatively, it could mean that the value or event does not have shared meaning for everyone. It could be that there is little trust and the ritual, empty of meaning it seeks to symbolise, is hypocritical and used as a public front or image builder. If any of these scenarios were to be true, it would undoubtedly be better not to design rituals as communication devices as they can serve to draw attention to that which is espoused rather than practised (Argyris and Schon 1974).

Rituals can take on an important role when linked to shared organisational values and goals. A good example of the optimal use of rituals was a fibre manufacturing factory which changed from a traditional 'managers think and workers do' design to a profit-centre principle. The pioneer profit-centre structure was run by employees on their own budget. All areas of management had to be 'bought in' by employees. It seemed when walking around that, literate or not, all these employees were certainly thinking. Every aspect of the business seemed to be interesting to a wide range of employees. To discuss market-share problems with a machine operator and human-resource issues with a sweeper would be nothing out of the ordinary.

The new organisational design in this case valued empowered employees and ownership of business strategies by all levels of the business. It valued high levels and quality organisation of production and a 'no secrets here' climate. Some of this would be evident from the company's structure and consulting role for managers, but inside the organisation certain rituals performed the function of constantly reminding employees and management alike about 'the way we do things.' Rituals which were in evidence here included the hourly newsflash. An electronic noticeboard was positioned near every profit centre. Each hour, on the hour, productivity results were posted. Every Friday lunchtime there was the ritual get together. Employees pooled various sums into a common fund. The canteen laid on a buffet lunch at a modest price and there was some sort of entertainment. As part of the ritual, qualifying managers would be given the bull's-eye award, which was humorous with more than a grain of truth in it. The Golden Award was given not only to those who had excelled, but also to those who had overcome some burden in order to be empowered. This was a sensitive way to ritualise feedback, particularly challenging feedback, between managers and employees. The hero of heroes was the CEO who, legend had it, suffered two nervous breakdowns and almost a divorce in the brave battle to allow the factory to become a profit centre. The rituals were a way of celebrating that the CEO was justified in having faith in the employees.

It is an important and vital part of the manager's work to understand the various roles that rituals play in developing and celebrating a sense of organisational identity, history and custom.

An important role for rituals is that of a cohesive agent. We could consider ritual as social glue. The Friday night beer, the fishing trip and the barbecue are more small-scale examples. The annual dinner and Christmas lunch are larger scale but no less important. Ritual as a help in barrier breaking plays an important role in organisational life, especially in Asian countries where 'face' prevents direct comment or criticism to a manager and sometimes a colleague (Bond 1989).

Rituals such as sports events, barbecues and networking/social evenings allow 'experts' other than technical or work-oriented experts to be celebrated. Swimmers, golfers, cooks, singers and joke tellers can be appraised and praised. The temporary redistribution of prestige and status helps to put work relationships in perspective. Informal meetings can also perform this function. They can be ritualised in such a way as to allow everyone to operate at one level. Strategic suggestions can be offered, critical comments made, seeds of ideas sown and personal harvests reaped outside the confining hours of the 'official' relationship. Formally, these are often designed as quality circles, team briefings, networking sessions and similar forums.

Sometimes in some cultures, there is a need to preserve barriers and the following example shows the power of ritual to both enhance or endanger values. Bill White, manager of an international hotel in Hong Kong, was very keen to share with his employees the friendly American style of management that he himself enjoyed when he was an employee. Developing camaraderie and breaking down status barriers were strongly valued in the American system. Bill had just been down to the hotel kitchen to launch the ritual of Management By Walking About (MBWA). He tried, not too successfully and not for the first time, to engage the kitchen staff in conversation about their respective families. The home culture of these traditional Chinese workers required the boss to be kept at a distance, to be depended upon and to mix with other taipans (important people). The MBWA ritual contravened deeply held cultural values and actually produced divided loyalties between organisational values and those of the home culture. See Figure 2.1, 'An employee's membership of three cultures'.

One of the strongest roles of rituals is to recognise and celebrate some achievement. Tangible symbols to mark the ritual occasion are usually given to commemorate the achievement. The symbols could be as extravagant as a gold watch or as modest as a cold can of beer. It is the symbol, not the item, which matters. And the achievement doesn't always have to be real. Rituals can be fun things where symbols are as likely to be given for two hours without swearing (or laughing) as they are for 25 years of service. Such rituals can be oases in the desert of fast-moving working life. Just for a little while, the mechanistic, practical, fast-oriented world we have become used to is suspended. Just for a while human spirits congregate. Emotion is okay. Humour is okay. It is okay to agree that human beings are pretty wonderful things and to feel a unison about cheering a winner. It doesn't so much matter how big the prize is. What really matters is that the team spirit is liberated and the human aspects of work are celebrated.

Rituals can also be used as signals that all is not well. When discussing rituals, people always draw attention to empty rituals. People are quick to judge when a ritual is real or when it is an empty gesture. Judging when a ritual is a waste of time is no easy matter. Managers have traditionally agonised over whether to turn a blind eye to such rituals as lunchtime card games, smokos and social conversations at desks, and now with new technology even competitive computer games during working hours.

At first sight, these examples look negative and time wasting, especially in today's competitive climate. But wait — it may not be so.

A manager really needs to know the prevailing climate to be able to judge the status of rituals. For example, if there is a custom of 'we value getting the job done in the time to a high standard and from then our time's our own', the social rituals may have been built by the participants as energisers, social reinforcers and identity builders. Employees could be demonstrating pride in their prowess of performing with time to spare. Fill that time up as a manager and what are you doing? Possibly eroding the work groups' sense of self-competition. If the rituals of card playing, smokos and so on are aimed at expressing a negative relationship with the organisation, then the language of the ritual will be loud and clear to those who can understand such signals.

Hearing and interpreting the meaning that rituals and symbols transmit comes easily, almost intuitively, to some managers. In other cases, they are aspects of a workplace language that need to be studied and learned. This is particularly true in the workplace of the future where negotiated and shared meaning between managers and employees gives a competitive edge. See Figure 2.2, 'Developing shared worlds of meaning'.

A popular ritual conducted by employees (and sometimes managers) among themselves is the rite of passage. Newcomers are initiated into the customs and norms through in-group humour. Being sent for a left-handed hammer or a long weight are two examples. The whole story, from the newcomer's eagerness to please to the gradual frustration and then dawning recognition that the newcomer has 'been had', will be gleefully narrated. The story will translate into folklore, and the culture and solidarity of the group in question will be reinforced.

A shipyard legend was Mick the Killer. The story went that if someone upset him or his squad, that person went overboard the ship (being built or repaired) on which they were working. In one go, legend had it, he hurled a riveter, welder and burner all overboard. Why did no one read about it in the papers? I wondered about this until I became a little wiser. Of course, the reason was that no one was ever actually thrown overboard at all. The story, like the fisherman's story, had somewhat grown. It wasn't the fact that mattered — anyway, what is a fact? It was the story that mattered, and its symbol of Mick and his group's strength and unbeatability that the workers appreciated.

Deal and Kennedy's (1982:3) story about NCR's chief S. C. Allyn is a wonderful example of stories that bind top management to every worker.

> S. C. Allyn, a retired chairman of the board, likes to tell a story about his company — the National Cash Register Corporation. It was August 1945, and Allyn was among the first allied civilians to enter Germany at the end of the war. He had gone to find out what had happened to an NCR factory built just before the war but promptly confiscated by the German military command and put to work on the war effort. He arrived via military plane and travelled through burned-out buildings, rubble, and utter desolation until he reached what was left of the factory. Picking his way through bricks, cement, and old timbers, Allyn came upon two NCR employees whom he hadn't seen for six years. Their clothes were torn and their faces grimy and blackened by smoke, but they were busy clearing out the rubble. As he came closer, one of the men looked up and said, 'We knew you'd come!' Allyn joined them in their work and together the three men began cleaning out the debris and rebuilding the factory from the devastation of war . . . A few days later, as the clearing continued, Allyn and his co-workers were startled as as American tank rumbled up to the site. A grinning GI was at its helm. 'Hi,' he said. 'I'm NCR Omaha. Did you guys make your quota this month?' . . . NCR's hard-driving, sales-oriented culture was still intact.

A General Electric senior manager tells the story of the rite of passage where typically a new graduate, complete with calculator, perhaps a suite of offices and a grand title visits the shop floor and is told to go and sweep the floor. This is, in effect, a lesson about how important it is to enter the real world and not to view it from the ivory tower of management. It concerns knowing a place symbolically as well as factually.

Managers as designers of rituals

One of the most difficult things for which to forgive a manager is when she/he does not recognise and actively participate in the management of symbols and rituals. It would be unheard of for a manager to be unable to read a balance or budget sheet. This would mean that he/she could not tell the financial health of the department or division. Yet not being able to read symbolic and ritualistic behaviours means that the manager is unable to read the social health and possibly not even able to penetrate the real life of the department. The manager who cannot understand the import of symbols and rituals may, without knowing it, be managing by default. This can end up not too far from management by abdication. It is relatively easy to design formal and official systems such as spreadsheets, standing orders and technical procedures. However, human environments are not so straightforward to design. They need to tap into the whole person — heart as well as head. See Figure 5.4, 'OKX in tapping the emotional and imaginal'. People are complex and they are social. They will have preferences about the ways they want to work together. There is no one best way. There is the way best suited to the culture, values, beliefs, rituals and ceremonies which have survived many permutations. The design of rituals needs very careful thinking about.

Stories

These stories make up that wonderful aspect of organisational life — folklore — as the examples below show.

The supervisor who was held in affection by his office colleagues was partial to a drink during work hours and was also an expert in naughty limericks. As clients passed his desk, he would either comment to colleagues that they wouldn't stand still enough for him to see them clearly, or with a solemn face and wildly twinkling eyes mutter a limerick so that only colleagues could hear. As he was supervisor, and as he often issued 'straight' instructions, his staff were caught out every time. It was said that he had a repertoire of three thousand limericks. He was the office character, drunk or sober, and his escapades were a focal point for office stories.

An example of how events quickly translate into organisational lore concerned a management development course. Participants had spent some time in generating their values and norms, which centred around professionalism and adult learning principles. There had not been too much opportunity for participants to unite as a group until something happened that caused immediate cohesion. A presenter, appearing for the first time to this audience, used a style that was not appropriate for the culture of the group. There was a sense of 'being back at school' and having a 'critical parent'. Participants who were 'selected' for criticism found themselves receiving support and affirmation from other group members, which was unspoken but almost tangible. Within two hours after the event, the story had passed into the folklore of the group. Being faced with such a definite example of behaviour which contravened the core values of the group generated a spontaneous desire to reaffirm and restate the values. The story of the actual event would serve as a shorthand to the group when values were challenged or supported in future.

Very often, stories and legends are underused in building and binding a culture. Learning how to proactively develop organisational folklore through the creation of meaningful heroes, symbols, rituals and stories is an important role for the first line supervisor as well as the other management groups. The only time this may not work, of course, is when there is a lack of authenticity. If the culture building does not take into account the values of the workforce, then the vision or direction will not be 'owned' by workers either. If, once the workforce's values are established, strategies are chosen which contravene them, then faith in the culture will be lost. If, further down the track, management style is incongruent with the espoused values, vision, mission and strategies, then the culture will be replaced and filtered through the lens of the manager's own world view (and think what would happen if a Theory Y espoused culture was left for reinforcement in the hands of a Theory X manager).

Matching organisational design to culture building

The finest skills in the world in designing rituals and symbolic occasions will not compensate for a manager who does not have a conceptual understanding of organisational design principles. Without this knowledge, it will not be possible to recognise the structural context in which she/he will be trying to launch change.

The work of Fred and Merrelyn Emery (1993) has been chosen to best represent crystallised organisational design concepts and knowledge. The *ecological paradigm* (Covey 1992), which basically celebrates the ability and decision-making power of the individual, is also highly compatible with the empowering philosophy behind the core values model. The work of the Emerys has been tried and tested for more than 50 years in Europe (25 of these years in Australia) in an Action Research setting, that is, learning about organisations through changing them. There is a rejection of scientific management principles and of autocracy-style bureaucracy in favour of the participative principles which characterise the models and cases in the work of F. and M. Emery.

There is a wealth of historical, theoretical and practical information for managers in the 1993 *Participative Design for Participative Democracy*. Some key ideas and elements of *participative design* and its predecessor *socio-technical systems* have been chosen to demonstrate the sort of preparation managers need in order to prepare their employees-as-individuals for a partnership in culture building and culture binding.

Participative design

Participative design did not suddenly appear, either as a concept or way of managing. The Emerys (1993) start the story with Lippit and White (1939) and their finding that there were three 'types' of organisational structure which influenced the lives of those bound by the structures: autocratic structures, *laissez-faire* structures and democratic structures. Autocratic structures produced hostility, quarrelling, scapegoating and damage to equipment; creativity and commitment were not evident and, of course, initiative would not be possible. *Laissez-faire* or 'go as you please' structures produced the above, plus a sense of being lost and inadequate. Democratic structures were almost the opposite in that creativity, commitment, vitality and co-operation were dedicated to the task.

Following a 'finding' in the coalmining industry (Trist and Bamforth 1951), a reinforcement of the idea that social structures can be as dominant in producing behaviours as technical structures was developed into a structural design known as Socio-Technical Systems (STS) (Emery 1978). This method of organisational design not only looked at social systems and technical systems but also looked at the relationship between them as a system itself. In order to understand socio-technical systems, and indeed organisational design in action, Fred Emery's Design Principles conceptual model is indispensable.

According to Emery (1993:102), there are two design principles or mental models of how organisational structures and systems should be designed. These are briefly explained below. Both are built around the key concept of 'redundancy'. The concept assumes that all organisations need to build in a certain amount of slack or redundancy into their systems if they want to be flexible and adaptable in the face of the unexpected. How organisations choose to go about designing redundancy into their systems is a symbol of their underlying philosophy and assumptions. In Figure 6.3, the assumptions are that senior managers should construct strategy, mission and vision, and hand them down as theory to workers. This would be in keeping with Design Principle 1.

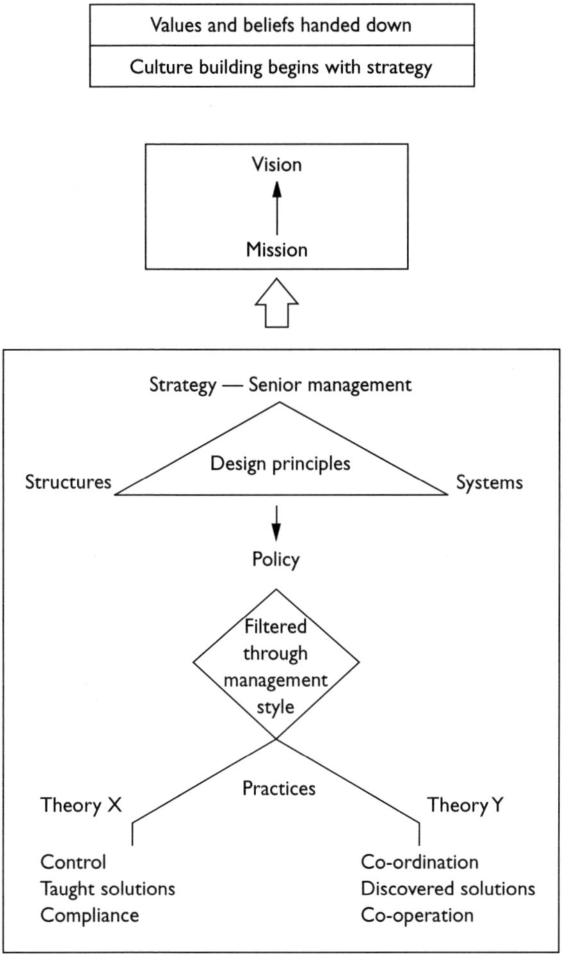

Figure 6.3 Philosophy handed down as 'theory'

Design Principle 1

The *principle of redundant parts* ensures that a part or person is easily replaceable should they fail to perform in the correct way. Extra parts or people will be on hand, ready to replace a part of the social or technical system as needed.

A key feature of Design Principle 1 is that co-ordination and control take place at *one level above* where the actual work is being done. See Figure 6.4. So does decision making and problem solving. Typically, supervisors will co-ordinate and control who does what, when and

Supervisor of supervisor (S)

Supervisor	Supervisor
E E E E	E E E E
T T T T	T T T T

E = Employee
T = Task
S = The locus of co-ordination and control

Figure 6.4 *Design Principle I*

how. Therefore, there is little need to develop employees in problem solving and analysis, decision making, interpersonal relations and presentation skills. As issues are passed up the line, employees must rely on others, such as trade unions, to present and argue proposals. The concept has developed in some organisations to the point where there are supervisors of supervisors whose major function is to co-ordinate and control the work of supervisors who are already once removed from the productive work on the shop or office floor. In this case, supervisors will often be found who, in practice, are really superworkers.

A second significant feature is the 'one task-one person' syndrome. This is where a person is responsible for his/her own task. This requires no flexibility or adaptability from the employee. Communication would be of a directive nature. Unless specified as part of a job, interpersonal skills would not be required. The front line employee is removed from decisions and goals other than those directly related to the job.

Design Principle 2

The *principle of redundant functions* designs the redundancy not into spare parts or people but into the constricting notion of functional tasks. Instead of tightly defining and prescribing one task per person, the functions are incorporated into a holistic job design where individuals may not be using all their functions at once in a job role, but they have the capacity to use them as and when required by the operating system. Importantly, co-ordination and control are kept within the boundaries of the producing group. Group members are also responsible for the interdependencies of themselves and elements of the tasks. Communication systems within the group resemble the more informal systems found in families and special interest groups. Following this principle, the work group is closely connected to the perform-

Supervisor (S)

W+W+W+W   W+W+W+W
T+T+T+T   T+T+ T+T

W = Work group responsible for co-ordination and control
T = Task in the sense a collection of social and technical tasks
S = Facilitator and cross-department co-ordination

Figure 6.5 *Design Principle 2*

ance and aspirations of the organisation. Replacing the control role of supervisors would be a facilitation, information gathering and educative role. See Figure 6.5.

There is an important developmental need for the manager or the supervisor who needs to move from Design Principle 1 to Design Principle 2 to see the shape of each design principle as a mental model or mindset. (Those using the core values model and/or wishing to emulate the success of the organisations described in this book would need to use Design Principle 2.)

For example, Design Principle 1 might look like a hierarchy, and usually problems/decisions are solved two or even three levels from the line of operation. See Figure 6.6 below. If a hierarchy

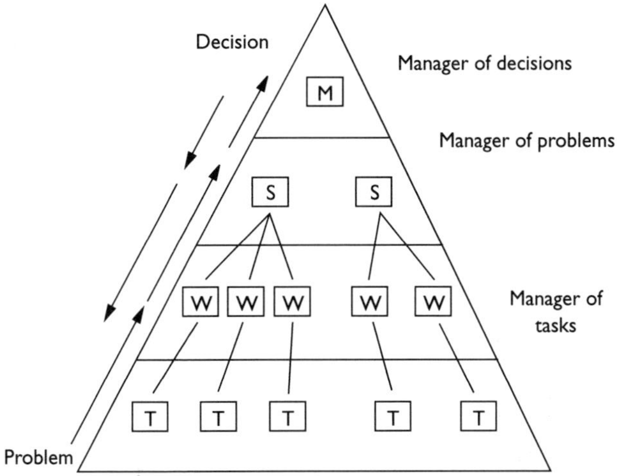

Figure 6.6 *Problems are passed up and down the line of control: Design Principle 1*

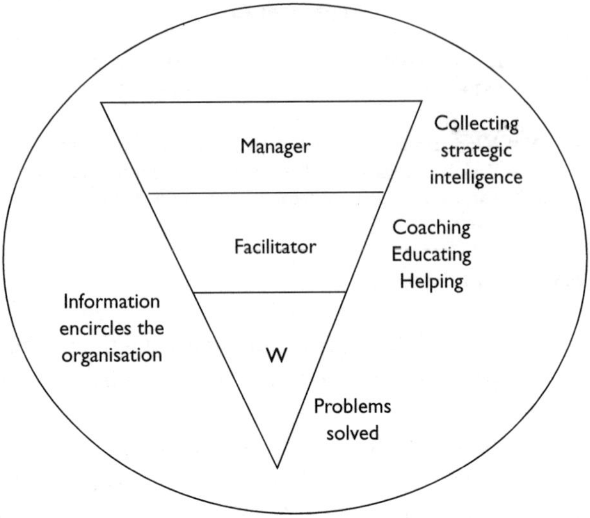

Figure 6.7 *Problems are tackled 'on site': Design Principle 2*

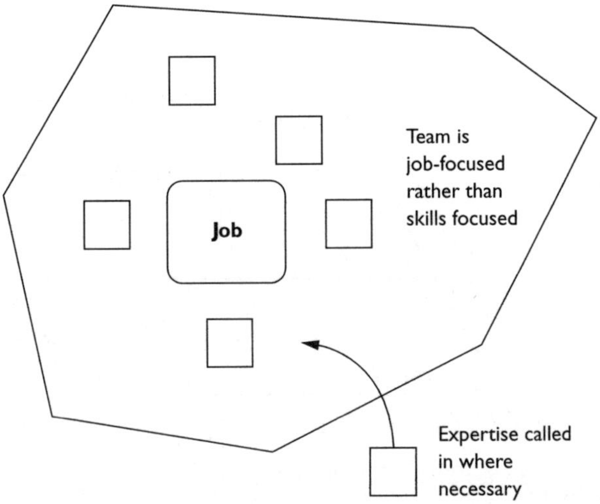

Figure 6.8 *Problems are handled inside or expertise is called in: Design Principle 2*

were to exist at all in Design Principle 2, it would probably look like Figure 6.7. Design Principle 2 might look like an amoeba where team workers become as one cell, grouped around job needs, pooling or drawing in skills and expertise. See Figure 6.8. A combination of multiskilling and drawing in of outside expertise would be an appropriate way of resourcing such a design. From this model, it will be clear the sort of developmental approach which is needed to secure obedience and compliance in the first model (Design Principle 1) compared with that needed to secure the co-operation and commitment of employees in the second model (Design Principle 2).

Development of managers, supervisors and employees

Managers and supervisors

The major drivers and reinforcers of culture in an organisation are senior management. A major role of managers at this level is to scan the environment for business intelligence and future opportunities as well as impending threats. A responsibility of senior management is to see and then convey the big picture to managers (should they still exist as such), supervisors and ultimately employees. Kotter and Heskett (1992) are also saying that maybe top managers need to redefine their role and revolve their organisational design and development around communication of the culture, core values and desired behaviours.

Once the leadership is there, the person who is on the interface between management and the front-line workforce has a pivotal role to play in building and reinforcing culture. In particular, looking at the potential role relationships that trainers or coaches have with trainees, there are many opportunities to identify and celebrate heroes and to design symbols and rituals which reaffirm the organisational values within this role. Trainers take the facilitator role. They instruct and act as friend, mentor, mediator, adviser, counsellor and liaison person (Flower and Brown 1983).

Experience with organisations shows that supervisors and managers are not always aware of the people skills, which are as essential as technical or accounting skills, in terms of being able to introduce change. The menu of skills most selected by supervisors and managers in workshops conducted by the author include those listed in Table 6.1.

Table 6.1 *Skills selected by supervisors and managers*

Skills	Dimensions
Criticism skills	• handling criticism • giving criticism • transforming negative to positive feedback
Conflict resolution skills	• becoming aware of own style • developing a repertoire of conflict-handling methods • educating subordinates to present an analytical and objective case to resolve
Negotiation skills	• becoming aware of own style • appraising other's style • solving problem • persuading • saying 'no'
Interpersonal skills/ Communication skills	• listening actively • encouraging behaviours • using presentation skills • having empathy • giving and receiving feedback • encoding/decoding messages
Group/Team building	• being aware of own team-building style • using group dynamics • using team-building models

Employees

Participative organisational design means a redefined role not only for many supervisors/managers but also for employees. Faced with the probability that employees will want to take some planning and decision-making activities, the responsibility for facilitating the development of a learning environment falls on supervisors and managers. Fostering an enabling climate, by helping employees to link ideas and experience to similar and different contexts, will be a feature of participative culture building.

Bringing employees into operational planning and problem solving is nothing new to managers. However, bringing them into culture building that leads on to strategic planning is different in two important ways. The time frame of operational work is usually the past or the present. Typically, current problems will draw on established ways of doing things. The human abilities needed in the operational framework are usually practical and some are conceptual — 'knowing, and knowing how to do'. Culture building is a very different activity. It goes hand in hand with organisational renewal and strategic planning (Lippitt 1982). The time frame is mostly future oriented, with data from the past and present only being used to extract what is valuable to carry forward. The human abilities needed in the first instance are emotional and imaginal (Heron 1989). See Figure 5.4.

Using the emotional/imaginal abilities, individuals and groups can visualise future scenarios which are not yet here. In particular, they can visualise the *feel* of things, in terms of atmosphere and relationships as well as practical operations. On this basis, it is necessary that a problem-solving framework is offered to employees which allows emotional and imaginal inputs, as well as the conceptual and action-oriented inputs. This may be an entirely new ball game for managers who, as controllers rather than enablers, have never had to worry in the past about whether employees' hearts were in it or what they felt about the implementation of solutions to problems. Responses from managers who have been presented with the hierarchy of practical, conceptual, imaginal and emotional abilities will say that they are very well developed in the first two and (in the work sense) underdeveloped in the third and fourth. The role which is likely to change drastically as organisations move to participative management is that of the manager or supervisor. The new role will have a heavy facilitation focus. The skills of releasing imaginal and emotional abilities in others will be an asset in participative management.

Facilitation skills in culture building

Basically, facilitation consists of a person, a structure and a process. The title implies values of making things easier, getting obstacles out of the way, and encouraging the elusive 'shared meaning', which is the basis for true democracy.

The facilitator is the spirit-tapper, who is more concerned with encouraging people to bring the spirit to succeed and to get it right, than to tell them what success is or what getting it right entails. The facilitator may be orchestrating inputs, reading non-verbal language as though it were a scoresheet, and constantly drawing out questions, opinions, criticisms and answers that will motivate group members to achieve their outcomes. Still, the intuitive communicator is almost certainly working within a learnable framework, using learnable techniques and processes.

Like any production manager, the facilitator is concerned with inputs and outputs, and also, of course, the 'true' nature of the task to be done. Facilitators usually agree on the following core aspects of facilitation:

- Generally, achieving more initial inputs almost always leads to more creative outputs.
- Sternly whittling down inputs that are not robust for the purpose leads to tightly focused outputs.
- Recognising the need for 'ownership' to ensure implementation further down the track, facilitators will go to great lengths to involve participants, be patient, and draw out the hesitant or self-conscious.
- Fostering a problem-solving approach is a built-in requirement of the facilitator's work. Defining issues, prioritising, seeking strategies or solutions, and evaluating their impact on contexts or people are the major activities of facilitation.
- Communicating in the sense of trying to penetrate several 'perceptual fields' (that is, personal realities) at once is the prized skill of a facilitator.
- Judging whether the group is a work group or a group in the grip of hidden agenda is also an ongoing, highly skilled activity.

Facilitation is hardest to do well in an atmosphere of non-involvement and non-participation. If the manager is to adopt the role of facilitator (and this will become the hallmark of the next-generational manager), then an organisation which supports participative management is a must. This is elegantly described by Spencer (1989):

> Our experience in working with thousands of organisations all over the world has revealed that a new understanding of participation is emerging. This new understanding can be broken down into four basic tenets.
>
> 1 Participation is an ongoing, integrated, whole system approach.
> 2 Participation is an evolving, organic and dynamic process.
> 3 Participation is a structured process involving learnable skills.
> 4 Participation requires a commitment to openness from everyone involved.

Facilitation using new technology

Since the 1980s, facilitation has been made more effective through the development of Group Communications Technology, and in particular Group Decision Support Systems (GDSS). The GDSS process has been used extensively with the core values model mainly because of human properties of the software (Lewis 1987, Lewis and Whiteley 1992).

The new technology began as GDSS technology and is now often referred to as Group Support Systems (GSS). In addition to the whiteboard and butcher paper in the meeting room, typically there are several notebook computers and a connecting computer (called a 'chauffeur' station). The chauffeur records the ongoing contributions, and usually these are printed *in situ* and relayed during the meeting to participants. The computers are used by participants so that the ideas of several people at once can be processed simultaneously and anonymously. Two special features of GSS software are that each participant's input is anonymous and each person has equal opportunity of input. These two features have the immediate effect of:

- being able to disassociate ideas from their owners, so that the idea and not the owner is the focus of discussion; and
- being able to ensure some ownership by each individual as no one has been left out.

A typical meeting room, set up for GDSS (under the design of Meeting Works software), is shown in Figure 6.9.

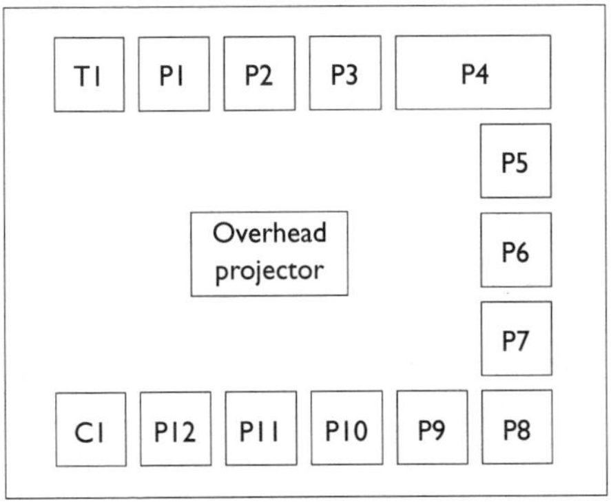

T = Timekeeping notebook
C = Chauffeur station
P = Participant notebooks

Figure 6.9 *A GDSS meeting room*

A structured process, expressed as 'tool modules' is as follows:

Generate	Electronic brainstorming
Organise	A means to discuss and organise items into categories clusters, headings and sublists
Discuss	The appropriateness and importance of items on the list
Comment	Using such things as SWOT (Strengths, Weaknesses, Opportunities and Threats) analysis, positive/negative implications of certain categories (often called the 'gut feel test' of a set of items)
Evaluate	Using a range of methods from simple voting to ranking/rating and the more complex weighted factors and multicriteria decision making (arrive at an outcome, a decision or a list of prioritised activities)
Cross impact analysis	Testing out the prioritised outcomes on the environment against other factors which could have an impact on their successful implementation
Review	An opportunity to revisit the outcome and affirm the idea of shared meaning and understanding by the meeting members

Some aspects of the technology are easily reproducible in low-tech meetings where there is basically the whiteboard and butcher paper available. These are the brainstorm, organise, discuss and simple voting elements and also, in more simple form, cross-impact analysis. Sometimes there are sensitive issues or the group which is meeting has not yet formed a high-trust environment. Then the GDSS 'anonymity' tool could be emulated by manual method such as nominal group technique (Delbecq et al. 1975). This method can also ascertain equality of inputs to help offset dominant/shy or reluctant participants. Sometimes a good process and model is almost as important as a good facilitator. This means that the supervisor and manager need to develop a repertoire of problem-solving and decision-making models and processes.

As organisations move towards participative organisational design, the employee will come into focus for training and development to learn the 'new' language and methodologies, not only of facilitation but also of many other management activities. As Emery (1993:3) suggests, a quite serious problem in achieving participative organisational and cultural redesign is 'a disregard for, or failure to perceive, concepts, an ever-present tendency towards fashions . . .'

Whether or not technology is used, it will be essential to bring together the models, frameworks, tools and techniques for culture building and culture binding. As the cases in this book show, both top management commitment and employee participation are necessary to drive the changes needed to rebuild a culture.

Useful concepts for the agent of organisational change

The following concepts have been chosen to help the supervisor or manager in the role of organisational change agent. All have arisen from a shop floor need or request. The concepts discussed are self-fulfilling prophecy, Action Research and self-development.

Self-fulfilling prophecy

The idea behind this theory of education is that if you set expectations (or prophecy) to a particular standard, you will unconsciously construct learning environments that will encourage the person to perform up or down to meet those standards. The workplace has similarities to the classroom environment in that performance is required, and attention, incentives and rewards are used.

> Rist [1970] provides a disturbing account of one teacher's behaviour in a black, urban infants classroom which was observed from the arrival of a new intake of children. Within a very short time of arrival *and without any objective evidence of the children's capabilities*, the teacher had allocated each member of her class to one of three tables which then received different work, different amounts of attention, different incentives and different rewards. The teacher had decided upon the seating location of each child on the basis of her perceptions of his/her social class origins and potential ability. Some three years later he found that almost the same differentiation existed between these children in their Grade 2 work and performance. The self-fulfilling prophecy had come true.
>
> Cohen and Manion (1981)

Trainer/Supervisor/Manager forms different expectations of trainees based on perceptions (which may not be substantiated).

↓

This will cause him/her to begin to treat apprentices/trainees/employees differently in terms of giving challenging tasks, coaching and encouraging.

↓

Trainees/employees can 'read' the prophecy from the different, often subtly so, treatment. Contextual clues and cues are used as signals of others' perception of their ability.
They respond in accordance with their 'reading' of the clues and cues, and judge their own potential as seen through Trainer/Supervisor/Manager's eyes. They will live up or down to expectations.

↓

Their behaviours and performance provide 'evidence' to the Trainer/Supervisor/Managers that their original prophecies were accurate.

↓

The outcomes of the different treatment will send some trainees/employees on an upward spiral of success but others on a downward spiral of failure.

Figure 6.10 *The flow of the self-fulfilling prophecy*

In the self-fulfilling prophecy, everything cascades down from that initial set of expectations the teacher/mentor has of the learner in the organisation (see Figure 6.10).

The evaluations of others are what we use to develop an idea of our 'self'. We accumulate evaluations of others in developing our sense of self. We develop an idea of who we are, that is constructed partly from the actions of others towards us. The unique set of interactions which each of us has with people (parents, teachers, friends, workmates) combine to give us an idea of the socially real self. Positive feedback if given authentically helps to raise self-esteem. Negatively given feedback (which is different from constructively given negative feedback) will probably lower self-esteem. So self-esteem is a social consequence of how we need to be seen in order to fulfil the expectations of others. See Figure 6.11. What does this sort of conceptualising tell us? It tells us that the self-esteem is constructed by oneself, depending on:

1 self-evaluation → self-expectations;
2 others' expectations;
3 resulting behaviour.

The growing idea of the self is fed by the responses of others to our behaviour. If the response, or feedback, is positive, the incentive to continue the behaviour is there. If it is continually reinforced, the

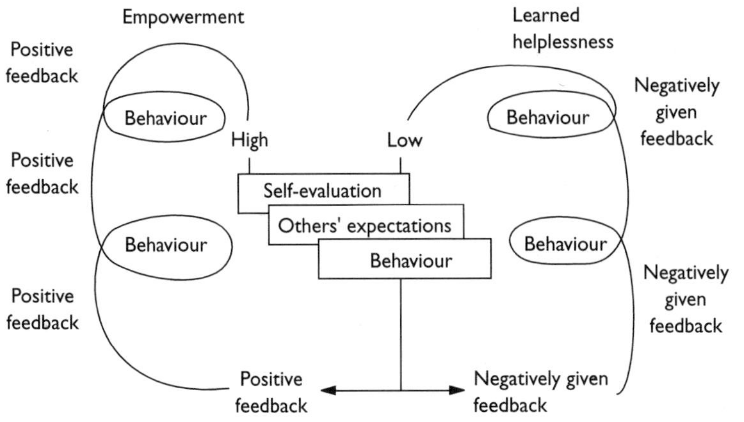

Figure 6.11 *The process of constructing self-esteem based on others' feedback*

incentive grows to the point of empowerment and, with it, a high self-esteem. Conversely, if the feedback is negative, there is a disincentive to repeat the behaviour. As negative feedback accrues, disengagement occurs so that the self becomes dependent on others in the certainty of a low self-esteem. In such a situation, low expectations of others from oneself could produce a self-fulfilling prophecy of failure.

Action Research

Action research in an organisational setting is usually described as a small-scale intervention in the functioning of the real world of work. This is an activity which is connected to any endeavour to introduce change in an organisation. It involves a close examination of the effects of the change intervention. Action research is basically an on-the-spot procedure to deal with a problem, a change or an issue in a specific location. An underlying idea is that the best way to know how something works is when you try to change it. The research is undertaken within the organisation by those doing the work or involved in the problem/issue. The researcher role involves a systematic process. The theory is rooted in participation and group planning, and pays particular attention to group dynamics (Tyson 1989:49; Dick 1991).

Characteristics of Action Research

Action Research is characterised by the following:

- It is practical.
- It is directly relevant to what causes change relationships.

- It produces functional and process knowledge (rather than theoretically rigorous knowledge).
- It is compatible with problem-solving techniques.
- It is empirical (based on observations, not on hypothetical, behaviour).
- It should be flexible and adaptive because it is part of a dynamic, ongoing situation.
- Because the 'researcher' is also a participant (part of the work situation), it is almost impossible to take an abstract/detached approach (something usually gets done).

An Action Research Process, suggested by Robbins, will be useful here. Robbins (1993b:678) defines Action Research as a change process based on a systematic collection of data, and then selection of a change action based on what the analysed data indicate. Its importance lies in providing a scientific methodology for managing planned change.

The process of Action Research consists of the following five steps:

1 Diagnosis	Information is gathered about problems, concerns and needed changes from members of the organisation.
2 Analysis	Information gathered at the diagnostic stage is then analysed. What problems do people key on? What patterns do these problems seem to take? The change agent [action researcher] synthesises this information into primary concerns, problem areas and possible actions.
3 Feedback	What has been found from steps 1 and 2 is shared with employees. The employees, with the help of the change agent, develop action plans for bringing about any needed change.
4 Action	Now the 'Action' part of the research is set in motion. The employees and the change agent carry out specific actions to correct the problems that have been identified.
5 Evaluation	The change agent evaluates the effectiveness of the action plans. Using the initial data as points of reference, any subsequent changes can be compared and evaluated.

Self-development

Personal strategy and goal setting is one method of becoming insulated against, and prepared for, sudden or radical change. This is because the lifelong learning orientation is not directed at, for example, one single structure, company or technique at work. Rather, it is directed at how a person habitually reacts within work situations with a view to changing undesired habits and retaining desired ones. Looking at how one becomes aware of oneself reacting to negative criticism, say defensively or aggressively and working out how to change this to agreement, acceptance or perhaps rationalisation, would be an example of self-development.

The central aspects of self-development need to be addressed before management development can really get underway. They include:

- an acceptance of the self as the source of motivation for learning;
- a belief in self-initiated action;
- a recognition that basically the self is the major decision maker in the learning or development process;
- a willingness of the self to take responsibility for decisions at all stages of the learning process;
- a self-independence towards using resources on a needs or opportunity basis;
- a willingness to give and gain the experience and learning that comes through group interaction;
- recognition that connections and modifications will need to be made between what is formally taught, say off-the-job, and what is reality back on-the-job;
- a desire to grow and develop, never being content with current abilities and capabilities.

Such a focus will empower the individual so that there is a growing independence in searching out and satisfying his or her own developmental needs. Suggested building blocks for self-development are shown in Figure 6.12.

A suggested model for self-development is the OKX model (Whiteley 1991). It is based on the premise that many managers will continually refine skills and techniques at which they are excellent (X) already. Conversely, they will (unintentionally and usually unknowingly) ignore skills at which they are not so good. To use the OKX model, design it into your daily organisational life. For example, take a range of activities which you seem to be doing fairly constantly, such as those

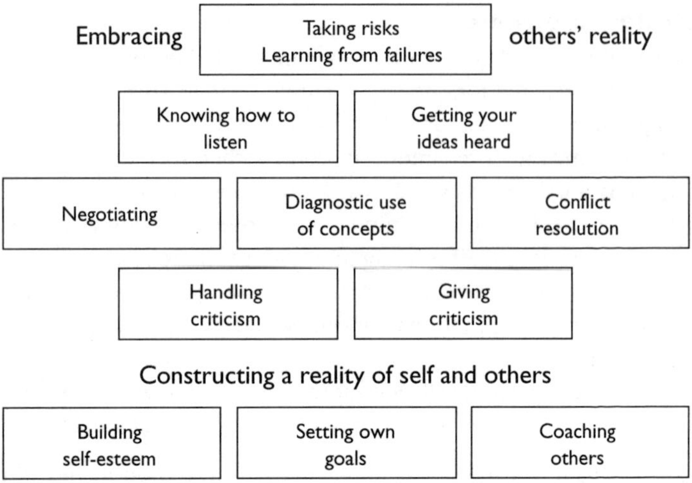

Figure 6.12 *Suggested building blocks for self-development*

Table 6.2 *Matrix of activities and self-development goals*

	Dealing with customers	Running a planning session	Member of disputes committee	Liaison with opposite number in another department
Analysing	√	√	√	
Listening	√	√	√	√
Negotiating	√	√	√	√
Building your esteem	√	√	√	√
Accepting criticism				
Taking risks		√	√	
Giving criticism				
Coaching		√	√	√

in Table 6.2, and put them in a matrix with some self-development goals.

It is clear from Table 6.2 here that the individual is consistently avoiding the whole criticism issue. Perhaps in the past, adverse experiences have been felt on the giving or receiving end of criticism. Perhaps the problem is cultural. Criticism causes loss of 'face' and so it is to be culturally avoided. If the cultural norms do not reject overt criticism activities and the individual is using an avoidance strategy, this is valuable information for self-development. It is clear in any supervisory role in which giving feedback is a central responsibility. If the cultural norms reject confrontation, however sensitive, then the supervisor/employee needs to make sure that criticism opportunities are grasped in the more informal situation. Alternatively, adopting strategies, such as using a mediator, third party or agent, allow objectives of feedback and culture to be satisfied.

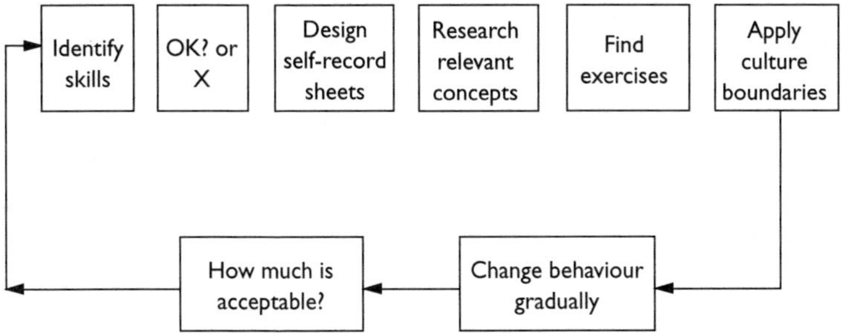

Figure 6.13 *OKX methodology*

The methodology follows a process such as that shown in Figure 6.13. This methodology gives managers and employees the independence to choose at least some aspects of their personal key result areas. Choices can be based on organisational circumstances and personal aspirations. Any source — academic, a practical role model or mentor — can be used as a resource to be 'dipped into' for knowledge, advice and guidance. As the learning is work-driven, the worry about ivory-tower theories becomes less likely. As the goal is initiated and developed by the manager for use in work, the worry about transferability of learning is almost removed.

Learning concepts

The learning concepts discussed in this section are the concepts of paradigm, attribution, perception, international culture and performance versus control.

The concept of paradigm

The concept of paradigm will be known to readers under many guises. Some will call it a 'mental model'. Some will call it a 'mindset'. Employees often use such terms as 'tunnel vision' and 'blinkers' to describe a colleague or manager's strongly held paradigm. All these descriptions are acceptable. A paradigm is a mental model but the model also dictates the right way to go about things. The rules of a paradigm dictate what it is legitimate to study and to question. It is a working theory which produces principles and, at the practical level, standard operating procedures. The following example below is one where a paradigm has been translated into a theory of management:

> When Max Weber based today's 'theory of bureaucracy' on principles of authoritarian hierarchy as the industrial age began, the concept was revolutionary because it brought great gains in rationality, efficiency, and order. Now it means almost exactly the opposite: irrational adherence to petty rules, inefficient and wieldy systems, and disregard for mounting chaos. The most damning thing a critic can say about an organisation today is to call it a 'bureaucracy'.
>
> Halal, Geranmayer and Pourdehnad (1993:4)

The power of a paradigm is evident by the very staying power it has, even when its principles and rules are obviously inappropriate. The power is evident in the struggle of managers who are trying to introduce new and enabling paradigms but find themselves locked in to the seeming rightness of the old paradigm. The old idea of bosses, of subordinates and superordinates, and of language such as 'reporting to your superior' appear unwittingly. A failure to recognise and work to change one's own paradigm could mean that designs such as horizontal structures, quality circles and networks are round pegs in square holes. They just don't fit. They take on the status of a fad or fashion. They cause the well-known groan of despair: 'Oh no, not another of the latest guru's recipe's'. Paradigms are foundations upon which the building blocks of the organisation rest. Often the response to changes in the environment is to replace the blocks without attacking the foundations. In the Australian Public Sector (APS) the risk of this is clear. The 'iron rice bowl' paradigm of security coupled with principles of rational and impersonal efficiency is no longer suitable for the goals of the APS (McCarrey et al. 1993).

There is an emerging paradigm that is well suited to the aspirations of the espoused goals of the APS of the future, which includes strategies such as competitive tendering and a strong market and customer-driven focus. It is the *internal market paradigm* (Bennis 1966; Halal, Geranmayer and Pourdehnad 1993).

> Internal markets are *meta* structures or *super* structures that transcend ordinary organisational structures. Rather than being fixed structures, they are *systems* designed to produce continual, rapid, structural change to manage the unusual demands of today's complex, turbulent world.
>
> Halal, Geranmayer and Pourdehnad 1993:4

The concept can be translated into a model, mindset or paradigm. The idea is to think of markets and market sectors instead of the traditional hierarchical organisational structure. Thinking about how much flatter or higher the organisation should be is often a reaction to prosperity and even management fads and fashions. This is not the way marketers think of their market segments or sectors in the long term. Rather, they set out to sense and service their customers' needs, and in doing so to understand how the customers perceive the world. Instead of thinking of how much difference in structure and process should be designed, the need is to rethink altogether. In the market situation the market is controlled by market forces, rather than attempted controls over consumer choice.

The critical factor is whether an organisation merely changes its theory of management or whether it challenges its own assumptions and indeed its philosophy about the true nature of work, management and employees as consumers of the organisational product. Are some of the common phrases we hear such as the need to be customer focused, to have a customer charter, and to give excellent service accompanied by organisational structures and reward systems to match? In the Australian Public Sector (APS), people still often define themselves as a 'level three' and so on rather than by the role and contribution currently being made. The APS appears to be talking about a new paradigm when it outlines radical new theories of management (Western Australia, Parliament, 1994) but it could be that the new policies are an attempt to loosen up a rather institutionalised Public Sector. In other words are we seeing a new paradigm or not?

The answer is important because paradigms have very practical consequences. If the paradigm has changed, then it is at this level that employees and managers need to be given the whole picture. People instinctively ask why: Why are we going into competition with the outside world? Why are we losing our security? Why are the requests to be creative, innovative and autonomous being made when reward hierarchies are the same and the decisions about pay, work times and reporting systems are still made by 'superiors' on our behalf? In the absence of a strong paradigmitic or mindset statement at the very outset of organisational change, the way is left open for as many attributed motives for change as there are people to implement it.

If vestiges of old power, control and authority systems are kept in place at the same time as new principles are installed, then either there is not a real change in mindset, or there is and the process of change has not begun with organisational design. The nature of managerial work needs to be rethought. New tools, methods and competencies need to be developed. An organisational design which is in harmony with the internal market paradigm is the profit centre with an emphasis on profit sharing. Managers, contrary to the fearful comments to be heard, do, or can, have a role in the internal market paradigm. They, as well as leaders, are 'keepers of the values' of an organisation. They can take roles as educators, mentors, facilitators and advisors; in other words they can see to the learning within the organisation. Planning or launching change then cannot be separated from the concept of paradigm. A paradigmitic change is a change in philosophy and assumptions (Whiteley and Levantard 1994).

It follows that the existing value base from which the organising principles flow, and from which the mission is defined in its particular way, will represent a different mindset from the one needed to succeed in the new reality. Simply put, a cultural change will be necessary. If it is deep cultural change as in the case of classical bureaucracy to internal markets, then correspondingly deep and enduring mechanisms need to be put in place so that the change can take place over time. Replacing personal paradigms or mental models is what the organisations in the bureaucracy case would be asking employees and managers to do. This can be *learned* to some extent but it should also be *felt*. That is why the developmental needs for managers should include developing methodologies for releasing the imaginal and emotional, using tools of culture binding to develop shared vision, and recognising that strategy implementation rests upon being able to answer 'why' questions convincingly at the philosophical level (a level which employees are heard to operate at much of the time). It also rests upon ownership and commitment, the two going hand in hand. Development needs for everyone should include developing synergy — allowing differences to become a valued extension of each other — rather than championing one's own perspective.

The concept of paradigm is an appropriate one to lead into Part II of the book. As well as the learning devices such as roles and questions which accompany the cases, an overall approach of thinking about the paradigms of the organisations involved and the various ways in which new models and principles are imparted would be a good way to use the case material and methodology.

The concept of attribution

It is not possible to 'see' another person's thinking, motivation or decision-making processes. All we can see is that person's actions or behaviour. The actions or behaviour act as the clue behind the thinking or intention. This forces us to infer what the person means or intends by the outward action.

Attribution theory suggests that we attribute meaning to other people's actions from within our own framework (or construct of meaning). Furthermore, we judge people differently, according to the meaning we give to a set of behaviours. In particular, we attempt to see whether the behaviour was internally caused (that is, under the control of the individual) or externally caused (that is, as a response, often forced, to outside pressures). Before making the judgment we would see whether the person's behaviour was distinctively different from normal, was consistent over time with normal behaviour, and was different from others' behaviour in the same circumstances. If the person showed poor performance and this became the normal pattern for him/her, and others with a similar set of circumstances consistently performed better, then the person might well be judged to be responsible for the poor performance. If, however, the person normally performed well and at the level of others, and the poor performance was distinctively different from his/her usual performance, then one could look to outside causes (such as the stresses of a change program or fear of redundancy) as a likely cause of the behaviour.

This theory is vitally important because if problem behaviours are attributed to the person's internal ability, effort and/or motivation then real causes of poor performance could remain undetected. These could include poor supervision, an inhospitable climate for the person's cultural needs, poor materials/machinery or management interventions such as training or change programs. Attributions are judgments. What can cause errors of judgment? What has been found in organisational life is that there is a tendency to overestimate internal factors (that is, the problem is with the person) and underestimate the external factors (that is, the problem is with our systems and processes) (Kelley 1972). This is called *fundamental error*. There is the tendency for individuals to attribute success to internal factors such as ability and effort, and failures to external factors such as bad luck or things like 'the supervisor has it in for me'.

What does this mean for managers? Basically it means that the same phenomenon, such as poor performance, cannot be attributed to the same cause in two cases. Each case needs to be carefully investigated to see the plausibility of the attribution being made concerning the particular employee's behaviour. In order to do this the manager will need to understand the concepts of perception and selective perception.

Perception

Perception is like an individual lens. The lens is self-built and is a particular way of looking at the world which results from how individuals filter and process information through the senses. See Figure 2.4. The way someone might process the scene of an accident at work to give it a unique meaning might be different if he/she was a safety officer, a mate of the injured person or the company nurse. The role of the person is only one factor which determines how we construct our own individual realities or perceptions. Past experiences colour the interpretation of information coming in. Take the introduction of change as an example. Say, in the recent past, change was introduced as the new long-term opportunity for everyone to become empowered and enabled. Let's say that in practice the structures and processes which preserved the status and decision-making power of the chosen few were retained. The next time a change strategy was introduced it may not be interpreted in the same trusting way as the previous one by some individuals (but it may by others).

Take three people walking around a factory. One is a personnel manager, one is a production engineer and one is the young male operative who is showing them around. They see a young attractive girl in tears at her machine and several colleagues are gathered around. The personnel manager may be interested in what the behaviour symbolises and see the supportiveness of the colleagues as a central feature of the scenario. The production engineer may be interested in the costs of downtime and he/she may see the scenario in terms of the lost production consequences by counting the number of people (production units) who are off the job. The young operative may perceive the distress of the girl and her need for (his) comfort as the thing that figures most in the scene. The features that stand out are 'figure'. Those which have melted into the background are 'ground'. One person's figure may be another person's ground. Therefore, it is not possible to see any event or activity in organisations as it is. It is necessary to see the event or activity as the other person construes or perceives it. Other things which colour the perceptions are personality, values, beliefs, attitudes, culture, stereotypes, contexts and how people dress and speak.

Of particular interest to managers is the way people *selectively perceive*. The concept is called *selective perception*. Our processing abilities are the way we filter information and incoming messages. Like panning for gold, the question is what is going to be filtered through as dust and rubbish and what will remain as nuggets of gold. The message that is sent through one person's filter may be perceived as important, clear and of interest to the receiving person. The receiver, filtering the message through his/her own filter may *select out* the key points intended by the sender and *select* such things as the imputed motives of the person sending the message, the reputation of the sender and even the medium through which the message is sent. The task of the manager is to make sure that the essential elements of messages are not selected out by the receiver. This means acknowledging that a communication does not take place when the message is sent but when the sender has some confirmation of meaning from the receiver. It also means that it is necessary for the sender and receiver of a communication to enter into the world of meaning of each other. A message needs to be encoded so that the receiver can decode it through his/her perceptual lens. This means that managers need to research their internal clients (that is, employees) for their ways of 'seeing' organisational information.

International culture

This book has emphasised culture at the organisational level. There is another level which affects how people at work might perceive the same phenomena differently. This is culture at the societal level. A good example of this is that in Australia people would talk about fairness, justice and equity. They talk about these values both implicitly and explicitly. We could say that they are the cornerstones of Australian society. One obvious way to see this in action is to take note of how pay structures are designed. The ground rules are that systems should be (and be seen to be) objective, equitable and relatively fair. How the concept of fairness is derived may be different in almost all cases, but the fact that organisations will try to arrive at fair processes and outcomes will be common to most. In other countries such as those with a Confucian ethic and especially in organisations which are 'traditional', the value of fairness may be irrelevant. The value of harmony and 'face' may be of more influence in shaping peoples' perceptions of quality of working life.

Hofstede (1980) has offered a way of testing some important dimensions of cultures, one against the other. He uses four dimensions: individualism/collectivism, power distance, uncertainty avoidance, and masculinity/femininity. These were derived from responses from 160 000 managers in one multinational organisation. (This may sound a little biased but the theory has since stood up to worldwide scrutiny.) There are other dimensions which you would want to study if you managed or did business in Asia, such as *modes of activity* ('doing' or 'being'), *time orientation* (does the organisation do business from the point of view of building on past relationships and future relationships or does it operate in the here and now?), and *space* (how is space used — privately, publicly or to give people prestige/take prestige away?) However, the four dimensions Hofstede defines are very useful for diagnosing differences in outlook between people of other nationalities.

Individualism/Collectivism

How do people define themselves. Do they define themselves as individuals or as a collective persona? The answer is prescribed by the social rules of society. In an individualist society, one can imagine that a preschool child would be rewarded and recognised for finding his/her way, say, to the correct coat peg or maybe the library shelf. If the child asked to take a little friend along, this may be allowed but the intention would be to make him/her independent as soon as possible. The idea is to look after oneself and, as one grows older, immediate family and friends. Not so in the collectivist society. Here there are both tight social groupings which carry reciprocal responsibilities and, on a wider scale, the notion of becoming involved in any team or group enterprise which is needed for a purpose. The small child would be seen holding hands with at least two other children and would be rarely seen not doing so. Finding things out would be done together and the reward would be for sticking together.

How are members 'controlled'? In an individualist society, personal achievement is rewarded; the idea of one universal set of values for all to aspire to (such as democracy) is to be shared. Self-determination as well as personal performance are the bedrock of organisational values. Self-respect is important. Therefore, controls are usually internal such as guilt.

In a collectivist society, the emphasis is on facilitating group performance. The Japanese have a saying that the nail which sticks out will be pounded down. People expect that group members will support them, help them and share with them and in return they will receive succour and support from the group. Tell a person from a collectivist society that she/he did a wonderful job, especially when group members are there. First the person will feel a loss of face and then will vehemently refute the compliment saying something like 'Oh no, it was a team effort. I only played a small part'. Control is simple — shame. This is externally imposed, and a lacking in the collectivist (or caring for the group) area would disturb the natural harmony of things. The punishment is that the person loses 'face'.

Power distance (high or low)

A typical low-power distance situation is where the tea trolley person gets into the lift with the CEO. This is a good opportunity to tell the CEO what is currently wrong with the organisation, how to do it better and what might be preventing things from working. The CEO would not take this amiss and may even use the information selectively. There is a sense of egalitarianism and this seems particularly evident in Australia.

A typical high-power distance situation would be where the only person to approach would be an immediate 'superior'. This would be accepted as legitimate as much by those at the power-receiving end as the power-wielding end. High-power members accept unequal distribution of power and also accept that this carries responsibilities of support and 'buffering' by those higher up the hierarchy.

How can you do a simple test for this? To what extent is it acceptable to bypass the boss and go higher up? In a low-power situation this would be much more tolerated than in a high-power situation.

Uncertainty avoidance (high or low)

How much do people feel threatened by ambiguous situations? Those who feel highly threatened are said to have a high level of uncertainty avoidance. An observation of many human resource management systems is that they may well exist to prevent ambiguity (rather than achieve strategic goals). High-uncertainty avoidance is characterised by documentation, standing orders, formal administration systems, tenured/secure jobs and an evident desire for stability. Low-uncertainty avoidance is characterised by a high tolerance for ambiguous outcomes and often a tolerance for less formal administration systems.

Masculinity/Femininity

Masculinity would be a high degree of assertiveness, the acquisition of material things and often an objective approach to people and relationships. Femininity emphasises the 'soft' or people-oriented aspects of relationships and there would be a blurring of the male/female role categorisation.

These dimensions solve some of the mysteries about why some people respond to the same managerial initiatives in different ways. In particular, reward systems can gravely offend people if they are geared to group instead of individual performance and vice versa. The familiar, easygoing Management By Walking About (MBWA) would be highly offensive in a high-power distance situation, especially if you try to break down barriers (when barriers are the thing employees prefer). Imposing things such as performance appraisal forms in a low-uncertainty environment would probably accrue lip service and in certain cultures a tendency to protect the other's 'face' by giving an average score. The lip service would be because there would probably be more fluid informal (less certain) methods in operation. Where management is highly logical and rational, characterised by systems rather than relationships, it would be best to ensure that employees actually do prefer the more masculine type of existence.

Hofstede's book gives the findings of around sixty countries (and this can and should be taken as indicative only). The benefit is that the dimensions do reflect values which are relatively stable aspects of life.

The concept of performance versus control (by David Napoli)

In managing organisations we make a fundamental choice. Do we want performance or do we want control? Most people will respond by saying they want performance. However, when their structures, processes and behaviours are analysed it becomes obvious that control is what they are seeking. Take organisational colleagues talking of the bottom line and budgets. These are usually used to express control. They are attempts to bring certainty and predicability into our organisations. There are some fundamental differences between control and performance which are expressed through organisations in the ways shown in Table 6.3.

Table 6.3 *Control-focused and performance-focused organisations*

Control-focused organisations	Performance-focused organisations
• Organisation pyramids value control above all else. Organisations are inward looking. Predicability is valued.	• Focus is on the customer and organisations are outward looking. Improvements are always being sought. Responsiveness is valued.
• Whole departments are created for control purposes.	• There is reduced or eliminated dependence on inspection.
• To lose control is to lose everything.	• To give control is to get control.
• As long as we are in control who cares what else is happening?	• Focus is on service and contribution to the whole.
• External controls are emphasised.	• Self control is emphasised.
• There are rules (which are inflexible).	• There are guidelines (which allow flexibility).
• 'No surprises' leads to the illusion of control.	• Surprise is essential to high performance. All learning is preceded by ignorance, followed by surprise. It is surprise that develops energy and motivation.
• People avoid individual responsibility.	• People act as if it is their business. They don't blame the boss, system or the product.
• Performance assessment is from above to someone.	• It is appreciated that in reality we know it is not possible to accurately plan and predict. The individual seeks assessment from customers and participants in the process.
• We feel our survival is in the hands of others.	• Our survival is in our hands.

Refer to Chapter 13, 'A new regional bank'.

Part II

The cases

7
Introduction to the cases

Part II practises the ideas and concepts in the first part of the book. The intention is to make you, the reader, part of a living case. In some of the cases you will find a role and problem set out in the boxed text. In other cases you may be asked questions. Each of these cases is real. Each is current. Each of the organisations is embarked on a journey of creative change. Therefore, by taking a role and answering questions, you can take full advantage of simulation.

The companies and people who have so generously contributed their experiences share one thing in common. They have a dedication and commitment to transforming the human endeavour in work to one of mutual profit. Some have proved that there is still a place for trade unions. All would agree that the conventional role of the manager has gone. They have also proved that to compete with the rest of the world, almost every role in organisational life as we know it needs to be redefined. The P.I.C.S. (WA) case shows that sometimes it is necessary to start again.

The cases demonstrate the top manager's role as a visionary and culture builder. The case organisations also exude the idea of 'continuous'. Without exception, the people in every case in this book gained real learning from self-appraisal; from dealing with problems; and from a willingness to try, to risk and, in some cases, to pick themselves up and start again in the face of what could be termed depressing drawbacks and resistance.

Case study method

The case study method has become a valuable learning device to expand and *extend the experience* of people far beyond the scope of their daily work experiences. It allows simulations and experiments to be developed and tested without running the risk of bearing the consequences. (This is both a strength and a weakness, of course, as the release from living with the consequences can make for more bravado than may be wise. It is a caution that nothing can replace the need for careful analysis of all aspects of change management in real situations.) The case method is more than an example or exercise to illustrate some proved theory. Indeed, in this book some of the case organisations are actually contributing to the formulation of new and emerging theories of managing change within their industries.

A value added in case work is the opportunity to see *what worked and what didn't work* and some likely causes. These causes can range from environmental (social, economic, political and legal) pressures put on the organisation, to internal pressures such as people, resources, structures and systems or 'soft' causes such as mindsets/paradigms. Using cases allows us to rehearse things such as criticising people or their actions without the people being there. Testing various methods of giving sensitive feedback in a case study group is relatively safe. Studying cases is best done in group settings. Here, various preferred solutions can be sounded out among diverse personalities (and set against the solutions chosen by the case organisations). Also, conflict which certain suggestions may produce within a group can allow *feeling* as well as *thinking* to enrich the study.

Because of the need to chart the way through a case, often having to fill in gaps and imagine information that is not explicitly given, the linear approach and the 'one solution' are discouraged. The idea is to generate as much data as possible about the situation including ideas and concepts as well as the facts as they appear. Problems can be identified. Then, and this works well in a group setting, *a range of possible solutions* are generated and the solution most likely to be accepted for implementation (rather than the one which is administratively perfect) can be tentatively suggested.

Each reader or group is expected to have a special area of interest, as the organisation is going through a particular type of change. The models appropriate to that interest, such as the problem-solving example given later in the chapter, will be useful. However, experience shows that the following activities are central to the ability to study cases (Tang and Whiteley 1991:18) whatever the perspective:

- situational analysis/problem identification;
- data collection, analysis and synthesis;
- analytical and critical thinking (Whiteley and Levantard 1994);
- intuitive thinking and imagining;
- willingness to challenge assumptions;
- ability to make judgments;
- prediction of a range of outcomes, not only the logical ones;
- ability to make decisions and consider likely outcomes;
- appreciation of 'soft' systems and processes such as culture building/communication/information/climate building and the ability to transmit ideas and concepts;
- commitment to the monitoring and evaluation of decision processes and outcomes.

Figure 7.1 shows how the individual and the organisation come together, often through work groups, to provide input to the solution of problems. As they do, the undercurrent of organisational life means that the managers need to have sensitive behavioural competencies.

A sequential process for studying cases would include the following:

- Scan the environment to take in the background, variables and contextual impressions.
- Decide the nature of the issue or problem that has faced the case organisation.
- Work out the type of influences and impacts upon the problem/issue. Are they environmental, people-oriented, resource-related, structural or a mixture?
- Apply the creative problem-solving method to generate some alternative courses of action or problem solution.
- Predict the likely outcome of one solution over another, taking into account the organisational culture and climate.
- Estimate the resources, organisational design systems and climate needed for this solution to work.
- Envisage any implementation problems and how they might be resolved.

Although the above points are generic to case study, the cases in this book have been chosen to fit the themes of managing change through culture building, resting on a core values framework.

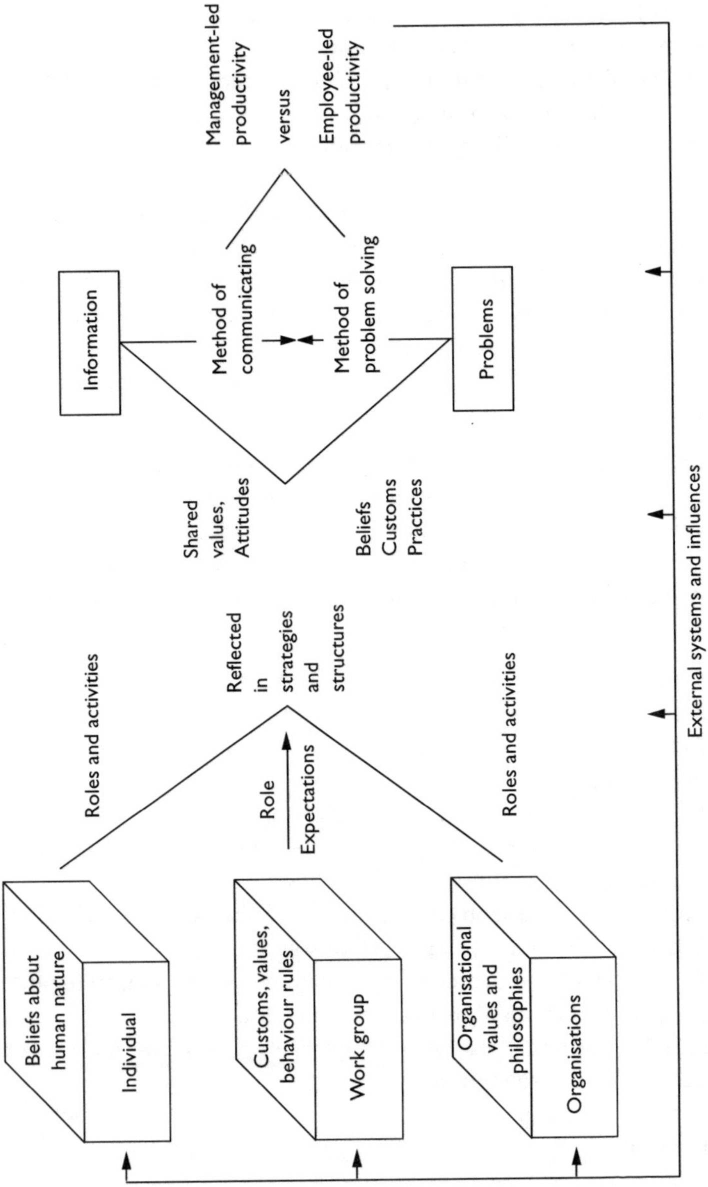

Figure 7.1 *Individual, work groups and the organisation come together*

Tips for using the following cases

The following tips are particularly suited to this book's theory and cases. There are two types of case in this book. One type is where cases are designed in two parts: the problem and the outcome. The first part invites the reader to take a role in the case organisation. She/he is invited to 'see' the organisation and the way it has developed. As a learning point, the reader is invited to stop and develop some plan or solution to the case so far. This is an essential part of the learning. To avoid the frustration of not knowing what came next or how the reader's ideas match the organisation decisions, the second part (the outcome) of the case is an account of what actually happened. The second type of case is a descriptive case history where the organisational experiences are described and questions are asked.

The theme of this book is managing change, particularly change in organisational values. Each case needs to be examined with the core values in mind. It would be useful, therefore, to have this copy of the core values model ready when going through the stages of analysis and problem solving, which is a feature of the case study method. See Figure 7.2.

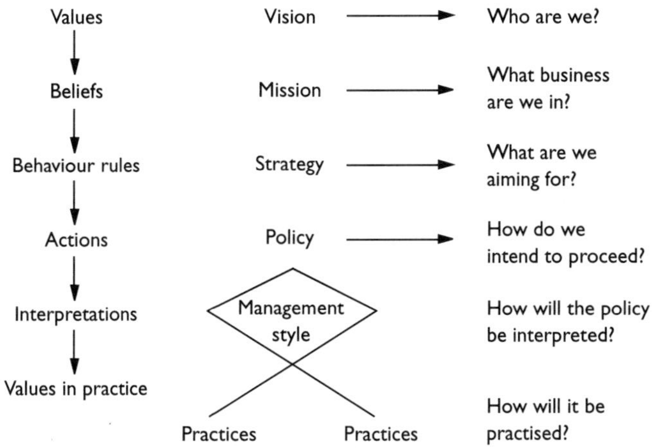

Figure 7.2 *Organisational and management style*

There is also an implied relationship with strategic change as an organisation changes its culture. A change in culture is no less than radical change (Dalmau and Dick 1991). A useful tip here is to think of tactical or incremental change as change which can operate *within* the current culture, structures and systems/processes that is the mental model or paradigm.

More radical change which is going to transform the very heart of the organisation will require that changes are installed *outside* the current culture, structures, systems/processes and paradigm. It will be unlikely that deep change can be made while retaining traditional power and authority structures, and functionally bounded systems and processes. Analysis of these cases will entail using some imagination. From a few short sentences in the case history about what the previous management scenario was, it will be possible to build up an idea of how the past and prevailing paradigm affected and pervaded the aspect in which you, the reader, are particularly interested. What is the legacy or 'baggage' left by the old paradigm? It will be helpful in doing this to refer back to, or make notes about, the various management paradigms which we in the developed world have inherited. It is essential to remember at all times that on-the-surface responses about changes to new paradigms can be deceptive. The values established in building other cultures will have been translated into operating systems and 'institutionalised' into daily practices.

To reinforce this it would be useful to take each of the major human resource functions and apply the 'rules' of the prevailing paradigm (for example, Taylorist 'rules' suggest that 'workers are rational/economic beings'; 'managers think/workers do'; and 'one best way'). The major functions would include recruitment and selection, socialisation, work redesign, and the 'performance three' (training/development, performance appraisal, reward system), as well as soft systems such as culture-building, communication, motivation and leadership.

Problem-solving example

An example would be to take recruitment and selection where the prevailing paradigm was one where 'managers should manage and workers should get on with the work'. The paradigm would be well expressed in Emery's Design Principle 1 (see Figure 7.3).

In keeping with this paradigm, recruitment and selection would be a 'remote from the shop floor' activity. A typical scenario would be where a department is asked for its staffing levels for the month/year. The staffing would be expressed in terms of functional tasks or trades, for example X welders, Y labourers and Z typists. The recruiting section may judiciously rearrange the figures submitted by departments on the

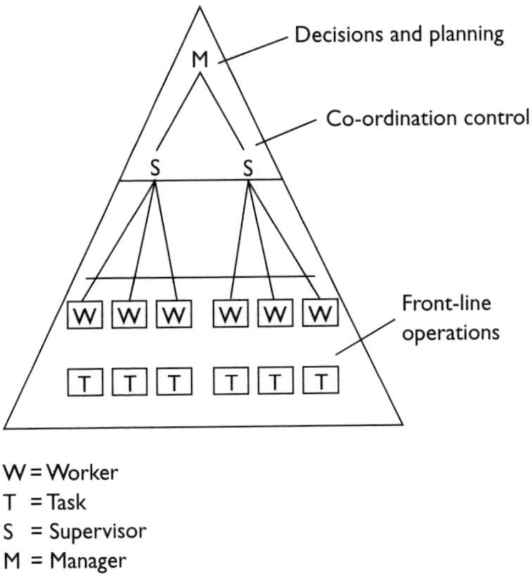

Figure 7.3 *Design Principle I (hierarchy principle)*

basis that people always ask for more than they need in case they are given less. There would be job descriptions, usually based on KAS (knowledge, attitude, skill), and these would be translated into internal and external advertisements. There would be little investigation into the values of the proposed applicant at this level. Little attention would be paid to the culture and norms of the placement group. There may be reference to the 'staffing plan', but it is unlikely that recruitment and recruitee requirements would be linked to the strategic plan.

From the outset the recruiting people, work-group members and prospective candidate are dancing alone and to different music. The aim of the recruiters is to produce a valid and reliable system. The aim of the work group is to do the best with what it is given and then hope. The aim of the applicant is to get a job first and then to penetrate the mysteries of the workplace as soon as possible. (Of course, the work group then has a clear field for socialisation into group goals. This is because, in the absence of an open communication system about organisational goals, the group becomes the main source of information after the first few days or weeks of induction.)

Good case questions arising from seeing the paradigm in action would be about who owns the recruitment process; who matches the needs of the job and group to those of the applicant; and who is conveying the initial set of expectations about work life at this organisation and are they the same people who will be satisfying them? The answers need to be set against an optimal way to recruit people in another paradigm and compare the two against some benchmarked or Best Practice standards described in the cases.

Before going on to the step-by-step approach to case analysis, it is important to know which perspectives are of particular interest and which models help the analysis process. For example, if the perspective was problem solving it would be useful to have a creative problem-solving model ready to apply to the cases.

Whetton and Cameron (1991:189) outline stages of creative problem solving as preparation, incubation, illumination and verification.

Preparation entails a flexible approach to data gathering, problem definition and the generation and exploration of alternatives. These processes are also used by 'rational' problem solvers but are generally constrained by such things as a logical, linear and factual approach to problem elements. With creative problem solving, the bizarre is a candidate for the feasible and the imagination with its fun side and far-ranging scope is unleashed in the vicinity of the problem. 'Flexibility in thinking is critical to good problem solving. A problem solver should be able to dance around the problem like a good boxer, jabbing and poking, without getting caught in one place or "fixated"' (Whetton and Cameron 1991).

With problem recognition the question is whether the problem is a symptom or a problem which needs to be solved. If it is a problem and it can be identified, can it be classified, that is, given a name? Several techniques can be used for this purpose; for example, focus groups, data analysis, force field analysis, and problem-related key words analysis. Each of these techniques has a central goal, which is to flag or signal the nature of the problem by giving it a name. Connected to this stage are causes and issues — what are the causal connections (until the root causes are discovered).

Exploring alternative solutions in creative problem solving means letting the intuition come in and allowing an *incubation* stage 'in which the mind combines unrelated thoughts in the pursuit of a solution. *Illumination* . . . occurs when an insight is recognised and a creative solution is articulated. *Verification* . . . involves evaluating the creative solution relative to some standard of acceptability' (Whetton and Cameron 1991:189).

If studying the theory and cases in this book from a problem-solving perspective, it will prove useful to have a problem-solving methodology to hand. It will be equally useful to have a strategic change, communication, information technology or organisational design model, if these are the perspective(s) of interest.

Step-by-step method

The step-by-step method below is suggested as an additional way of approaching the cases.

Step one

Read over the case story ('the problem' in the two-part cases) and jot down the general details, for example:

- This is a food manufacturer.
- It is small to medium.
- It is paternalistic, still in the reins of the original entrepreneur, but is it getting too big?
- Trade unionised relations are not so good — will have to change.
- It is a fairly mature organisation.
- It seems keen to change.
- I am picking up an atmosphere of co-operation.
- I can sense problems looming ahead on the reward front.
  etc.

You are looking for an overview and a sense of what is being depicted as the story develops.

Step two

What seems to be the plot? What does the company seem to be striving for? What is the vision and mission (if they are apparent)? What are the forces that are driving the change? Can you relate them to your own or imagined experiences? What might be the case as seen from the different perspectives of workers, managers, trade unions and customers? Are there likely to be any mismatch of expectations or values, and if so at which level in the core values model are they likely to be?

Step three

Analyse the following in more detail:

Values	What are the espoused values? Are they imposed by senior management or constructed by the key stakeholding groups?

Strategies	Do the strategies harmonise with the values? Who owns them and why? How are they (a) generated and (b) communicated? Do the methods reflect the values?
Structures	Are the structures authoritarian, hierarchical or moving towards participative and horizontal? Do participative styles stop short of rearranging the hierarchies of control?
Systems	Are the systems technical in nature, with people managed as in the engineering metaphor, where the utmost accuracy and precision is sought and there is little tolerance of error? or Are they social where there is a strong emphasis on relationships? or Are they socio-technical — a blend of both? or Are they participative and heading towards being democratic?
Processes	How are things done? Are the processes ones which will gain the sort of climate needed to achieve strategic goals?
People	Who are the major players? Are employees included as key stakeholding groups? Are relationships in keeping with optimising the human resource or is most of the learning still done by managers?
Roles	Is there a McGregor's (1960) Theory X or Theory Y interpretation of management/worker roles? Are people likely to take the roles they are given or can you see why they would make them into something else?

Step four

What are the strengths and weaknesses of the organisation as you have analysed it, concerning what you, in your given role or through questions, have been asked to do?

Step five

Produce your plans, suggestions and so forth as requested in your role brief or questions.

Step six

This step applies only to the two-part cases. Compare your solutions with the outcome — what the company did. What might you do differently in terms perhaps of timing, the items in step three or other decisions the case reflects?

Step seven

Extract learning points, methods and reading references. Support your points with theories (which can also be tested against contemporary management practices).

Step eight

Reread Part I and place the models and concepts in concrete settings. This will happen continuously rather than in a step. It is better to cross-reference the book and cases on a consultative basis.

Step nine

Reflect and develop your own models and working theories, which you can then test both in your organisation and against management theory. In particular, this should be possible in the areas of culture building and managing change.

Step ten

Check against the core skills and process outlined in the case study introduction and see which have been exercised in studying the cases.

Notes for managers

The book in general and the cases in particular help the manager to move from the general work of vision and mission statements to the specifics of what to do about them once they have been generated.

The cases are useful in that it will usually be possible to compare some characteristics with the manager's own organisation. The cases draw pictures of structures and systems, design teams, communication systems, and very practical things such as time frames, resources and sequential processes. For the practical manager, the book is both a blueprint and an explanation of why things need to be done in new ways. For the theoretical manager, this book is a very modest iceberg-tip. The next move is to study anthropology, which is where most of the research and culture was undertaken prior to its migration to business and management.

Notes for lecturers

There are many issues and problems unfolding in the cases other than the ones which revolve around culture. The cases can be used to stimulate discussion on many human resource management issues. They can also be used as case scenarios for Total Quality Management and internal marketing. Less evident applications, such as design opportunities in Human Resource Information Systems (HRIS) and the use of information technology to redefine the manager's daily activities are built into the cases.

Notes for supervisors and trainers

This set of cases rests on the premise that the supervisor/trainer role is the one which mediates much of an organisation's values. The opportunities to spot heroes, and to celebrate successes and efforts (including unsuccessful ones) through rituals are open to supervisors and trainers more than anyone else. By studying the cases and using the core values model, supervisors and trainers will no longer think of KAS (Knowledge Attitudes Skills). They will think of KASVAL. They will have new 'eyes'. These eyes are looking to see what the conversations and behaviours symbolise. Do they symbolise commitment and caring? Or do they symbolise a 'Do as I say, not as I do' situation? Given that we can't always see ourselves as others see us, we can begin to include insight into the meanings of employees' actions and reactions.

To help employees take an active part in their own work-related decisions, supervisors and trainers need to promote problem-solving, presentations and project-management courses for employees. Where enterprise bargaining workplace agreements and with them consultative committees are on the horizon, these become key result areas for employee development. The cases demonstrate how much a feature of organisational life these skills and abilities have become.

Finally, to all reader groups, the cases provide a methodology for recording the past and current situation in one's own organisation. A final reminder — reality is negotiated. Sometimes hard differences have to be faced and somehow converted into acceptable new realities.

Where certain concepts are appropriate, cases will be prefaced by key concepts to help you. These are not the only concepts to bring into use as the case develops, however, and they are to be used in conjunction with models and concepts from your area of interest in managing change.

8

BHP Iron Ore

The case of the Mobile Equipment Workshop (MEW)

Peter Bell, Manager Personnel

As part of your assessment for a management post with a mining organisation (not BHP) you have been given the case history above. The first question you have been given is: What Best Practice phases do you think should follow for the MEW to achieve its goals? You will be expected to indicate some content within the phases, and maybe some anticipated problems.

The problem

Background

> The Best Practice approach, utilising the techniques of benchmarking, has forced managers and employers to address the direct and indirect barriers to improved performance. In effect, it has forced both groups to look at the workings of their department through 'new eyes'.
>
> Peter Bell, Manager Personnel

Using the idea of Best Practice demonstration and the accompanying federal government support (which it capped by a ratio of around 4:1), BHP Iron Ore targeted the area of operations at the Mobile Equipment Workshop (MEW) to use the technique of benchmarking to establish goals and targets for Best Practice performance. However, what commenced as a management technique soon developed into something much more. At BHP Iron Ore, management had, over the years, attempted to improve workplace productivity by using a number of different, but traditional, methods. These had varying degrees of success but none was embraced with any degree of enthusiasm by employees. The Best Practice approach seemed to be an exception to this. The reasons were perhaps obvious. It sought the active participation of employees in the planning, design and construction of a better and more productive workplace. In doing so it unlocked a wealth of knowledge, experience and energy which BHP's systems had previously left untapped. The *process* of benchmarking provided data for comparison and, when employees were given an active role, it also became a *mechanism* for their contribution and involvement in workplace change in a manner which had not been seen before.

BHP selected this workshop (the MEW) not because it is the world's best (in fact management knew it was in the bottom quartile of performance when measured against comparable mines), but because BHP knew it had the people and equipment that could make it the world's best. Thus, the project was to attempt to demonstrate how the MEW could go from below average performance to equal or better international benchmarks in a set period of 12 months.

The Mt Whaleback Mine is the largest single open-pit iron ore mine in the world. These days, approximately 120 million tonnes of materials is moved per year, of which 25 million tonnes is high-grade iron ore. All of this material is moved using an assortment of large electric shovels and what is termed 'mobile equipment' — 190-tonne and 240-tonne rear-dump trucks, tracked dozers and large front-end loaders.

BHP's business depends on the amount of material that is moved and the efficiency with which this is carried out. At present, the major constraint on this production process is the availability of BHP's mobile equipment, particularly large haul trucks. 'Availability' is a measurement ratio which indicates the amount of time an item of equipment is available for use in the production cycle. For the remaining time that item is used for planned maintenance or repairs due to in-service breakdowns.

At the beginning of 1992, a general aggregate average of the availability of haul trucks was 73 per cent. Within 18 months this figure grew from 73 per cent to 80 per cent, reaching a high of

82.5 per cent in 1993. This was accompanied by a substantial reduction in maintenance costs per operating hour. The number of unplanned maintenance hours (breakdowns) went from 80 per cent of total number to 50 per cent.

This level of performance had never been previously achieved at Mt Whaleback. In addition, this performance target would have had to be achieved within an area which had 230 employees, five unions, a history of troubled industrial relations and a workplace 'culture' which has traditionally been very resistant to change.

This is not to say BHP has put all its faith in a single method of improvement. A range of traditional means to achieve performance targets, such as engineering modifications, award restructuring and changes to work methods and arrangements (for example new shift systems), have been introduced and have progressed. However, it was recognised that these traditional approaches were not enough, in themselves, to reach targets of international Best Practice. This would require something more and BHP believes that the systems it has developed, which are based on the technique of benchmarking, can deliver what is required.

Best Practice approach

The Best Practice approach seeks to improve business performance over a set time frame. It does this by identifying what is international Best Practice for a particular work process or activity, analysing and identifying what factors lead to that performance, and then *adapting* them to the enterprise's particular circumstances. What distinguishes this approach from traditional good management are two factors:

1. The performance criteria are based on world class standards, not just one's own past performance or that of local competitors.
2. Employees actively participate in setting the performance targets, analysing the gap in current systems and being involved in problem-solving teams which identify and implement solutions.

The *process* of benchmarking as it developed at BHP Iron Ore involves a whole range of activities. These include:

- identifying what and where is world's Best Practice;
- understanding its own performance relative to standards of Best Practice (the realisation, by managers and employees alike, that 'we' are performing badly in terms of objective, comparable measures can be a positive and powerful motivator in itself);

- understanding the processes that comprise BHP's business and identifying what are the key factors that 'drive' or influence performance;
- analysing the factors that have led to world's Best Practice including visits, if appropriate, and determining whether they can be adapted to BHP's own workplaces;
- applying these data and this analysis in the form of initiatives and action plans that close the performance gap.

The outcome

Phases in a Best Practice program

Phase one: Management training and commitment

- For the change process to be successful, the commitment of senior management is an essential first step. This is necessary not only to secure the appropriate resources and personnel, but also to ensure the acceptance and help of middle and lower level managers. BHP's experience in the MEW has led it to believe that *this is the single most important factor in a program to bring about workplace change*. If management aren't convinced that a change is necessary, and are not *seen* to be committed through their actions, then there is no chance of those on the shop floor of embracing anything other than token change.
- Organisation structures must also be reviewed. If it is necessary to make changes, these should be undertaken *before* the change program is commenced.
- Although a framework for benchmarking can be put in place, performance improvement will not happen automatically. It must be *led* by management. BHP has found that it is very difficult to teach managers and supervisors leadership. This means that in some cases it may be necessary to make some personnel changes to the areas where the change process is to be trialled.
- Before any training for shop-floor employees takes place, management and supervision personnel should undergo training so that they are thoroughly familiar with the purpose, concepts and detailed processes involved in benchmarking. This is particularly important if the existing work group is to develop 'ownership' of the program.

- BHP did not possess the expertise to be able to carry out this training and so some specialist consultants had to be commissioned to design the program and run it on site. In this, two programs were developed: a one-day session for all employees, so that they could be exposed to the general concepts and techniques; and a two-day program containing more detail for those 25 to 30 employees who wished to have higher involvement.

Phase two: Employee training and commitment

- Management must explain, in clear terms, just what the purpose of the change process is. If there is a chance that there will be a reduction in numbers as a result of the process, this should be spelt out *before* the program commences.
- All employees within a particular work group (at BHP Iron Ore this is generally 100–150 employees) should undergo the benchmarking training (a one-day training program on concepts and general techniques was developed) so that they all 'speak the same language' when the activities begin to take place. However, BHP has learned that participation in benchmarking activities should be *voluntary* and should seek to involve only those employees who are committed, interested and prepared to make contribution. BHP has found that it is not only wasteful of resources but can even be counter productive to attempt to 'force' all employees to participate.
- Generally speaking, with a work group of 150 people, 25 to 30 of these step forward to be actively involved.

Phase three: Setting objectives

Objectives must be set, which have measurable performance improvement at their centre. But these objectives cannot be management's alone; they must have perceived benefits for both management and employees. For the MEW, these benefits were:

- increased mine production through equipment availability, as summarised in the aggregate measure of 73 per cent to 85 per cent plus;
- improved safety performance;
- all MEW employees understanding the business of the workplace;
- direct employee participation in international benchmarking exercises.

Phase four: Developing a methodology

Developing a methodology involved:

1 establishing a representational group from each classification and work process — at the MEW, there are fitters, electricians, trades assistants and foremen;
2 understanding what currently exists.

Before benchmarks of international Best Practice can be usefully set, the detail of work processes and performance as they currently exist have to become known. This is accomplished by utilising the 25 to 30 high-involvement employees in directed small-group activities, to carry out:

- mapping and analysis through business modelling, which tracks all the significant costs through the major production processes using DuPont modelling techniques;
- identifying and surveying customer/supplier relationships with the department (for example, the 'customer' for the MEW is the Mining Department and its truck drivers, and a conceptual analysis is undertaken which, in itself, draws employees to reassess work processes;
- 'process mapping' all of the major maintenance and planning activities in terms of time and resources.

All these activities were in turn subjected to Pareto and process flow analysis. This was done so that BHP had a clear picture of what actually took place in the MEW, while members were now aware of the main 'drivers of the business'. It is, of course, impossible to benchmark all activities, so in the design of benchmarking projects, it is these 'drivers' that would be concentrated on.

Phase five: Selecting benchmarking partners

Selecting benchmarking partners is a complex and time-consuming administrative process. For the MEW, it involved compiling information on what organisations were world's best by the following:

- Personal experience — being an international mining company, BHP necessarily has a lot of employees who have had experience at mining operations in other countries.
- Supplier recommendation — we wrote to every supplier and asked the question: 'Who are the best maintainers of our equipment in the world?' This involved some thousands of letters and

subsequent responses. Of course, we had to allow for a certain degree of selling skills but, nonetheless, we built up a data base on Best Practice enterprises. Not all were from the mining industry, and there were a few surprises. Two US examples were Disneyland (hydraulics maintenance) and Dade county school bus system (maintenance planning) which has over a thousand school buses to maintain.
- Management literature.

BHP then made a short list of potential benchmarking partners and wrote to each of them. This involved an explanation of the objectives, together with the offer to reciprocate on the sharing and exchange of information.

Phase six: The benchmarking questionnaire

- With the help of consultants, BHP developed a questionnaire which was sent to the benchmarking partner some two months before the benchmarking visits.
- Initially, the questionnaire was a very comprehensive document of about thirty pages. However, it was found that there was a degree of resistance by some companies to completing such a lengthy document, together with the problem of our own people's being overwhelmed by so much data. BHP have since reviewed the approach to the questionnaire and now it is about twelve pages long.
- The questionnaire covers the following broad subjects:
  - communications;
  - recording maintenance operations;
  - worker input levels;
  - total quality initiatives;
  - change management;
  - safety.

Phase seven: Benchmarking visits

- BHP has always focused change on achieving employee involvement. As such, it has taken an unusual approach to the selection of employees for the benchmarking visits. The prime determinant was to have the people who would be called upon to actually implement any changes to be exposed to the examples of Best Practice. In this, BHP had teams of seven employees. In the MEW, they would include:

  - 2 metal tradespersons;
  - 1 electrical tradesperson;
  - 1 foreman;
  - 1 person of non-trades classification;
  - 1 'customer' — usually a foreman from the Mining Department.
- BHP dispatched six of these teams to centres of Best Practice around the world:
  - 2 teams to the USA;
  - 1 team to Australia and Papua New Guinea;
  - 1 team to South America;
  - 1 team to Japan;
  - 1 team to Europe.

The teams did not confine themselves to other mines but visited industries of different kinds. (However, in retrospect, this was a mistake. Analysis showed that the really significant data came only from the mining industry and from mines in the USA. Added to this is the high cost of investigating industries that might have information of only marginal interest.)

Phase eight: Implementing solutions

The purpose of benchmarking is to identify solutions to operational problems. The next phase of this process is to *adapt and implement* these solutions to one's own operational circumstances.

To do this at BHP, the benchmarking teams collate the information into three streams:

- items which can be implemented immediately;
- items which require more detail analysis such as costing, engineering and management approval;
- items and issues which are outside the ability of department employees and management to change (usually those with industrial relations implications).

Each workgroup then takes a performance improvement project and, using a project management type framework, carries out the required work under a set time frame.

Problems of the program and Best Practice approach

The program and Best Practice approach has generated a lot of energy and enthusiasm, but it has not been without its problems and setbacks. These have included the following:

1 Resources
   a The program is extremely consuming of resources. At Newman, BHP Iron Ore has received $111 000 from the federal government but the organisation has spent over $830 000 of its own money to date. But perhaps an even more important consideration has been the amount of management time required. This has far exceeded estimated expectations.
   b One of the biggest resource problems has been expertise. All these approaches were new to BHP and BHP has had to rely heavily on consultants while the in-house expertise was developed.

2 Industrial relations
   From September 1992 to December 1992 the union with the largest representation in the MEW withdrew its participation. This was in support of claims for a general wage increase covering all employees. Of significance was the fact that the union members actually working in the MEW did not support the move to withdraw participation. After some months of intensive lobbying by these employees and the company, the ban was lifted.
3 Scope
   This experience has taught BHP that it is not good to be too ambitious and complex in the scope of issues raised and performance areas targeted for improvement. Fewer, simpler and more focused projects seem to produce better results.

Questions to consider

1 What are the similarities between BHP and other cases in this book regarding (a) the need to change, and methods of changing organisational culture; (b) benchmarking methodology; and (c) constraints which have to be faced on the industrial scene.
2 What environmental factors make a favourable climate for organisational change in contemporary Australia?
3 Which elements of BHP Iron Ore change methodology would transfer to service organisations, particularly those in the Australian Public Sector (APS)?

9

Underground Chemicals Limited

The case of the bloodied bins![1]

by Joseph Garcia

The Problem

Background

The company, Underground Chemicals Limited (UCL), is a large natural resource-based company headquartered in the United States. UCL has holdings in oil, potash, soda ash and bauxite throughout the Americas. UCL's historic strength has been in processing and delivering its product to customers, and so the engineering and transportation functions lead the company's direction.

> You, Bill Jones, work one of UCL's soda ash operations located in the American Rocky Mountain West. Your story really begins with the setting up of a new mine and processing plant in an environment where management shows a keen interest in creating and maintaining a safe workplace.

It is spring 1988. A second mine shaft is completed and the surface processing mill quickly reaches full capacity. Tragedy strikes in early summer! An underground miner gets caught in some equipment, dragged through an ore crushing machine, and is later found ground to bits on the conveyor belt up the line. The entire mine is shocked by the tragedy. An investigative committee is launched to discover the cause of the miner's death. Upon thorough study, the committee

[1]This case uses as a base an actual set of events that occurred in the mining industry. The names of the individuals and the company have been changed for purposes of confidentiality.

determines that the miner received the minimum required training and was poorly prepared in terms of learning to focus effectively on safety issues. Apparently, in the interest of getting the mine to operate at full capacity, safety efforts were kept to the minimum required for the entire operation. The committee report suggests that this accident is only the tip of the proverbial iceberg. Fearing another possible tragedy local management, with the full support of corporate headquarters, commits to developing a more comprehensive approach to safety training and performance.

The safety projects

Winter 1988 marks the initiation of phase one of the safety projects. An operation-wide safety training and awareness program for all hourly employees begins. The program is more extensive than the required federal and state training requirements. The company prepares every worker in both hazard awareness and safe practices material in the classroom and at the job site. In addition to this training initiative, you, Bill Jones, and the safety director, implement a safety-feedback bulletin board for both underground and surface operations. In each case, the name of the most recent accident victim, his or her immediate supervisor, and the nature, cause and extent of the injury are posted near the employee change rooms.

You strongly believe that making accidents visible is part of the feedback and learning process that will help UCL employees to work more safely. Meanwhile, supervisors absolutely hate having their names posted on this board of infamy. The employee grapevine is rife with stories about so and so and their accidents and how that particular supervisor runs a loose ship regarding safety. The usual tale is that the boss wants productivity at any cost and employees are pushed beyond their limits.

In spring of 1989 you bring a consultant into the operation to design and conduct supervisory training with an emphasis on safety management. The program includes modules on communication that praise safe work habits and general management principles. You yourself also conduct some of the training. Following this, you decide that a safety-incentive program should be implemented in the organisation to complement this new set of training activities. First you distribute 'UCL Safe Employee' stickers to every employee who has an accident-free week. These are to be worn as marks of distinction on hard hats. The stickers become an instant success! Employees display them proudly on their hard hats. In several months most employees have enough stickers to cover their entire hats. This is a good sign, which is consequent (you tell yourself) upon your hard work. Your own investment, late nights and threat to your marriage has been worth it. The consultant will be pleased too, you think.

As a result of these efforts, minor and lost-time accidents have decreased by over 50 per cent in December 1990 and productivity continues to meet expectations. Another intervention is introduced in January 1992. At the end of every month, the unit with the fewest accidents is awarded a free steak dinner for their employees and their families. The dinner includes a recognition ceremony and the awarding of a handsome 'Safety First at UCL' belt buckle for each employee in the unit.

By June 1992 the UCL facility has reduced accidents another 40 per cent! You are very, very happy and filled with pride at the result of your efforts. The facility has become the best in the company and has gained industry recognition for its improved safety record. Furthermore, government agencies now refer other companies in need of assistance to yourself and the soda ash facility management. 'Bill the Guru', you think in your less modest moments.

At a management team meeting in August 1993, you give your report with new and even more impressive statistics. All at once, Tony Spinks, Surface Operations Production Manager, breaks up your presentation, saying: 'I remain unconvinced! Why is it that in the mill, where we have not had a lost-time injury reported since we started the steak dinner program, I frequently see blood-soaked towels in the toilet waste bins? Something is not adding up! Who is monitoring this situation? Are all of these safety programs a sham? What is happening here? What if someone who is hiding an injury sues on finding out later that he/she has a permanent disability because no encouragement was given to seek timely treatment?'

That night you have a nightmare that it is raining bloody fingers, toes and faces. You shoot up in bed, wide awake and trembling. You decide to be totally honest with yourself and write down what you think may have happened as a direct result of the design of the safety system (and particularly the reward element).

What might you have written?

The outcome

This is what might have happened, using the core values model.

The change in employee behaviour was produced by a straight *stimulus, reward, reinforcement* device. The stimulus was a goal in the form of a hard safety statistic. The reward was public fame, positive reinforcement or shame (negative reinforcement). The approach was mechanistic: 'We say jump — you say how high?'; also it was depowering. It certainly wasn't investigative. Workers were performers not learners. Rather than try new experiment for better ways to be accident free and healthy, they would play safe and look for the pat on the head (and it filled Bill with shame to write this) to avoid the public kick in the teeth.

The message which would have ultimately reached the workers was that the bottom line is everything, and that they, like the safety statistics, were nothing more than bloody numbers.

'Tony Spinks has hit the nail on the head, even if I could ring his neck,' thought Bill. 'Ego's are at stake here. Group against group. Who would mention small wounds when the steak dinner competition meant gaining or losing face? Only the brave. Okay — now, fortunately, I've got the courage to go back', Bill decided. 'I can use the core values model and this time I'm going to start at the beginning'.

One year later, Bill was in the management meeting. So was Tony, whose attitude had changed. Tony said, 'I think I owe you an apology Bill. I've been hearing some excellent reports from your workers. You seem to have installed the concept of a safety culture as part of the daily language. If you can't beat them into submission with numbers you're killing them with theory. Is that the game? Only joking. Your new lingo has reached my division, so you'd better give me the lowdown on your culture operations.'

'Sure', said Bill, 'but we're just beginning. We are creating a new vision together, based on the philosophy it has taken us six months to design, and that means all of us. It's "Continuous improvement — step by step — in an Honest Environment".'

'Can you sketch out your process for me, Bill?' said Tony 'and a couple of the other managers are pretty impressed at the turnaround. Can we get together over a beer and exchange ideas?'

Bill reflected that in just a year a simple model, a bit of knowledge, a bit of self-criticism and a lot of faith in the workforce had put him back on track again. All of a sudden, he felt excited about the safety road ahead. He sent this message in response to Tony's request.

Dear Tony,
I am delighted to receive your memo showing an interest in our safety culture. It was you who caused me to stop to re-examine what I thought was 'good training' when it was little more than good conditioning. You had correctly intuited that people were more interested in performing for an audience than in learning and creating a safety culture themselves. Although we have a long way to go, we will be sticking to the same process. I have outlined the model we are using and the process to bring everyone into the culture. To show how simple the model is, I've copied it onto a beer mat. I hope you like this beer mat. It's the only one-sided mat I could find.

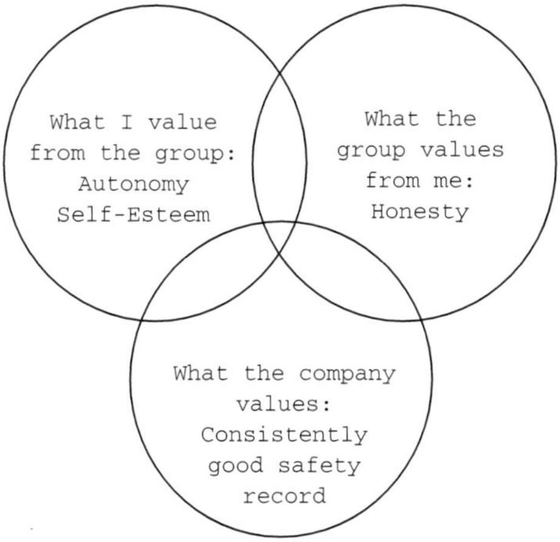

Here is how I did it Tony. I used the following process.

Workshop one
I presented my core values, and positive and negative examples of behaviours which support or contravene them. For example the positive example on the autonomy value that I gave was when I am away longer than expected and something new comes up on the safety horizon – it could be legislation. The employees translate this into what it means for us

and add the instructions to the manual, making sure that everyone has a copy. The negative example on the autonomy value that I gave was when a job was stopped because there was no direct instruction to cover it. The way to go*could* be implied from past experience but there had been a dependency on me to run with it.

The group, facilitated by me, did the same. It presented its core values and preferred behaviours. This means that I now have a blueprint of 'approved' behaviours (which I actually prefer because we get off personalities and onto events and actions). For your interest, I have included an example. On the value of honesty, the group gave the following example of positive behaviour: A group member has a renowned temper. His performance has been dropping. He comes in belligerently and asks why his performance rating has dropped. You are honest with him, risking a row and even maybe a walk-out; after he has cooled off you go back and work things out. The negative example the group gave on the value of honesty was when things such as staffing cuts are rumoured and no one can get an honest answer about the details.

Workshop two

This was a safety officers facilitation workshop. We all went on a training course where we learned how to negotiate a shared meaning between the group, other groups (like yours) and the group management. This entailed a lot of discussion and debate, and working through issues. The outcome was positive, but we felt we needed a bit more depth on some aspects.

Workshop three

This workshop was held to go through some concepts and develop some tools to help with building our safety culture. These included:

- Self-development
- Action Research
- Culture building

The surprising thing was that there was no shortage of participants. Everyone came along. Yes, Tony, every single person. We're all in the game together.

What we now have to do is to look more closely at our various marketplaces to find out what our internal and external customers want. We need some more resources and so we have decided to hire ourselves out as consultants. We reckon we could run the three workshops ourselves now. Seriously, we are pleased that others are interested in the safety culture, Tony, and we'll be willing to share what we know any time.

Cheers
Bill

Questions to consider

1 What is the difference between a safety program and a safety culture?
2 Regarding a safety program and a safety culture:
   a Which is the most difficult to achieve?
   b Which takes the longest and why?
3 What are some other areas of human resource management that employ the *stimulus, response, reward* method of conditioning? Discuss the benefits and possible drawbacks of this method of management.

10

The Commonwealth Industrial Gases Ltd

Gas Cylinders Division

with Richard McBurney and Peter Lee

The problem

Background

Gas Cylinders is an Independent Profit Centre (IPC) within Commonwealth Industrial Gases Limited (CIG), Australia's leading supplier and manufacturer of gas and gas-related technology. It was first established in 1973. In its 'first life' Gas Cylinders aimed to supply the Australian market with state-of-the-art high-pressure aluminium cylinders. The cylinders span several markets: medical, sports (diving equipment), industrial and social. Now Gas Cylinders, based in King's Park, Sydney, and employing around 110 people, exports 50 per cent of cylinders produced to Japan and South-East Asia.

The Gas Cylinders mission and philosophy, described opposite, embody over ten years of preparation, culminating in the decision, by August 1990, that the company needed to develop a new vision and philosophy. This would reflect significant changes in the way that management, the union and employees would need to relate to each other.

It is this philosophy, or declaration of the 'true' nature of working life as expressed by those involved, which continues to evolve and to serve as the focus for the continuous development of Gas Cylinders.

Gas Cylinders mission and philosophy

We strive to become a model business through satisfying customer needs, providing a desirable working environment, ensuring a good return for shareholders and conducting our business in a socially responsible manner.

1. all decisions will be consistent with our mission statement.
2. We will take a team-based approach to addressing issues, solving problems and making decisions.
3. Our approach will be one of continual improvement.
4. Each employee will have the opportunity to meet individual needs and objectives while meeting organisational needs.
5. Applied skill and knowledge of individuals will be recognised.
6. All individuals will know how they are performing as team members. They will also know how the business as a whole is performing.
7. Safety of employees and the community will be a high priority.
8. Each employee will be provided with the necessary tools, information and training to do the job right the first time.
9. Teams have the authority to meet their responsibilities, including stopping to fix quality-related or safety-related problems.
10. Job-related mistakes are opportunities for improvement.
11. The business will endeavour to offer appropriate personnel and social support services.
12. It is an objective that all employees be afforded equal status regarding conditions and opportunities.

Twenty years has seen changes at CIG Gas Cylinders. (A theme which runs through the lifelines of many successful companies which have undergone fundamental change is that it *does take time*. The time can range from five to 25 years, but the exciting thing about the cases in this book is that the end result is not a change from one specific point in time to another. It is a change from the past to a present which is constantly evolving.) As with many companies, it took an accumulation of situations and events to produce the feeling that Gas Cylinders was losing opportunities fast in a very inhospitable climate.

In 1977 Gas Cylinders began to collaborate with Luxfer Gas Cylinders, a subsidiary of Alcan, CIG's aluminium supplier, in what we know as benchmarking. Luxfer is a world leader in cylinder manufacture with one plant in England and two in the USA. Gas Cylinders explains benchmarking as follows:

- Benchmarking is a way of comparing performance by looking at the Best Practices of other companies and organisations both within and outside Australia.
- Benchmarking encourages continual improvement by determining how much a company needs to improve to be a world class performer.
- As information is exchanged and standards achieved, benchmarks are progressively raised.

The work done with Luxfer was comprehensive and cogent, and benchmarking changes were going to hit at the heart of organisational life. If certain improvements had to be made in major areas such as those below, existing customs and practices were going to be severely threatened. The two companies identified key areas with potential for improvement. These included:

- labour productivity;
- quality;
- organisation structure;
- material use;
- safety;
- finance;
- manufacturing lead time;
- product cost structure;
- engineering development;
- stock levels;
- marketing techniques;
- maintenance.

Gas Cylinders and Luxfer designed measurement techniques that enabled management to compare the individual plants' strengths and weaknesses and to set realistic targets. To improve their operations, both plants exchanged information regularly and conducted site study tours. For example, a major strength at Gas Cylinders plant is producing large cylinders. By world standards this is considered a complex operation. Gas Cylinders was able to provide Luxfer with information on how to improve its technology. In return, Luxfer was able to help Gas Cylinders to reduce total work hours needed to produce each gas cylinder. An essential feature of benchmarking is reciprocal information and ideas sharing.

Figure 10.1 shows the resulting improvement in productivity made at CIG's Gas Cylinders plant.

Figure 10.1 *CIG Gas Cylinders sales history*

The outcome belies some very sensitive and difficult issues which had to be managed, not the least of which was performance measurement. Arguably, one of the most contentious 'old days' management/worker battle zones was performance measurement. Following the benchmarking with Luxfer (which was highly innovative for the 1970s), problems with the introduction of new standards and performance measures arose. They were related to the prevalent 'them and us' mentality in the industry in a climate which often showed high-industrial dispute and low productivity. By the 1970s, performance measurement had become a concept which carried 'baggage' in the workplace. Scientific management principles, described earlier, caused the division of the human worker and management, fostering the well-known 'them and us' performance relationships. When the jointly designed (Gas Cylinders and Luxfer) measurement techniques were introduced, process workers did not understand why performance was being measured or why changes were being made. Gas Cylinders recognised that workers did not understand the new performance processes; therefore, the only ones who could 'own' them were senior and middle managers. The issue for Gas Cylinders became: 'What is needed for *all of us* to succeed in business?', and to make the concept of 'them and us' as meaningless as possible.

One important strategic decision, from which the others flowed, was to crystallise value or philosophical statements such as those below.

A business can succeed only if everyone involved works together.

From this value would come a belief — this time a belief in ability as well as interest.

We believe that all employees have a common interest — the success of the company.

Implied here is another very important belief about the workforce:

Every employee has ability and competence. Each person can contribute equally at his/her own level.

Common Interest Program

Easy to say, but most employees (many of whom have heard such rhetoric in the past) might say, 'Put your money where your mouth is: We're used to sharing the pain — what about sharing the gain? You want us to change from "Don't think — do it" to "Do think and we'll all do it", so what is the reward?' One way of introducing rewards was an initiative called the 'Common Interest Program' (CIP). It was introduced in 1982 and was seen, not as a one-off initiative, but as the first step in workplace reform. The Board of CIG Ltd (parent company) had decided to institute and support the reforms at Gas Cylinders. The aim was to lift production and reduce the likelihood of industrial disputes. Also, by reducing unit costs it was clear that opportunities for export existed.

Under the CIP, productivity gains would be shared equally between Gas Cylinders and its employees. However, *this was based on team work*, not individual performance. Furthermore, each employee could contribute to any decisions made which affected the company and its performance. The Common Interest Program was designed with three important components: a committee which includes employees from all levels of the company, ground rules and a mathematical model.

The committee

From 1984 to 1989 the committee had ten biannually elected members including five shift workers from the aluminium and acetylene cylinder plants; maintenance workers; foremen and supervisors; office staff; management; and a personnel officer. (This has evolved into a somewhat more informal set of communication devices such as team meetings and fortnightly team co-ordinator meetings.)

Ground rules

The ground rules included guarantees of various employment conditions for employees and specified rules for distributing profits under a new pay structure. The following rules were agreed by the representative committee:

- Productivity increases will not mean lost jobs.
- Health, safety and welfare standards will be maintained.
- The gains will be split 50/50 between CIG Gas Cylinders and the employees when there is a profit.
- An equal monthly dividend is paid to all employees.
- Dividends will not be paid to employees on unpaid absences or compensation.
- There will be no pay deductions for productivity losses.
- Plant changes are made only by consensus.
- Productivity gains arising from capital investment are excluded from the agreement.
  and
- A committee representing all company levels will meet monthly to make management decisions.

The mathematical model

When the program was initiated, a special mathematical model was used to calculate future gains and losses, based on past performance. The hours needed to produce a cylinder, and the number of reject cylinders were also analysed.

Since the model was introduced, all improvements made to the production process are measured, to ensure that they do contribute to productivity. The model is also used to calculate productivity-related dividends.

The program was put on a six-month trial. It is important to know the risks which were being taken. The outcome could have resulted in any of the following three:

- continued industrial relations 'consultations', which did not achieve too much except have unsettling effects on both management and the workforce;
- lip service where the right noises were made and documentation was completed, but no real gains were visible;
- a real in-spirit acceptance where 'hard' and 'soft' (that is, productivity/savings and motivation/morale) gains were beginning to show.

In effect, the outcome accepted was the third option above. At the end of the six-month trial period, Gas Cylinders was saving $25 000 each month, retaining half for profit and distributing dividends to employees averaging $100. Even so, Gas Cylinders felt it could develop real partnerships with employees even further.

> You are one of a small team of senior and middle managers at Gas Cylinders. You were always committed to benchmarking and you have experienced some magical moments of transformation from some of the old industrial relations ways to what seems to be a coming together of management and employees.
>
> It is 1991. You have lived through some pretty incredible times at Gas Cylinders. You have seen managers give and employees receive shared power and decision making. You have seen a workforce skilled in making aluminium cylinders become expert in making decisions, solving problems, developing processes and learning various statistical techniques. You have seen productivity rise and disputes fall. You have seen the *quality* mentality replace the *reject* mentality. You are reflecting on these changes, not without some complacency until you remember why you are sitting in the boardroom awaiting the rest of the decision makers (who now include workers as well as senior and middle managers). You have been called to discuss the ultimate in accountability — how to give workers control over operations. This is more than control over issues which affect their own machines and output. This is control over every part of the business: quality products; high productivity; customer service; and workers' own skills and abilities, and their continuous development and motivation/morale.
>
> Develop your personal plan for achieving this. Does it look anything like the one that follows?

Self-managing work teams

What Gas Cylinders did was to design a program for developing *self-managing work teams.*

The self-managing work team program was introduced at Gas Cylinders in July 1991. This program has four main features:

- hierarchical management structures moved to team-based support;
- an increased focus on customer service;
- training and multiskilling; and
- salaries and production goals for all employees.

Gas Cylinder's plans allowed two to three years for the introduction of the program. The program was designed to give employees more control over Gas Cylinders' operations which improve quality, customer service, productivity, skills and morale.

Steering and design teams

Employees were asked to volunteer for a 'design team'. The team's brief was to design an appropriate self-directed work teams program and introduce it to Gas Cylinders. Members included a production manager, a personnel superintendent, a maintenance supervisor, a maintenance electrician and four operators.

A steering team was established which included the general manager, engineering manager, the union organiser and a night-shift operator. This team's role was to oversee the design and protect the team from outside influences as much as possible.

Both teams were fully briefed on the theory of socio-technical systems (STS) which entailed the following: 'rather than separate analyses of the social structure and the technology, the new [STS] approach examined both, and the relationships between them as a system in its own right' (Emery 1993:141). The Technology Transfer Council and overseas companies which had used the model provided practical advice on applying the model to Gas Cylinders' operation. The teams held workshops to identify a company mission, a set of values and, most importantly, a list of reasons for change.

The program

Two studies formed the basis of the program:

- an employee survey which analysed job satisfaction, communication, ambitions, team participation and sources of dissatisfaction;
- a technical study which closely examined manufacturing processes in the plants.

Once written, all employees were asked to vote on whether to proceed with the program.

Work teams (special interest)

Teams were formed in the manufacturing areas. Foremen were moved into team-support functions and their responsibilities passed onto controlling teams, organised by elected team co-ordinators. Co-ordinators were rotated every six months so they could develop a broad understanding of the entire business. As co-ordinators became more experienced, they were to be rotated more often.

Because the production team was responsible for the delivery and quality of the gas cylinders, it was seen as being closest to the customers. However, to perform effectively the production team required information, resources and skills provided by the other teams. As the production team had a heavy responsibility, more trust was instilled in it and there was a deliberate move away from close supervision.

Training

Developing responsibility and asking employees to take on wider roles automatically meant that further training was needed. Providing people are able to use their new skills and knowledge, a higher level of job satisfaction is evident as a result.

Three types of training were undertaken: social, technical and business. Social training included team building, communication and interpersonal skills. Technical training involved establishing standard operating procedures, maintenance, training methods and problem-solving techniques. Business training was provided in key areas such as skill upgrading and quality management practices, and how Gas Cylinders operated as a company.

Reward for responsibility

People now have new and wider responsibilities in the team structure. All employees receive salaries based on varying levels of individual responsibility. Pay has been adjusted to correspond with these varying levels. For example, a cylinder technician's salary was calculated by annualising and averaging hours normally worked, including overtime. (Profit sharing initiated in 1982 still applies.)

In return, teams are asked to meet specified production and quality goals. If employees do not need to work overtime to meet these goals, overtime does not need to be undertaken and the take-home pay is not altered.

However, in spite of these achievements and the introduction of the self-managing work teams, problems arose concerning the special interest groups and design team concepts.

The problems of undermining special interest groups and fears about elitism

You have been worried for some time about the rumour mill. As an experienced manager, you know that every company has one. It doesn't matter how much you have all grown together as managers and workers, one thing will always remain: Management can hire, fire and transfer workers. Of course, this is no longer true, given employment protection legislation and, in this company's case, its allegiance to the workforce. Your friend who is from the shop floor and has been a major help and support through these years of fundamental change tells you that there is undermining of the special interest groups.

A second problem developed during the design phase of the change program which related to the perceived elitist nature of the design team. In this environment most people wanted to have a say in the way that the new system would be developed. Others were fearful of change and did not want anything to change. In practical terms it was not possible to have everyone involved in all segments of the change, and although this group was representative of the workplace many people were not happy. They were jealous of the volume of information design team members were being exposed to, as well as the amount of time spent away from jobs in the plant. This was a very highly empowered team. Members were being asked to develop a new work system which would break free from traditional shackles, rather than tinker with the edges of the existing system. Underlying fears about elitism within the employee group and the results of relative power were understandable, given the work and effort that had gone into breaking down barriers with management. 'Were we seeing a different type of management?' was a question suggested by a delegation who wanted to discuss the elitism of the design team.

How would you handle these kind of problems? (See 'The outcome' on page 171.)

As well as being prepared for problems, managers need to be prepared for the fact that not all initiatives will come to maturity straightaway. In 1984 Gas Cylinders decided to formally adapt and apply an approach which would de-emphasise past and current negatives and emphasise those things being done right and a 'future' orientation.

Program — Total Quality Control

Gas Cylinders believed a quality approach represented a better way to manage, as opposed to dissatisfaction with historical or current performance. This prompted an outlook of continuous improvement.

At Gas Cylinders, quality began at the source or production level of the cylinders. Cylinder technicians were encouraged to participate in the quality program through salary restructuring and productivity/quality targets. Also, it was important to take quality control beyond shop-floor and product-inspection functions. Quality principles in customer service and administrative functions were seen to be just as necessary to the Gas Cylinders division.

Main features of Total Quality Management

The main features of Total Quality Management (TQM) are:

- training in statistical measurement techniques, to check the quality of production and customer service at every stage and set quantitative goals for improvement;
- Deming's Principles, which focus on systems, the theory of variation and statistical thinking, leadership in planning, predication, learning, measuring and monitoring.
- Quality Circles, where a range of employees are invited to make suggestions for improvements in areas outside their normal fields of work; and
- charting on the shop floor, which is an organised and structured way to solve problems as a group.

TQM, following Deming, suggests systems, a statistical approach and the sort of activities undertaken by a TQM leader. Central to all of these was a framework called FADE (Focus, Analyse, Develop and Execute), shared and understood by all, for solving problems. FADE has become as essential in the Gas Cylinders 'toolbag' as a spanner or calculator.

The four stages: Focus, Analyse, Develop and Execute (the FADE model) are explained below.

- Focus — First the team must generate a list of problems, and then select one problem and define it in writing.
- Analyse — After deciding what further information is needed, statistical data such as measurements and patterns should be collated, and the factors causing the problem defined. (Defining the cause(s) of a problem often automatically leads to its solution.)
- Develop — Alternative solutions are listed, and the team agrees on one solution and develops an implementation plan.
- Execute — After gaining management and shop-floor commitment to implement the solution, it can be put into place and its effectiveness measured.

The year 1987 brought the idea of value-added management. Japan was an example of the competition. Unlike its reputation in other areas, Japan had high production and time cost in its manufacturing. There was a chance for competition. Could Gas Cylinders adopt an approach to win? Several ideas were put into place. Just-in-time management eliminated all non-profit-making activities. Stock, tooling changeover times and customisation were improved. For example, a policy stock change was to keep no stock of finished goods. Another was that production was to be driven by customer pull, not production push. As a result, stockholding was reduced by two-thirds. Production time was reduced from 27 days to 10 days. Also there was a significant reduction of work-in-progress.

TQM has matured and developed within the Common Interest Program (CIP) environment. The CIP was a symbolic program. It symbolised partnership, and one usually chooses partners as people to trust and respect. It symbolised a recognition that there were abilities and competences to be tapped. It symbolised that managers were prepared to be first assistants, coaches and counsellors rather than judges and juries. The company success through meeting targets, improving quality and demonstrating synergy was more important than providing status props to managers. It symbolised the importance of the team, of equal contribution and of pulling together for success. However, this was not without its problems.

The problem of first-line and middle management

In a productive atmosphere such as that below, and largely achieved by self-managed work teams, the question had to be faced of how to deal with those foremen/managers who may have progressively felt they were somewhat superfluous. Gas Cylinders:

- produces around 205 000 gas cylinders annually;
- exports over two-thirds of cylinders produced to Japan, South-East Asia and New Zealand;
- manufactures composite cylinders, aluminium cylinders and acetylene cylinders in a variety of sizes;
- supplies cylinders for beverage gases, medical and industrial gases, as well as fire extinguishers and scuba tanks;
- distributes cylinder parts including valves and accessories;
- has produced over two million gas cylinders since the plant first opened;
- in 1986 received an Australian Export Award for outstanding export achievement, from the Australian Trade Commission and the Confederation of Australian Industry; in 1991 received an Australian Export Award from Enterprise Australia and also in 1991 was awarded a Total Quality Management Encouragement Award by the National Business Bulletin.

How would you approach this problem of first-line and middle managers in such a successful and self-managed team environment? (See 'The Outcome' on page 171.)

Returning to TQM, Gas Cylinders, building on the quality values has, over time, infused practical principles, models and measuring techniques. Because of the underlying philosophy of TQM (that we are all someone else's customer and we need to treat customers as we would like to be treated), the production partnership mindset is as liberating as the old 'measuring' mindset was constraining. Why? Because tools such as TQM are still only tools. The values and principles which govern how and to what end tools will be used determine whether these tools are enabling or constraining. For example, worker involvement without reward would soon take on 'them and us' connotations. Using statistical techniques to measure degrees of variance is fine. However, if 'learning' results within the desired variance were punished, the technique would be perceived as demoralising and threatening.

With several wins but with the problems of the design teams and special interest groups still left to solve, how would you build on the achievements below if you were given the challenge of doubling performance from these already stunning achievements?

- Productivity has increased by 220 per cent.
- Return on funds has increased sevenfold between 1982 and 1992.
- Manufacturing lead time has been reduced from 24 days to 6 days.
- The company has developed an export market — today, over two-thirds of cylinders produced are for export.
- Labour turnover has dropped to 5 per cent.
- Absenteeism has been reduced to 3.5 per cent.
- Stock levels have been reduced by 72 per cent.
- There have been no strikes between 1982 and 1989 and few since.
- Employees receive comparatively high wages plus an average monthly dividend.

The outcome

Problems of special interest groups and design teams

How did Gas Cylinders manage the problems of the special interest groups and the design teams? The story of the problems are told by a Gas Cylinders person responsible for helping to solve them: Peter Lee, Cylinder Technician Team Co-ordinator.

A problem existed right from the first day of the program where it was mooted that this was just a way of getting rid of the foreman. Much false information was spread through the rumour mill. This information was widespread and difficult to combat as people were being exposed to this information more often than they were to the facts, and because the design team members were busy with their design work. Also, we have three fixed shifts which means that night shift and to a lesser extent afternoon shift had limited opportunities to discuss the information with the people in the know.

It was on the informal basis that much of the undermining had to be overcome. Members of the design team were continually reassuring people on the one-to-one basis of the facts. The finality of the work was a one-day off-site session where the plant was closed, and open discussion was encouraged with senior management, the union organiser and the design team. It was here in public forum that many of the issues were put to rest. A vote of endorsement was gained with more than three-quarters of our people voting in favour of the change.

The problem of first-line and middle management

First-line management

How was this special group managed? One of the pluses in the history of Gas Cylinders was that the first-line supervision level was always hands on. Those who were displaced in the traditional sense were not punished through the new structures by losing out financially. They kept their monetary reward. Of course, some would inevitably feel a loss of status and so there were some losses. Still, the majority of foremen remained on site. It was essential that there was substantial and continuous reassurance about such anxieties as people losing their jobs. Internal consultants, together with managers, made many presentations. No people would lose their jobs. Those affected would be given roles in the new process. Some people accepted the new roles and some didn't. However, it has been possible to retain most of the people and to create new roles for them.

Middle management

Middle management change was tricky. The status of middle management in the traditional sense had disappeared. Two or three managers who did not like the new direction did, in fact, move on. For those who may have suffered but were prepared to hang in, some concrete help was offered. The type of help offered is given below as tips for those involved in similar change.

It is advisable to clearly define managers/supervisors' roles and establish them from the word 'go'. Some approval may be lost but, if treated right, the individuals will continue to contribute their managerial and foreman skills. The chances will be greater if they are made strongly aware of how valued they are and how valuable their skills are to the organisation.

The most impacting change is that of the foreman/supervisor role. Therefore, it is necessary to recognise, respect and celebrate these roles. It is essential for senior management to brief managers and foremen/supervisors whose status and roles will be altered *before* everyone else. In particular, the following must be reinforced throughout the process:

- They have an important role to play.
- Their skills are highly valued.

In order to support people who perceive they have something to lose, the following must be achieved and time and effort must be devoted to see that this happens.

A high-trust environment must be fostered. A communication system which is comprehensive and regular must be developed. A supportive industrial relations climate (which may take time especially if unions believe management are 'conning' employees) will need to be nurtured. Employees must be educated on where to go. (Gas Cylinders used the design team concept to achieve this in ways that the employees could understand.) Always, shop-floor employees, unions and management should be involved in continuous change. Always, a thorough and vigorous analysis of technical *and* social systems *and* the relationship of each to the other needs to be undertaken.

Be gradual in managing change. Many concepts such as those of self-empowered teams are new and unfamiliar. They cannot always be taken on board immediately. The idea is to install the concept over time. If possible, it is a good idea to take people off site and explain the implications of the changes which are likely and foreseeable. If an organisation is really serious about including the workforce in decisions, it will allow people to vote on whether or not to embrace the changes. Gas Cylinders did this and the 'Yes' vote was over 75 per cent.

Above all, the advice from Gas Cylinders is to take enough time. Even with its impressive record, Gas Cylinders is still developing on some fronts such as continuing customer focus and a real flattening of the managerial structure.

When asked how would you get grassroots and, say, union employees to change their ways, these were the tips from Gas Cylinders:

- Take time to address the question: 'What's in it for me?'
- Make sure that both sides of the change equation are balanced when asking people to take on new and different roles and even different values. In particular, the effort-and-reward ratio must be reflected in dollars.
- The dollar is a major tool in breaking down barriers.
- The dollar is a way to show good faith and is a key to common interests.
- The dollar is a tool to start a process and break down barriers in improving productivity.

Essentially, if the organisation gets to some version of that shown in Figure 10.2, and asks itself appropriate questions, it is well on the way to success. The model shows the need for a three-prong approach. The first target area is communication. When reading Figure 10.2 there is no sense of change which has been introduced with a fanfare then left to grow or not on its own. There are several types of communication, but most important is personal communication. There are internal devices, often heavily represented by management and the union, such as the consultative committee and advisory teams, so that information can be two way and, most importantly, expressed through the decoding system of the receiver (see Figure 2.3). Central to the whole change process here is the concept of involvement. There is the facility for two-way communication at all times and opportunities for problems and issues to have value added as various groups within the cycle contribute to the change process. The cycle of involvement, in turn, is made possible through structures. Firmly embedded in Design Principle 2 (see Figure 6.5) the team structures shine through the whole Gas Cylinders' organisation.

However, there are always dangers and Gas Cylinders particularly recognised the danger of 'plateauing'. The idea here is that when you plateau and become 'comfortable' there is an urgent need to *revitalise*. Substantively, Gas Cylinders has used an annualised pay scheme, and a weekly hours and overtime mix, and has developed the idea of

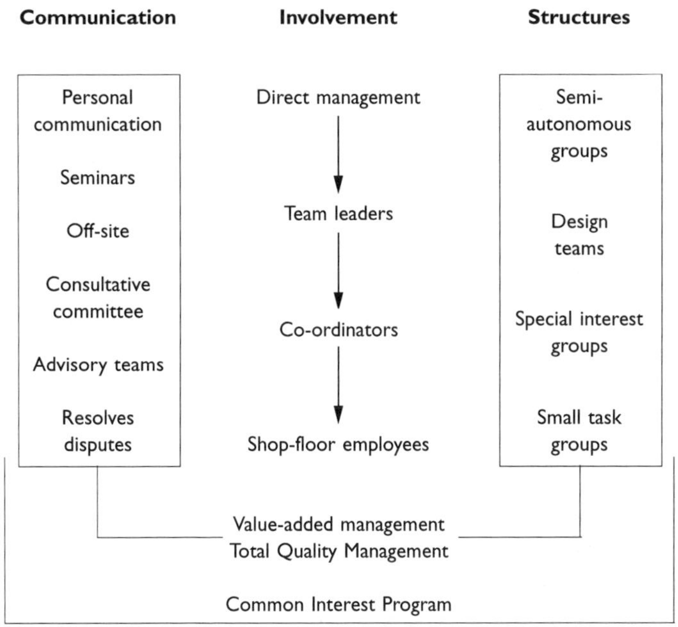

Figure 10.2

facilitating teams to look at the broader picture than theirs. Table 10.1 also helps those involved to see the evolving picture of achievement in many different areas, four of which have been selected to illustrate the model. The important thing about the model is the methodology and the thinking behind it. For a truly strategic climate it is necessary for everyone, not just management, to 'see' what is going on elsewhere and to have a sense of developing achievements at increasing levels. The idea is to chart activities which can be translated into goals. The picture evolves over time so that continuous improvement can be seen and with it a sense of achievement. The goal-linked activities can be as broad and as narrow as is appropriate for the particular organisational setting. As Richard McBurney, the originator of the methodology says, 'it needs to be made unique and translated into line activities and ways of doing things and can be as broad as you like'. The content in Table 10.1 uses some generic examples to give the general idea.

Table 10.1 *An evolving picture of what is happening and what is likely to happen next year*

	Involvement	Training	Safety	Stock control
Activities Level 1	Team is often actively involved in cross-functional improvement.	Teams validate skills training.	Housekeeping standards agreed to and documented.	Conduct cyclic counts with 99% accuracy.
Activities Level 2	30% of team actively involved in cross-functional improvement.	Teams identify time required for training independently.	Housekeeping standards adhered to daily. Near misses reported reliably.	Developing skill to use stock control information system.

Source: Developed by Richard McBurney

Questions to consider

1 What elements of this case might be transferable to your organisation?

2 As a result of studying this case (and others in this book), you can see that there is a predictable difficulty for managers who, under participative management, will have their roles substantially altered. Synthesising the various interventions taken by Gas Cylinders and others, how could you pre-empt some of the difficulties?

3 Organisational life is dynamic as environments and markets put pressures on internal management arrangements. If the key areas for improvement were changed, which, if any, of the key design features of Gas Cylinders could most easily be altered?

11

DuPont (Australia) Ltd

with Graeme Longe and Kathy Wiedner

The problem

Background

Central to DuPont's thinking, from CEO Richard Warburton to site managers such as Phuong Tram and operator John Martin is the idea of workplace culture. Restricted ways of looking at a company's position in the wider world, sometimes with the result of overestimating one's competitiveness overseas, are not part of the mindset. Nor is a fatalistic acceptance of the 'them and us' (managers against operators and vice versa) mentality. The message from the CEO is clear and unequivocal, as is shown by the following:

> My experience is that most people — shop floor and management — are eager to participate in the day-to-day running of their workplace. This is especially so if they feel that their involvement will contribute to their job security, job satisfaction and their personal career aspirations.
>
> If operators and unions can be convinced of the sincerity of management, my experience is that their resistance will soon turn into support.
>
> In a recent interview in *Business Review Weekly*, the head of the Industry Commission, Bill Scales, was quoted as saying that he did not think that 'business people have yet understood the extent of the flexibility within the labour market'. He said that in his experience, senior worker representatives and the leaders of individual unions were prepared to be very co-operative with responsive management.
>
> The message that key union officials have given Bill Scales is that, if a company has a long-term vision and can explain to

union members how they will benefit, unions will do their utmost to clear labour restrictions from the company's path. Scales said he was surprised that so few business people were responding to what he saw as 'a great preparedness within the union movement to shed past practices'. Frankly, so am I. This is the very basis for workplace culture change.

Focus on management

However, 'them and us' can't be just wished away. Barriers to change can come from all key stakeholding groups. In most companies there are four key groups, who all play a part in developing and changing workplace culture: senior managers, middle managers, operators and unions.

The role for senior managers at DuPont (Australia) Ltd is clearly stated as part of the CEO message:

> CEOs need to recognise that ruling by decree is not a sign of strength. Instead, they must recognise the need to consult, to encourage teamwork and to delegate responsibility. In other words, you need to change the corporate culture from one that is fundamentally confrontational to one where management and labour work together towards common goals, for mutual benefit.
>
> Traditionally, the leader was a teller, a planner and a controller, who was burdened by year-end performance evaluation, and totally oriented by business results. What is emerging and desirable is the teacher, the coach and the counsellor — the facilitator who develops a work team.
>
> This team understands new techniques such as continuous improvement through measurement and ongoing benchmarking and sees, almost as a 'condition of employment', the need to develop such core values as people development, safety, customer satisfaction, the well-being of fellow employees, the need for shareholder returns and the enterprise's role in the broad society. When I see a leader with such a team, it reveals to me one important thing — that leader has been able to build trust.
>
> Now let me ask, how much are you prepared to build trust with your employees? Think for a moment about your decision-making style. How comfortable are you with delegating responsibility not only to junior executives and managers but

also to shop-floor people? Just how in-touch are you with the factory floor? Would you feel comfortable expressing your concerns — or your encouragement — directly to your workforce?

What about changing your management style? Are you prepared to be less of an enforcer and more of a coach and counsellor? Are you prepared to spend less time meeting with executives and more time meeting with process workers? Would you be comfortable eating your lunch and socialising at the staff canteen — every day?

Senior management, today, is primarily in the business of managing a *corporate culture.*

Many senior managers have developed values and beliefs about leaders where senior management rules with a rod of iron. If workers disagree, you then have a dispute which management toughs out and wins. In DuPont's view, such beliefs, and the actions which follow, are a recipe for disaster and such actions could produce an avoidable dent in the corporate image.

Managers cannot escape responsibility for managing change. Change *can* be seen as an erosion of the managerial prerogatives of making decisions, 'leading' and withholding 'strategic' information. Yet the success or failure which results from the implementation of change is solely the responsibility of management.

> You are a DuPont manager. You are pretty sure that you are going to be put in charge of managing a site which is part of the Operations Division. You are surprised because you and your fellow employees thought the site would close. Just about everything was wrong at this site — low productivity, quality not competitive, and poor morale.
>
> You have heard the CEO speak before but you are very alert now to gleaning his and anyone else's views on company values, philosophy, processes and tips for better management. You have been able to secure a short interview with various top managers and also to find out more about the workplace reform, core process concept and some of the implications of the flatter organisational structures and task teams. Sitting in your office, reviewing the notes (below), you think you see a design which just might work.

Notes from the CEO

This is what the CEO said:

> I would like to tell you that it is the *culture*, not the organisation, which is the focus. The better the culture, the better the relationship between labour and management, the more competitive you are.
>
> You can be in no doubt that here senior management, managers like yourself, and workers have agreed to give our workplace reform their best shot. That is a commitment and we have gone to considerable time, effort and expense to see that all parties are in no doubt about the need for change. It is our job to translate this need into a set of expectations. It is vital that we build a climate of mutual trust. This means identifying key issues and problems in managing labour relations, and bringing them out into the open. By recognising the need to change the culture of your site to reflect the corporate culture, you have already recognised that things can be done better. So, bringing out issues, sitting down with your people, and talking over their concerns reflect our corporate values. Manager as coach, counsellor, teacher and facilitator who can build a team will help the whole team to realise our core values, which are:
>
> - safety, health and environmental affairs;
> - customer satisfaction;
> - the well-being of employees;
> - the need for stakeholder returns;
> - DuPont's role in the broader society and overseas.
>
> Let me ask you some provocative questions in a supportive way. Up to now, has your major focus been on supervising and controlling processes or on building trust. The former, I suspect. So, how do you go about building this trust? I can recommend that you look at your decision-making style. How comfortable are you with delegating responsibility to junior staff even when they're experts? How in touch are you with the inside-out reality on the shop floor. Are you included in the jokes and skits? What are the jokes telling you? Do you recognise the company culture in there, because the 'I got one over the foreman again, stupid b . . .', tells you a lot about how we are perceived. Do you make the time to encourage directly,

and give/accept criticism in the spirit of learning? Most importantly, how do your workers 'see' things? How are they negotiating their workplace reality?

You are part of that reality. Find out what workers expect of management. Share with them what you expect in return. Invite them into your reality in real terms. Give them information, maybe on our current constraints on new capital expenditure and our market fluctuations. They can see why we need to pull together for profitability. Invite workers into strategy or management meetings. Look at the current 'pain and gain' equation. What is happening that threatens our core values? You'll probably find sick leave, absenteeism, labour turnover and morale and a 'parallel line' communication system (the two lines never meet). Sickies are a good barometer of morale and, may I say, cost industry more than strikes. In fact all the above reflect a 'strike in spirit' and usually a silent one which is all the more difficult to put right. Let's say you get your communication right. You talk. You listen. You assimilate with your workers. You discuss and try to solve issues. Then you go away and develop your strategies and goals, maybe even your processes and procedures for achieving them. Who is displaying power? You. You are using the symbols of your position and your office door to say to the workers, 'Well, you are interesting to talk to. I've probably picked up some smarts in talking but the real power lies here — where the decision-making and design come in.' You have created a psychological hierarchy. Each knows his/her place. So, when you come to implement our appraisal system, which revolves around mutual goal setting and timetables for such things as productivity increases and changes to work practices and such sensitive areas as 'how much supervision', you may be sure that your workers will not feel empowered as partners.

These basic ideas are all about good employee relations. If you get them right and succeed in developing and rewarding your teams, they will go forward with you towards our benchmark aims to achieve the following objectives:

- a management emphasis and leadership dedicated to quality, and quality in all areas;
- improved productivity from a fully integrated approach, not just to one particular thrust such as reducing staffing levels; and

- teamwork at all levels.

On a closing note, I can't overstate the case for putting time and effort into forging empowered relationships; involving your workers in decisions; training workers; and inducting workers into our core processes:

- safety, health and environmental affairs;
- people development;
- supply chain management;
- quality management;
- facilities planning; and
- metrics (performance measurement)

↓

We all support the customer.

> Now, outline your vision and plan for reforming your site. You manage eight supervisors who manage eighty workers (skilled, semiskilled and operatives).

The outcome

Looking back you remember that one of the first things you did as site manager was to think through the meaning of 'enabling culture'. This, you decided, was the essence of the CEO's interview. Here are some of the ideas you came up with, particularly thinking of the workers — the operational staff.

We need to encourage the workers to participate within the business. Then they will become part of the decision-making process for the business. As a result of that they will influence or control their own destiny. As the business develops the people, the people will develop the business. They will help it grow and become secure.

You then reflected on the traditional way things were done in Australia:

- People were (and felt) extensions of the supervisor.
- They were the supervisor's arms and legs.

- There was no ownership of the work process.
- There was an income-earning view of work, resulting in the attitude of 'I'll put in my shift — no more, and less if possible'.

You thought of a typical worker your colleague recently supervised. We'll call him Bob Wilcox. He'd been on your mind for some time, nibbling away at the edges of your conscience.

Bob comes to work on time, or maybe late, whatever; he won't be seen to be early. As a person he uses specific skills as told by the supervisor. You see that to the supervisor, Bob is the sum total of the skills the supervisor wishes to use. Even of these, the supervisor will use only a selection. The supervisor exercises the option to use the skills selected as he sees fit.

You ask the supervisor, 'Is this productive, fruitful and beneficial to the business?' He's likely to shrug and say, 'Who knows?'

Yes, you muse, workers are dependent on the supervisor (who may assume that he has a knowledge of people skills). The worker will, sooner or later, say, 'Where is my future?' The worker has no say in which work impacts on him or his skills. There is no way he can even express his superiority in other ways because no one asks for voluntary conversation other than his peer colleagues and his mates.

Yet, looking back, was the supervisor entirely to blame? Supervisors usually stand out because they are individual contributors — superworkers. They probably had a record output, got more out of a machine and, as a mate, showed people skills. Such supervisors in the old days were promoted because they stood out among peers as star performers. You yourself were one example.

What did the old days bring though? The old days brought:

- unproductive output;
- low quality;
- high industrial relations disputes;
- negative industrial relations;
- low personal esteem.

This state of affairs would inevitably continue until the pressures come to boiling point. It would take the spectre of losing jobs for change to be recognised. New days would come. See Figure 11.1.

The new days would include the idea of change and 'life for all'. This becomes the mission. The overall problem is: how do I do it? Many hours of thinking, reading and talking things over resulted in

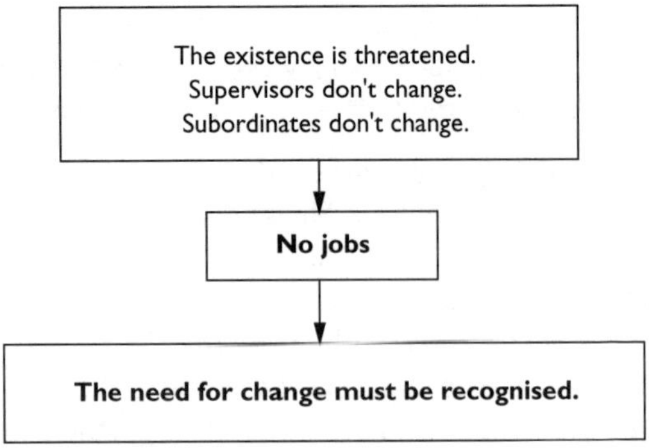

Figure 11.1 *The need for change*

the following models and solutions. If you wrote them down in some sort of sequence this is how they would look.

Solution 1: Change the environment

This solution is based on creating an environment for the acceptance of change. It operates on an individual level and involves the following:

1. Take the supervisors away from the scene.
2. Develop leadership and 'bigger picture' skills.
3. Convince workers that continuous improvement lies through people and teamwork.
4. Decide on a personal style which will encourage participation.
5. Emphasise the fact that *you can't make people participate*.
6. Instead you must *create an environment* so that worker and supervisor are on the one team. Develop *mentally* — the quality of thinking other than work-specific skills is the key.

Solution 2: Team skills model

This solution operates at a team level and involves the following:

1. Understand yourself.
2. Understand how your behaviours can help or hinder people.
3. Work out how you can replace a team supervisor with a team member.
4. Set up a chain of events — you prepare for change. You create the environment for others.

5 Encourage risk taking and promote failures as learning experiences.

Figure 11.2 shows two methods which the leader/supervisor can use to achieve change. The challenge is to let go, so that others can grow and be prepared for change. The idea applies both to those above supervisory level (leaders) and to those below (operators). The change represents a change in values from things which are event-driven to those which are continuous. At the core of this is the value of enablement and self-management.

This model shows an episodic approach and a continuous development approach to change. In an episodic approach, when the enthusiasm fades, the leader needs to be ready with the next 'new' thing to *do*. See Figure 11.2. In the continuous development approach, progress starts slowly as people learn to take risks and

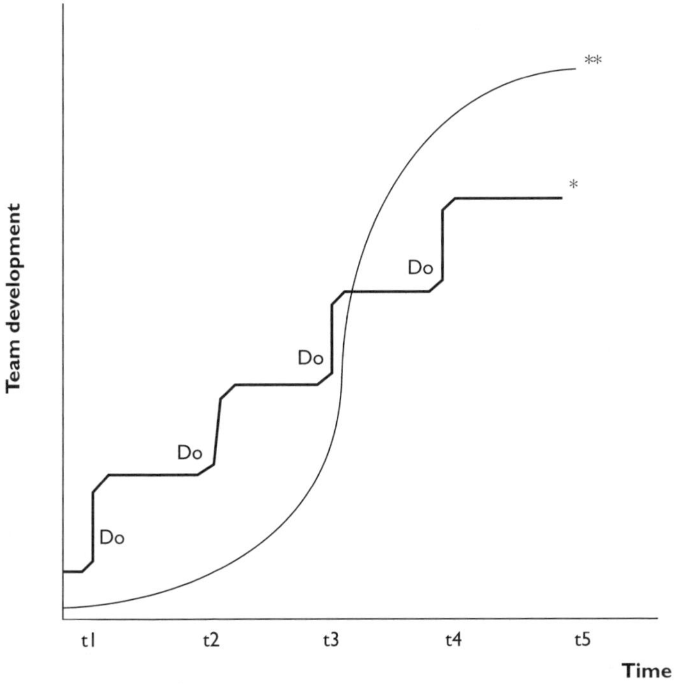

* Episodic approach
** Continuous development approach

Figure 11.2 *The episodic versus continuous development approach to achieving change* develop responsibility. The continuous growth is towards self-management. It depends on ongoing training and development (see solution 3).

There is a way of looking at the three areas of work (functions), self (free will) and team (thinking about being) which DuPont found useful. Figure 11.3 illustrates the sense of balance or harmony needed in relating these three very important areas to each other.

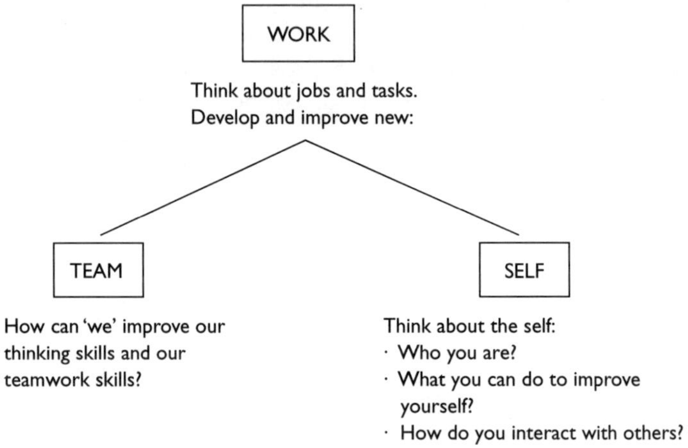

Figure 11.3 *The relationship between work, self and team in achieving change*

An important mental model which explains the way vision/principles, authenticity/values and motivation link together is shown in Figure 11.4. DuPont says that this simple model is based on two equally simple concepts: means and motivation. Both have to be present to be able to achieve any significant change.

The motivation axis begins with the ground from which to start and build upon. It ends with some of the goals around where we are trying to go: what we hope to achieve, the position we are trying to occupy, and what we hope to achieve by that. In this case we chose authenticity as the ground and a hierarchy of values as the goal (or the motivating force).

Having articulated our motivational forces, it is necessary to focus on the means of achieving this goal. Here you must determine the instrument by which you can move towards your goal and those things you can use to measure or assess whether you are employing the appropriate means to that goal. It ends with the direction

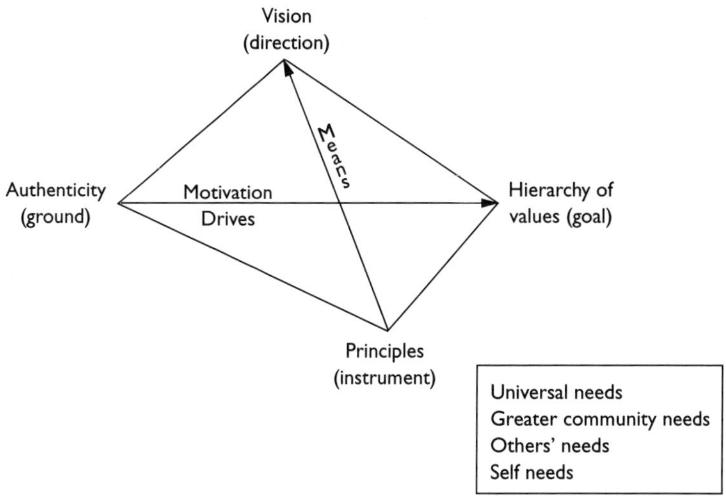

Figure 11.4 *Driving the vision*

required to get to the goal. Direction includes notions of who is going to provide the direction; the different steps in going from ground to goal; and how we deal with those potential diversions from ground to goal. Here we chose principles as our instrument and vision as our direction.

Solution 3: Ongoing training and development

Drawing on the experience of other DuPont managers who were further down the track with change, the following cautions on ongoing training and development are in order.

1. Be patient.
2. Provide a non-threatening environment (and understand the role changes, for example from manager to leader).
3. Providing a non-threatening environment will emphasise the need for change.
4. Don't let leaders stagnate through leading one team. Create opportunities for leaders to rotate through different teams.
5. Develop principles around the mission.
6. Explain what will be happening, when and where it all fits in the big picture.
7. One key learning point is that supervisors must receive their training after leadership and before shop-floor operators.

Supervisors perceive that they have more to lose than leaders or shop-floor employees. The most effective training of operators is that done by their supervisors. Therefore, it is imperative that this group has as much reassurance and knowledge as possible.

8 Critical to the success of developing good leaders are the following activities.
   a coaching;
   b counselling;
   c meeting skills;
   d influencing skills, that is, how to get others to do the work without offending and how to allow others to do work without becoming offended.

9 Do not take a deep corporate slice to train when you are starting. Wait until leaders have been trained, supervisors have been trained and *then* take the training to the people. (There will be challenges here because supervisors and operatives will initially develop separately and will have to learn how to come together to agree problems and implement decisions.)

10 Foster a 'thinking about thinking' approach. People have to learn to think about the quality of their thinking. From this thinking will flow a commitment to lifelong, continuous learning.

11 The following team ideas have helped DuPont to map the essential issues into some musts for developing teams:
   a To develop a team model, the first need is to have a volunteer mentality. Once voluntary teams come together they become responsible for determining what is required for their own training and development.
   b As people determine what they need for training, they will then look to their leaders for resourcing and leadership.
   c This creates an essential loop in the leader's own development as represented by the double-loop learning model.
   d People will voluntarily design phases and groups for training.

As these solutions and ideas began to work, the leaders were frequently asked to give tips to other areas. Single-loop and double-loop learning is explained in the following:

> This [experience] created an essential loop in the site manager's own development as represented by the double-loop learning model. In single-loop learning, we learn to maintain the field of constancy by learning to design actions that satisfy existing governing variables. In

> double-loop learning we seek to change the field of constancy itself. Double-loop learning does not supersede single-loop learning. Single-loop learning enables us to avoid continuing investment in the highly predictable activities which make up the bulk of our lives; but the theory builder becomes a prisoner of his own programs if he allows them to continue to be unexamined indefinitely. Double-loop learning changes the governing variables (the 'settings') . . . and causes ripples of change to fan out over one's own theories in use.
>
> Argyris and Schon 1974:17–19

12 Upon reflection, leadership was the most important factor influencing successful change. The following are some musts on managing change:

a *Leaders* must believe in change, be 100 per cent behind it and be authentic. Leaders must demonstrate commitment — losing this is losing everything.

Leaders need to take the long view because old habits die hard (remember, be patient). Success is incremental, only measured by hindsight. Leaders need to ask themselves: 'Where are the most pressing needs and what can we do to satisfy them? How can we develop programs to prop up the gaps that are emerging day after day?' (It is important not to be afraid to look for gaps.) How can we (as leaders) grow because supervisors' growth depends upon us, just as the operator's growth depends upon the supervisor's growth.

Above all else, leaders are an energy reservoir. They pour in the passion for 'the teams which own the processes' and the idea that *everyone* is a company leader.

b *Supervisors* are key communicators. Therefore, the communication process needs to be well understood by this group. As part of this process, the customer becomes the focal point of the communication strategy. Communication needs to be well understood. Customer requirements lead the way, and the customer replaces the leader as the focal point.

c *Operatives* are key players in managing change. The chain of leaders, supervisors and workers needs to be strong. Within the more enabling climate, operatives can bring in their brains from the doorstep where they had traditionally left them. Accordingly, operatives can learn about strategy. They can help develop new processes and operations. Operatives are the ones who open their own processes. They can be encouraged and developed to actively question and query. It is from them that the real power of continuous improvement comes.

Unions

Over the past ten years unions and management have reached a point where unions such as the FMWU (now Liquor, Hospitality and Miscellaneous Workers Union — the LHMU) use DuPont as an example to demonstrate to other companies their achievements of workforce empowerment. At that point the process has been facilitated by the partnership of the union and the organisation. Following site consultations with all staff, DuPont and the LHMU issued a joint statement on increased productivity and efficiency improvements.

The existence of strong relationships of bipartisan commitment has helped accelerate the process of change.

Industrial democracy came about as a result of the core process training, and it is the task teams that have been primarily responsible for the rise in improvements. Empowerment has led to the task and operational groups having total autonomy for the tasks and role which they themselves set. The union and management are committed to the encouragement of leaders, and it is this commitment that will lead to achieving Best Practice in team building and leadership.

Questions to consider

1. The CEO of DuPont suggests that there is a great opportunity and willingness for unions to clear the path for workplace culture change. What sort of role do you think unions would need to perform to make this happen? Which of the traditional sets of expectations about unions would be high on the agenda for change and why?
2. Supervisors and front-line managers seem to play a key role in managing change. Having read the DuPont case, what sort of transitional change program would you set up for supervisors in your own organisation (not forgetting any key concepts they might need to know)?
3. How could you transfer a model such as the DuPont model of 'Driving the Vision' to your own organisation? Why would you need to take into account the uniqueness of the way your organisation does things?

12

Kellogg (Aust) Pty Ltd

with Bill Richards

> You are a newly-appointed manager of Information Services in Kellogg (Aust) Pty Ltd. As part of your orientation, you have been sent to get first-hand information on the company's recent development.
>
> You are lucky enough to be given a personal briefing by one of the managers who was instrumental in the company's turnaround to become a successful global competitor. Here is the story as the manager told it.

The problem

The need for change

Kellogg (Aust) Pty Ltd has operated in Australia since 1924. It is 100 per cent owned by its United States parent organisation. The company has a senior management group in which Finance, Consumer Affairs, Sales and Marketing, Customer Services Manufacturing, Sales, Human Resources and Information Services are represented. These managers report to the Australian managing director. The company typically employs around 830 people. As can be seen by the start-up date, the company is very definitely a mature 'brownfield' site, where the organisation is mature and there has been time for processes and systems to become embedded into custom and practice.

Throughout its history, the organisation has managed to hold its own nationally. Even so, by the 1980s things had started to become difficult. Machinery had become older, management–employee relations had become poorer, and demand for the product had become matched by demand for overtime and strategic power at the employee level. Management style was traditional with managers managing and employees working, all in their own domains and mediated by the Craft Unions (unions), of which there were around thirteen in all.

By the early 1980s, the potential for looking at the future could fall into one of two categories. The future could look bleak if things went on as they were; however, the future could look rich and exciting if dramatic changes were made. There was hope for the latter because of some excitement, resulting from the opening up of the Asian market and, even further, the accessibility of the global market because of technology and telecommunications. What was needed was a *renewal* — a rebirth of just about every aspect of the business, from plant and machinery through to human resource management and employee relations. This realisation came around 1984–85. Such frightening statistics as 100 stoppages of various kinds in 1986 proved also that there had to be a better way of doing things with unions, firstly to achieve higher productivity and secondly because they were not going to disappear. Drastic action was called for and drastic action happened.

The company took union representatives off-site, attacked the accrued log of claims outstanding, and came up with a set of processes and rules for doing business. A negotiating committee was formed with one representative per major union. The members received training in negotiation and communication. By 1988–89, a 'single site' industrial agreement had been negotiated and 'ten commandments' produced in Kellogg (Aust) Pty Ltd Registered Industrial Agreement known as 'The Blue Book'. Unions' needs were listened to. The company had advocates, expertise and technology. The unions were given the same access as their company partners plus a meeting/work room equipped with a phone, fax and a computer. There was no magic genie waving the wand of consensus. Even though both parties, employers and unions, did not like parts of the emerging agreement, they reminded each other 'but we agreed . . . together we must . . . '.

The manager telling the story revealed that the journey to continuous improvement does not happen overnight. In the Kellogg's case it took years to break down past experiences. 'The change process is not risk-free. One makes mistakes — one consolation being that there are always less problems and issues to tackle', the manager said with feeling. At Kellogg's the undertaking of change meant no less than a change in the whole company culture. The manager suggested that no one person can be responsible for a change in culture. It has to be a team effort with union, management and employees all participating and being involved.

Landmarks show the continuous nature of the change in culture. December 1989 was the achievement of a single-site agreement for collective bargaining purposes. March 1990 was the ratification date by the Industrial Relations Commission of this agreement. In 1992 Kellogg's achieved Best Practices status as an employer.

Black Friday

Landmarks often mask hardships and drawbacks. For example, take 13 October 1989, often referred to as 'Black Friday'. This was the first time the company, through management, were allowed by the union to communicate with the mass of the workforce about anything under direct negotiation. There were 600 people to whom the message of change was to be communicated. In order to do this, Kellogg's closed down the plant. A meeting was set up at 11 a.m. at the local RSL (Returned Services League) club. The objective of the meeting was to explain to the workforce the impact of the new site agreement and the flexibility issues which were being requested as part of the wage proposal. The managing director, director manufacturing, director human resources and the plant manager all presented from their various perspectives, giving data and information to support their message. Management's expectations were very high and the managers assumed that having heard this information about their future with the company, the employee support would be unanimous. However, this proved not to be the case. The expectations were not realised for the following reasons. Firstly, there was difficulty in influencing such a large group made up of so many different nationalities (around fifty) and languages (around fifty-five). Secondly, the presenters did not put the proposal in the language of the people. Thirdly, the timing of the communication may not have been optimal.

Following this setback management reflected on the experience and agreed to use the media to sell the company information to employees. (After all Kellogg's used the media for its other customers, and employees were important consumers of the company when thought of as a product.) If management were to influence employees this could better be done by face-to-face meetings in smaller groups. Thus management decided to adopt the philosophy of 'media to inform' and 'face-to-face to influence', using media to support the latter as needed.

What Kellogg's management also learned following the Black Friday experience was that people have basic questions:

- What do I have to do in this new situation?
- Why do I have to do it?
- What is in it (change) for me: monetary and other benefits?
- What will happen tomorrow? (Will I still have a job?)
- How will the new changes affect my future? Will I still have security?

Change strategy

Because of the findings about what concerned the employees, the wage negotiations became a vehicle for our change strategy. This was in keeping with our desire to (a) improve the industrial relations environment and (b) become internationally competitive and in doing so be able to satisfy the needs of the employees. By 1990 the change strategy was ready to be presented to the workforce. The manager recalls the organisational talk as presented to the workforce:

> We are here in Australia and have a sizeable share of the Australian market. However, it is a mature market and the opportunities for growth are rather limited. Therefore, to increase market share, the company has decided to focus on Asia. In doing so, we need to concentrate on three key drivers:
>
> **Quality**
> **Cost**
> **Reliability**
>
> recognising that these will make us internationally competitive if we do them well.

Figure 12.1 is the corporate mission that now provides the focus for employees, managers and partners. The manager confided that he knew who had the key to improvement — the employees themselves. So, we conducted 42 sessions with around 15 people in one session, all sessions being held in the same week. The one-week target meant shift-by-shift sessions around the clock. The message was clear. It was to open up our new direction and give our new vision: 'Our growth is in Asia'. Management followed the philosophy of using media to inform and face-to-face to influence. This was

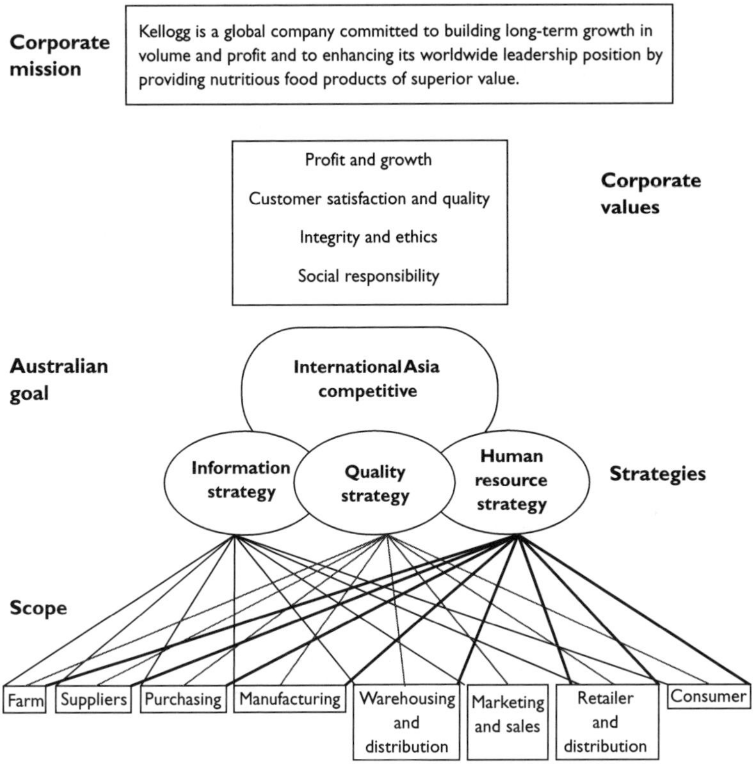

Figure 12.1 *Integration with corporate strategies*

achieved by a three-part video interspersed with face-to-face explanations. Given the communication challenges experienced earlier, we gave each employee a copy of the video. (This method is still followed when videos are used as part of a presentation.)

The manager pointed out that, of course, there were difficulties. There was plenty of historical 'baggage' in the form of 'them and us' attitudes. While unions in most industrial sites tended to be reactive rather than proactive, did it have to be that way? What was it that they reacted to? We came to the conclusion that it was:

- something management *said*;
- something management *did*; or
- something management *said they would do but didn't*.

If management were to move to an employee relations as opposed to industrial relations environment (something like that shown

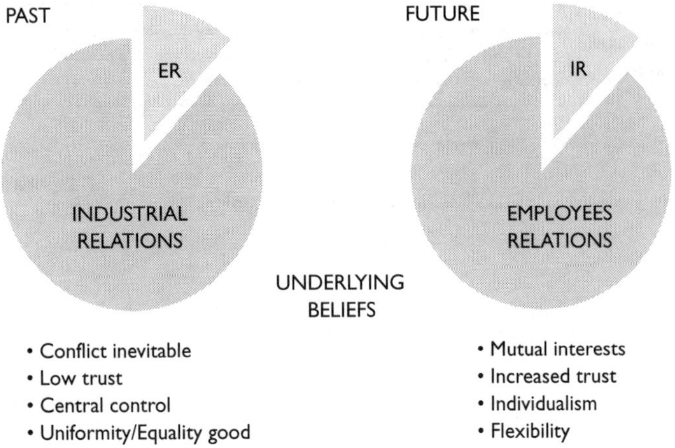

Figure 12.2 *Kellogg's enterprise bargaining: Direction Management*

in Figure 12.2), then management needed to change and it also needed to lead the change.

While the managers were technically very good, they *were* technical people with very good technical skills. They had little experience with conceptual skills and leadership/people skills. Basically, we had good managers but underdeveloped leaders. We had to think: 'What is our culture?' The development of people at all levels would feature in the new culture. The old culture needed to be disseminated. We judged that some core skills deemed mandatory for 'leaders' anywhere in the world included:

Communication
Problem solving
Decision making
Leadership theory and practice

So, we designed a leadership course (which is described later). The managing director and the senior management team were the first participants to go through the course. The Leadership In Management course (LIM) was about vision and it provided a base for setting our strategic direction. In particular there was a determination to make sure that the leadership concept and skills became cascaded from senior management leadership to shop-floor team building (see Figure 12.3).

The LIM (see Figure 12.4) was, and is, founded in a set of long-reaching principles of work and management as follows:

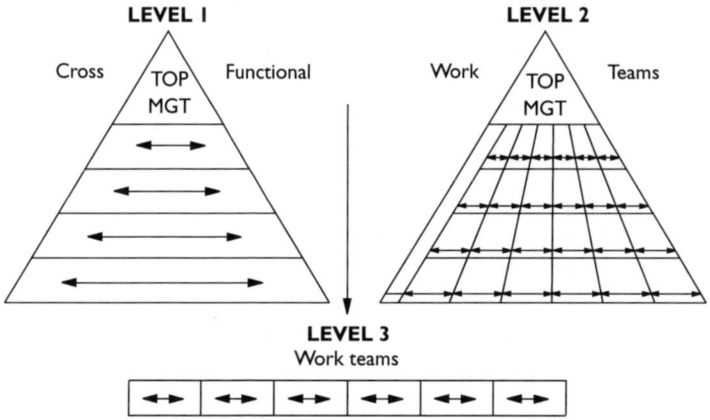

Figure 12.3 *Kellogg's course cascade*

- top down;
- self-development;
- conceptual framework;
- experiential learning with expert facilitation;
- skills relevant, transferable and reinforced;
- consolidation.

The core values of the Kellogg's approach were very evident in the choice of the above management principles and processes. They embodied senior management commitment with the value of personal growth and development. The recognition of employees as adults was very evident in the choice of content and methods employed in the leadership in management course and in the soft skills training (see Figure 12.5).

Course(s)	Content
1 Classroom lectures	• History, philosophy, theories of leadership • Structure of style and functions of leadership • Team building
2 Visiting speakers	• Leadership in practice — military, medicine, sport, commerce
3 Classroom simulations	• Demonstration of superiority of team over individual
4 Outdoor projects	• Practice of leadership functions and team building
5 Personal challenges	• Extending the comfort zone

Figure 12.4 *Kellogg Leadership in Management*

1 Effective interpersonal communications skills
2 Building trust
3 Problem-solving skills
4 Building teams

Figure 12.5 *Soft skills training*

Leadership was consistently promoted in a selective and holistic way. Aspects such as planning processes, lateral thinking, thinking outside 'the box', and flexibility in applying skills were fostered. We wanted people to learn to challenge themselves.

However change programs are never neat and tidy. Always there will be things running in parallel. For example, in 1989 we did a skills audit on all employees in the plant. Between September 1989 and May 1990 we negotiated with unions to move employees from the previous classification system of 99 levels to a new 14-level system. All this, plus constant communication about the need for change, the impact of change on employees and management, and about our successes, was happening. Our increased ability to learn from our mistakes was a necessary backdrop to the comprehensive change program.

> You leave the manager having received excellent verbal account of the changes. Also, the manager has kindly given you a file, which contains a summary and description of two of the company's change initiatives that have been developed during the change program. The file includes notes made at various meetings which the CEO held with management and unions to express important company concepts. You decide to analyse the file and jot down the essentials so that you will be ready to play your part in the management of future change.

The file

The file begins with a model of the Kellogg's manufacturing system (see Figure 12.6). This gives you a fair idea of the flow of processes as well as how values, such as being a learning organisation, are incorporated into the more functional areas.

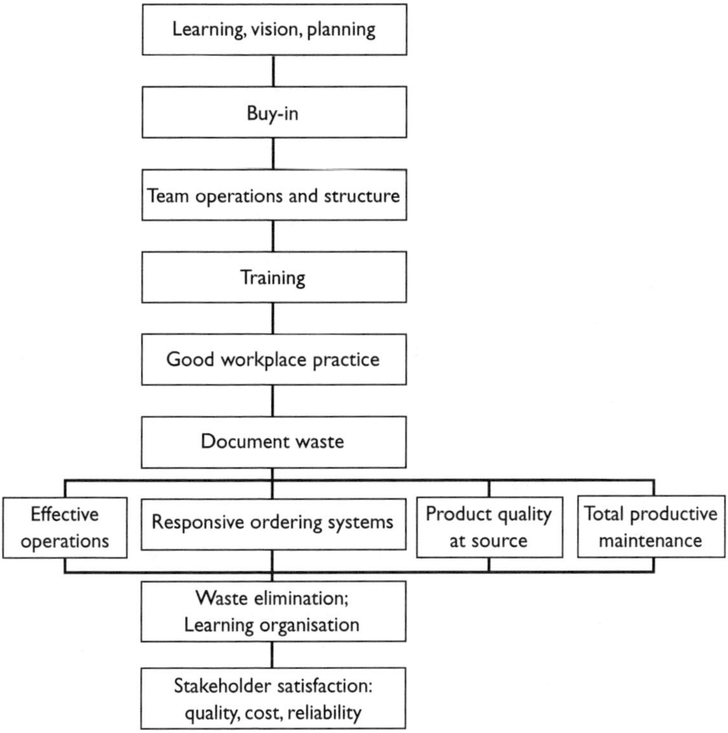

Figure 12.6 *Kellogg's manufacturing system*

> You know already, from your selection interview, that the company has thought deeply about what it means to be competitive in a global context. The company must be quality committed, cost competitive and reliable. The central theme, almost the byword of the company, is a wholehearted dedication to customer satisfaction. As an Information Services person, you are particularly interested in processes and systems, designed to achieve the behaviours and skills changes necessary in both the shop-floor and management areas.
>
> In the file are more details of the LIM initiative which you were told about and which serve as a vehicle for circulating and using important information.

LIM is an experientially-based course. It is conducted in an outdoor centre. Participants can leave familiar settings (and comfort zones) and concentrate on such things as the benefits of working together in teams and in doing so create shared experiences and use common nomenclature. The importance of the transfer of both team and individual skills in the workplace is emphasised because behaviour will change only if the newly acquired skills are supported and reinforced. This makes it a team-building approach with a difference. For a start it embraces not only managers and supervisors but also suppliers and partners. Accordingly, the following objectives make sense. In keeping with good training practices, the course is structured at linked levels.

Level 1 course objectives

- Demonstrate the value of good planning, clear communications, assessment of resources, humour, team spirit and a sense of camaraderie.
- Provide situations where teams effectively master the skills of co-operation, leadership, lateral thinking, planning and delegation.
- Demonstrate the skills and techniques for building and maintaining high-performance teams.

Level 2 course objectives

- Consolidate Level 1 skills and build on them to enhance leadership and team-building skills.
- Demonstrate the value and skills involved in conducting a thorough appreciation before constructing the plan.
- Provide a non-threatening environment where the theoretical skills of appreciation and planning may be applied to practical situations.
- Build 'in house' teams.

Level 3 course objective

- Link top to bottom. How to do that became a design issue. Many of the employees had never been part of a team.
- So they were shown what high-performing teams could do.
- Using the same environment as the leadership courses, the objective became to reinforce:
  - — shared experience; and
  - — establish a shared nomenclature throughout the organisation.

The above objectives were achieved through a step-by-step approach. The first step was the merging of key principles with the anticipated stages of dealing with change which Kellogg's people may go through. Each information group (IG) needed to give the right sort of information for the right stages. In particular, 'Actions' and 'Follow-up' were key activities for dispelling mistrust. See Figure 12.7.

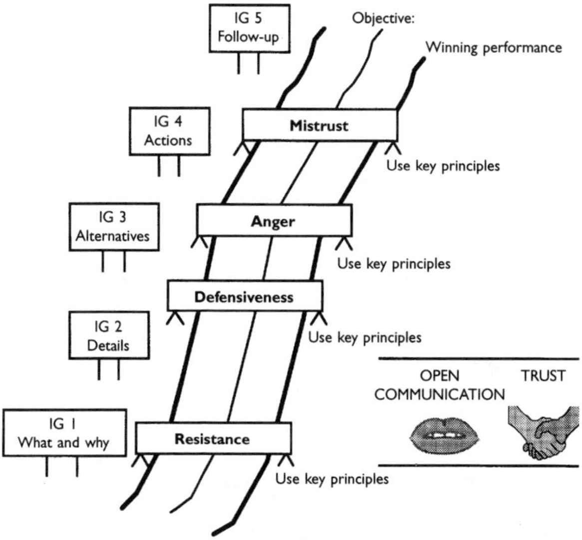

Source: Adapted from Byham and Cox 1988

Figure 12.7 *First step*

The second step in the change process recognised that training could not be considered as an isolated system. See Figure 12.8.

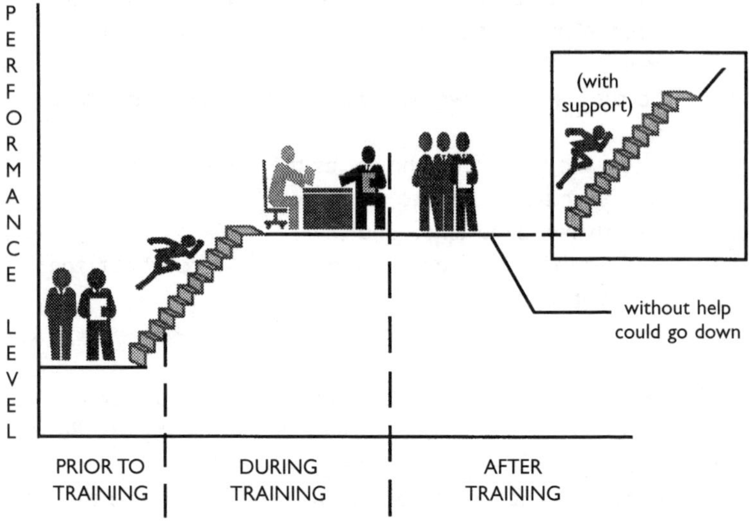

Figure 12.8 *Second step*

Step three (see Figure 12.9) is the integrated model which supports and is supported by step two.

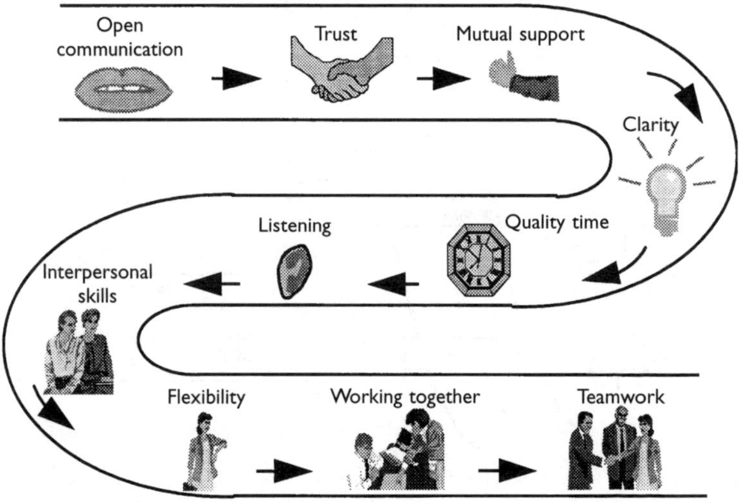

Figure 12.9 *Third step*

(The file shows that the CEO noted that some of the elements would be difficult and hard earned and that there would be setbacks. For supervisors and managers it would be seductive, especially under pressure of deadlines, to slip into old directive ways. There could be days where misunderstandings, falling down on promises and political playfulness may happen. The key to the long-term success would be not to dwell on these lapses but to build trust-in-general; to operate in a climate of mutual support which allows for setbacks and disappointments; to tackle rumour and ambiguity by going for clarity; to develop skills of analysis, presentation, listening and giving feedback; and to enhance interpersonal relationships.)

Building on the foundations already laid, what could you do in your role as the new Head of Information Services to contribute to objectives which the company has set itself in terms of the following?

- Kellogg's determination to become world class;
- maintaining a 'learning from our mistakes' culture;
- maintaining an empowerment process where there is freedom to act, information and feedback, skills and knowledge, and accountabilities right down to the shop floor;
- maintaining a quality-based management system;
- maintaining a climate of two-way honesty, firmness, fairness, friendliness and consistency.

Remember that the company sees that the key to successfully evolving the fabric and culture of the business is the way its knowledge and information services encircle the whole organisation. Information is defined as the fluxing agent required to bond the company's continual improvement ethos. The company sees the bonding process as involving not only the complete organisation but also its broad network of partners, customers and suppliers.

The outcome

Giving knowledge and information

The first activity appropriate to Information Services is to encircle the organisation with *knowledge* and *information*. This means that you need to consider every single individual as a leader. This does not mean creating information overload, with the fatigue and anxiety that this brings. Rather it means keeping in step with the Leadership in Management (LIM) and shop-floor team building, and fusing step-by-step and specific information into training programs.

Because the company is a learning and striving-for-progress organisation, any information and communication you give will need to follow adult learning principles such as:

- making sure Information Services people know why their information or communication will be of interest to the target groups;
- making sure target groups have got to the stage of accepting responsibility for their actions (this means making sure that inappropriate information is not given when the self-concept is fragile, (for example through the first step of the LIM program at times of resentment, anger and defensiveness);
- proactively seeking information from shop floor, union and management experiences to incorporate into 'learning communications';
- as far as possible tying information to goals, targets, plans or processes, or even company stories, heroes and rituals;
- keeping as close as possible to the chosen procedures and processes used in LIM and shop-floor team building, when giving information;
- giving information by working through social or psychological scenarios rather than objective, abstract ones (in other words, processing the technical and factual through a lens of cultural or social);
- tapping into ideas of well-being and quality of life (including life outside Kellogg's), and building on positive organisational self-talk.

Your third challenge is to enhance the empowering environment. The information and communication needs to address *who* should be empowered, *where* and by *what* information, and *how* the information should be imparted. Extracts from a speech the CEO has given gives a clear understanding of these elements.

CEO's speech

1	Formalisation and broad communication of the company's vision	**Where**
2	Active, consistent and demonstrative leadership	**Who**

3 Adoption and dissemination of a common nomenclature **What**
4 Activity to draw all human resources into the value-added chain **How**
5 Creation of a needs-based, problem-targeted information system.

Allow me to briefly explain these steps, and the logic implicit in this process.

Vision (the 'Where')
I mentioned earlier our Leadership in Management courses. One of the most commonly used lines in them is: 'If you don't know where you're going, you don't need a leader'. A not unreasonable proposition.

Fundamental to any activity is a crystal clear identification of eventual goals of what is anticipated or expected of the group, business and so on, of its resources and, most importantly, of the people it employs. All of us feel more comfortable when we know what is expected of us and what personal obligations we have when pursuing a particular course of action.

So at Kellogg's, a lot of emphasis is placed on letting everyone know where we — all of us — are going. We try hard to communicate the vision.

Leadership (the 'Who')
Leadership is a critical component of any change program. But its meaning in this context is often misunderstood. As I see it, leadership provides the spark and impetus for change to commence. The condition is simply demonstrated when someone initiates a push, a crusade or a striving for something better, and in the process captures the imagination and the productive capacity of stakeholders in the venture to undertake common and universal action.

To truly bring out change and to effectively *cascade* a refreshed business culture through an organisation, leadership must be exhibited throughout the *entire* business. In fact, everyone has the *opportunity* to demonstrate leadership, even if it is as simple as showing others a better way of performing a particular task. I deliberately said 'everyone'.

> Leadership is not just an obligation of the chief executive, his management team and the board. It's *everyone's*!
>
> Mr Konosuke Matsushita, founder of Matsushita Electronics, has told us that the core of management is precisely this art of mobilising and pulling together the intellectual resources of all employees in the service of the firm.

Your information plan

Given this inspirational speech you have developed your step-by-step information plan:

- *Step one*: Educate all employees and other groups outside, such as suppliers and partners, that the days of using information to control are over. Attitude change to the sharing of information systems is an important input in the change program.
- *Step two*: Managers who have not already done so will relinquish the role of being the regulator and co-ordinator of incoming and outgoing reports and data. Intelligence will be passed on to task or process teams, not on a predetermined (by manager) need-to-know basis but on a right-to-know basis. There will be continuing education in *attitude change* towards *information sharing*.
- *Step three* (in conjunction with human resource management): Performance monitoring will not require garnering and harvesting information to be used as evidence either in favour or against. In a trust environment, relevant information for particular purposes including discipline will be designed so that employees are not disadvantaged.
- *Step four*: Once these information accountabilities have been incorporated into the LIM and shop-floor team-building programs, the team structures can be used to workshop ideas and suggestions for 'The Ideal Knowledge and Information System', based upon the encirclement concept (see Figure 12.10).

With help you have devised a promotional campaign that will serve to symbolise the company communication plan to support a learning and progressive organisation of global competitive status, based on this company communication philosophy.

Communication, the need for factual intelligence and the galvanisation of the creative forces within the company, all flow from adequately handling the information and data resources within the organisation.

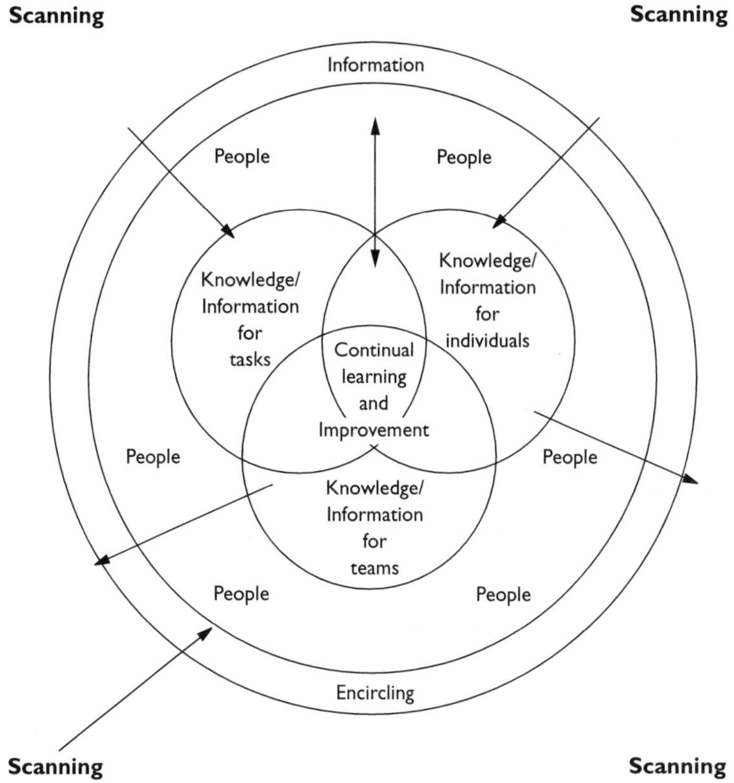

Figure 12.10 *The encircling model of information*

- *Step five*: Information Services will spearhead the generation and continuous creation of rituals, ceremonies, stories and heroes to reinforce the culture and values.
- *Step six*: Information Services will develop monitoring systems so that information and communication fit within the company culture/ethos alongside, and compatible with, the human resource systems.

> And you're ready. You have used the participative material and your own philosophical statement to build a schema — a model which is the blueprint for success in information services. Monday's the day you present it. Good luck.

13

A new regional bank

by David Napoli

The problem

Background

This case study is about an Australian regional bank which began its life as a building society, established in the 1860s. Throughout its history its public image was as a community-based organisation with a traditional management style.

In 1987 the society successfully applied for a banking licence — an action which significantly changed the way in which the former society was managed. It had to use a radically different legal framework to provide products and services previously unknown to the organisation. The bank was now competing in a very different market.

The architect of the change was the chief general manager. His drive and administrative competencies enabled the transfer to occur and the new organisation to be born. The early years were turbulent and the CEO concentrated on the structure and systems to ensure they could deliver the new services and products to the customers. He decided to focus on the development of systems and the technical skills of employees. Accordingly, he directed considerable energy towards establishing a comprehensive induction program for those staff directly in contact with the bank's customers.

In the early 1990s the bank, through the drive and energy of the managing director, attempted to introduce a participative improvement process similar to those created around the concept of quality circles. This meant encouraging groups of employees to meet regularly to consider improvements to the processes. Secondly, the bank introduced an employee-recognition program during that period to formally recognise employees for outstanding customer service or for significant innovations in the bank's processes. The employees had lived through a period where they were united by a single mission — to become a bank! It was a time of great individual commitment and a truly common and shared focus.

A takeover bid by another new, but larger, bank produced an additional bonding between staff. The situation created some unusual alliances. It brought employees and management together to secure the independence of the bank. The most surprising alliance, however, was between the union which covered the award employees and the new bank management. Collectively they fought the invader.

All of this turbulence in a relatively short period of time left the executive management of the bank with little time, or perhaps energy, to tackle a new challenge. The group did not keep up the commitment to employee involvement, which was born during the defence of their bank from the outside influence. (The comments which follow are the author's perceptions of the situation and do not necessarily reflect how others might see it. However, in the business of deciding when and where to intervene, one's professional judgment is generally all that is available.)

The human resources management functions

When this case history began in 1990, it became clear that the human resources function was seen as an administrative one. Internal customers also perceived the position as insufficient and ineffective. Successes were rarely celebrated and failures received a great deal of publicity; this reinforced the general view of the human resource role. A great deal of insecurity existed within the function.

There were resource shortages: employees strove to maintain a professional service with limited systems support. Many transactions were still manually processed which led to a considerable number of work hours regularly dedicated to the analysis of data and the preparation of reports. Because of the general perception that the quality of service was unreliable, increasing requests were made for reports and explanations. This clearly compounded the difficulties in providing a quality human resource management service with limited resources and 'stretched' systems.

The function seemed to lack a clear vision of what it wanted to achieve and a shared understanding of its purpose. Its lack of focus and direction caused confusion and anxiety among the directors and staff. There was a shared feeling of hopelessness. Staff believed that no one was prepared to defend them. Additionally, they felt uncertain about the purpose of their jobs and who they were serving. Human resources was a function in which staff were looking upwards and not outwards to their internal customers. Not many saw human resources as a legitimate part of the bank's overall management function. Certainly, for many it did not have an advisory, facilitatory or consulting role. It was an administrative processing operation.

A new position was created in order to separate the human resource planning functions from the administration processes. This enabled considerable improvements in the performance of the human resources function and allowed the human resource management systems to develop and improve.

The common purpose

Each individual executive had a vision for the bank. The managing director saw it as a 'boutique bank' in a niche market. Some executives, however, were desperately trying to re-create the banks they had left, while others were genuinely trying to create a new and exciting banking institution. Many executives did not enthusiastically embrace the managing director's vision either because it was not clear to them or because, in fact, they chose not to accept it. This possibly was a contributing factor to, or was the result of, a lack of genuine teamwork within that group. The managing director's dominance led many of the executives to be cautious to the point where decision making within their portfolios was limited to those areas deemed to be safe. The tactics used by the executives were political and often displayed symbolic self-interest. A high turnover rate among this group prevailed.

The bank

A management philosophy

The bank introduced programs to signal a managerial philosophy which focused on developing commitment through involving employees. However, this was generally regarded in a cynical light as theory and actions were often in conflict.

While delegation was discussed, the bank centralised decision making, often drawing it up to higher organisational levels. Important decisions such as those regarding redundancies or restructuring were undertaken in a climate of secrecy, while a program encouraging employee contributions to improvement and open communications were actively promoted.

The arbitrary and autocratic decision-making processes caused employees to question the moral and ethical values of the bank. There were no 'ten commandments' or other code of practice to guide behaviour. In fact, there was at times a feeling that the prevailing philosophy was survival of the fittest. At the same time, there was much teamwork, collective problem solving and working together. Predicability, certainty and a 'no surprises' mentality prevailed. Innovation, while encouraged, was risky. Control was the central value. This preoccupation with control was rationalised by references to market sensitivities as well as to the historically attractive product banks deal with — money!

Policies and procedures

In 1990 the bank established a set of highly centralised systems to control the outcomes of the decision-making process. The competencies of employees who were in contact with customers were continually questioned. The executive's view was that they were generally unable to exercise sound judgment, particularly in credit or loan decisions. Systems were seen as a means of controlling the unreliability of management. Paradoxically, employees were encouraged to build effective customer relationships by responding flexibly to customers' legitimate requests. Attempting to achieve this within a highly centralised and well-developed set of system constraints is at best a little difficult and at worst impossible. These circumstances led to poor staff motivation and assurance that they adopt the 'safe' position with respect to customers. Customers were often given negative responses to their requests because the managers either feared the consequences of presenting the cases or simply could not be bothered to act.

Employees had little faith in performance management and the remuneration systems to deliver justice. The performance management system was strongly biased towards quantitative targets. Qualitative issues such as customer service were not reliably evaluated and reported. The system was driven by the bosses who forced employees to look upwards and not outwards. This led them to a focus on 'what can I get from the bank' rather than 'what can I contribute?' Myopic self-interest prevailed. Manipulative and political tactics were often evident in each employee's actions. Self-interest and plain survival were the focus of many employees. Controls and checks were rife. Simple approvals required a number of signatures. Procedures were often unduly complex and sometimes activities were duplicated. The executive's view was that 'as long as we are in control, nothing else matters'.

Union relationships

The bank had a historically strong and supportive relationship with the Federated Clerks Union.

Banking business

Traditionally, the bank focused on housing loans. Since becoming a bank, this focus was expanded to business loans, for which there was an increasing number of non-performing loans. In other words, the borrowers were unable to service interest and principal repayments.

Employees

Employees often felt a sense of helplessness. Many were actively seeking new positions outside the bank but felt trapped by the economic downturn of the early 1990s.

The level of the employees' technical competencies was particularly high. A well-developed and renowned training process was in place to deliver those competencies. However, a means of effectively developing the non-technical process-related skills was missing, such as communicating with customers, seeking out information in an unintrusive manner and expressing intuitive information on behalf of the customer.

Fear and insecurity ruled. Employees often expressed the view that 'there is no security' and therefore we should 'maximise what we can get when we can'. This insecurity led employees to adopt manipulative tactics and pursue the myopic self-interest discussed earlier. Risk taking and innovative behaviour did not have an encouraging history. Therefore, employees adopted a policy of 'keeping your head down' and not attempting to disturb the status quo. A desire for safety prevailed at all levels. Cynical responses to continuous restructuring and redundancies reinforced the desire for safety.

Other work undertaken

During that period work was being done to improve the credit control processes, reduce the impact of business which exposed the bank to potential losses, and improve the job skills of employees. New banking systems were being developed to allow improved service and delivery. Rationalisation of the branch structure was also under way amid what was perceived as continuous restructuring.

The managing director's response

The managing director was aware of the need to focus on the issues outlined above. He created a new position of general manager, human resources, to lead the organisation through a change process in the management of its employees. The organisation recognised that the change from a building society to a bank had been successfully completed. The time had come to develop the other part of the organisation — the management of its employees.

Author's comments

The features of the organisation are presented for educational purposes only. It is not intended to be a criticism of the bank in question. The bank, it could be argued, is typical of medium-sized businesses in Australia and, similarly, the problems and solutions here could be constructed for many of them.

> Let's say you are taking up the position of general manager, human resources.
>
> 1 What is your analysis of the situation?
> 2 What do you see as the appropriate intervention points?
> 3 What strategic change processes would you put in place?

The outcome

Stabilisation of the bank's human resource management process

The first stage was to stabilise the current human resource management process. The reasons were twofold.

Firstly, reducing stress and time pressures, caused by operating unreliable systems and processes, was essential. Initially, such systems as pay processing, leave management and job evaluation were focused upon. Only by reducing and controlling variation in the systems could staff be freed to explore improvements in serving the internal customers of the human resource function.

Secondly, these systems had a profound and extensive impact on every employee within the bank. Improving the service and meeting their requirements built a strong base of support for the changes to be introduced in the future.

Other administrative processes were also improved, and were developed with the internal customers' requirements in mind.

Human resources management

Employees learned about the vision held, the purpose for that vision, and the values by which the human resource division would be managed. They embraced those ideals, concepts and values with varying degrees of enthusiasm. The cynics were prepared to wait and see if the actions would be congruent with the espoused theory. Management decided not to react to the cynical views but rather to let actions speak for themselves.

It was important to give all the employees in the division a feeling that the human resource management was clear about where everyone was going, and that it had a strategic plan to get there and a passion to achieve a highly professional customer-focused human-resource function. Establishing the division's credibility was a high priority.

Individual differences among employees within the division were explored and considered in optimising the match between individuals and jobs. As a result, it was necessary to restructure the division.

The planning model

A planning model based on the socio-technical principles advocated by Fred Emery and his colleagues was used.

Core elements

Defining these core elements begins by exploring the organisation's vision, its mission and managerial philosophy on values. This is the core of the planning process. It reflects management's beliefs about how people should be managed and work arranged. It reflects the relationship between the management's beliefs and the achievement of the bank's objectives.

The core elements do not provide detailed action plans or strategies but deal rather with the underlying principles. They serve as a guide against which to consider organisation decisions and thus ensure integration and congruency within the organisation.

Primary elements

The next level of planning deals with the primary features of the planning model. The technology in use, the systems, the design of jobs and the arrangement of jobs into work units are regarded as the primary characteristics to determine the organisation's effectiveness. At this point the technology is linked to the requirements of people expressed in the core element. Ask the question: 'What is the best way to design jobs so as to optimise the technology available to serve the customer's needs, and also reflect the management's beliefs about the way people should be managed and work organised?'

The demands of the technical system need to be considered in the pursuit of meeting the customers' and employees' requirements.

Organisation support features

This involves making decisions on the organisation's structure, supervisory roles, information systems, and recognition and reward systems in order to support and complement the earlier design decisions. The structure and specifications of the support features must be consistent with the core elements.

The implementation features

The next step is to consider the recruitment of employees, training, orientation, policies, procedures and symbols. Again, there is a need for these to be internally consistent with the design decisions taken at the earlier stages.

It is crucial to take an integrated or holistic approach. While it is not always possible to begin planning at the core level, this must be addressed early in the change process. The manager of the change process needs to speculate on the core element level items.

Although the initial intervention may occur within any area of the planning model, it is mandatory to consider all areas to ensure congruency.

The trilogy of lead interventions

Three points of intervention were chosen: job-evaluation system and process, competency-based pay for award employees, and performance management. These were implemented more or less simultaneously.

Job evaluation system and process

The first point of intervention was in the area of job evaluation. A new structure was developed and implemented with less levels to address some of the perceived inequities of the prevailing system. Jobs continued to be classified at the supervisory managerial levels.

However, they were grouped into families and a much broader classification system was introduced.

The process of job evaluation was changed to allow more input. Rather than rely as a small group largely comprising human resource management staff, the group was expanded to allow a broader range of people to become involved. A committee was formed. Obviously, this required education on the job-evaluation process for those who might not be 'formal' human resource staff. Additionally, managers who were responsible for seeking reviews of position classifications were invited to present their cases to the committee. Those presenting cases were also subject to questioning by the committee members.

These procedural changes worked to restore faith in the job-evaluation process — a process which ultimately influenced salary levels. This was a most visible change to organisation life.

Competency-based pay for award employees

The second intervention strategy focused on the pay and classification system for award employees. It involved the introduction of a system of pay directly linked to each employee-assessed level of competency.

This strategy represented fundamental change. No longer did people receive a rate of pay based upon the position they occupied. Rather, individual employees were assessed and paid according to their skills, knowledge and contribution. The process began with a presentation to employee representatives and union officials from the Federated Clerks Union, in which a personal management philosophy was expressed, a conceptual model of change presented and a process of employee involvement in its development guaranteed.

Working parties were established to address implementation issues. At the same time, briefing sessions were conducted with small groups of employees to explain the philosophical basis for the proposed changes and the implementation issues associated with them. In addition, an informal presentation was sought by the Industrial Relations Commissioner on these developments. This briefing of the commissioner encouraged the union officials to continue their support for the proposals.

While the workforce was developing an enthusiasm for the changes proposed, the middle management and some executives were beginning to display resistance. Resistance from this group had to be addressed. It was dealt with by continuing the presentations and allowing them to express their fears openly. At the presentations, fears were addressed and in doing so, new implementation issues were highlighted. Typical fears centred around the possibility of employees drifting to the top pay levels. There probably continues to be some managers who believe (without justification) that there is something desirable about a normal distribution. To have pay levels skewed towards lower levels is in some obscure way seen as abhorrent. Surely, if one is seeking a highly responsive organisation in which employees are empowered to respond to the reasonable demands of customers, then highly trained staff are mandatory. In the author's view it was lunacy to permit the bank to have staff who were not competent enough to be well rewarded to meet its customers.

'To achieve flexible customer-focused responses requires high levels of competency. High levels of competency can expect to attract higher levels of pay. A dynamic customer-focused organisation should be looking forward to its pay levels being skewed in favour of higher levels.' This was part of the logical counter argument to the resistance from the executives. Other points of resistance included issues about the mechanics of delivering training and assessing competencies of individuals. Points needed to be confronted here were firstly the insecurity of managers and supervisors regarding their own competencies and, therefore, job security. The second was the possibility that managers and supervisors had to face some real performance management issues. This meant facing issues such as telling their team members that they had inferior levels of competency which were no longer acceptable.

Furthermore, the reason that you deliver training to develop the competencies of employees is to enable them to make decisions. If employees were making more and more decisions at the point where the bank meets its customers, the role of management needed to change to one which focuses on improvement. Improvement covered both the development of competencies of employees and the systems in which they operate.

Other award and management-imposed restrictions were open to challenge as a result of this changed focus and new work arrangements. The introduction of a 76-hour fortnightly work cycle, standard hours of work throughout the network of branches, and changed overtime arrangements were but a few of the changes facilitated by this process. The new award bound both parties to significant changes in work practices and it initiated many other procedural and cultural changes within the bank.

Performance Management

The last intervention in the initial trilogy was to overhaul the performance management systems.

There were some significant changes introduced. Firstly, collecting qualitative performance data was given the same priority as the quantitative data. Recognising qualitative performance required more sophisticated ways of assessing it. No longer could the bank rely on managers and supervisors providing all the data for this assessment. The assessment required inputs from customer, subordinates, peers and managers.

Expansion of the database on which performance was measured contributed to a change in the culture. Previously employees were preoccupied with looking upwards to satisfy the requirements of their managers. The new process encouraged a focus on looking outwards in serving both internal and external customers. This culminated in a process where a meeting between the manager and the appraisee was held. Here, performance was agreed, plans for the next accounting period were developed, and individual contracts established. Support in terms of skills development and resources were negotiated.

The existing performance data were incomplete and, if available, were not particularly useful. The information comprised simple scales on which performance could be reflected. However, the data available demonstrated that central tendency was alive and well. The data therefore, were largely meaningless in terms of their ability to provide guidance for training and development decisions, career decisions and personal feedback. Lastly, the quantitative targets tended to create heroes and villains. The targets established were usually based on the result of past performance plus an arbitrary improvement factor. Because of the averaging of past performance and the arbitrary nature of the improvement targets, statistically we could expect to exceed performance in one period and fall below it in another. A crude reliance on quantitative targets prevented the process from delivering what it was set up to provide.

Greater involvement in setting targets was built into the process together with a better understanding of normal variation in the systems in which people work. In addition, a process was established to enable each employee to exercise ownership and control over it. The focus shifted from the process being used as an instrument for control, exclusion and inclusion, to one in which improving performance became each employee's passion.

Consequent interventions

As the changes at the practices and procedures levels began to affect the bank's management, it became more and more obvious that one could not throw a stone into the pond without the ripples going everywhere. The changes led to questioning by the executive and senior managers who began to feel an increasing loss of control. The lead interventions were expected to cause anxiety. Anxiety generally stimulates action and in this case it did. Workshops were called by the managing director to clarify and develop commitment to the bank's mission, vision, values and broad strategies. A small working party was assembled to establish a statement of the executives' beliefs and values about how people should be managed and jobs organised.

This produced the required statement of beliefs and values. However, there were no overt and deliberate plans to enrol the employees in the attainment of those beliefs and values. Rather, the actions of the executive were to be a tangible demonstration of the values. *This was a sound strategy for a relatively cynical audience.* A series of management development programs were developed and conducted during that period. As well as developing the skills of leadership to support the job design aspects of the model, this provided a forum for participants to develop an appreciation of the stated values. This orientation process was vital to the development of a critical mass of support for the changes from the middle levels of the bank.

Lastly, restructuring provided an opportunity to create a new function within the bank dedicated to pursuing improvements in technical processes. The socio-technical approach demands that the technical processes need to support the social systems (or management style and philosophy) and the social systems need to support the technical processes. Restructuring meant that technical processes were to be reviewed against the management beliefs and values. Issues of control, centralisation, risk and empowerment were to be the subject of consideration by the group reviewing technical processes.

Summary

The lead interventions were at the level of practices and procedures. This is usually the easiest area to begin with as they are the most visible. This step was followed by more strategic interventions which concerned themselves with the belief system of the organisations. The final set of interventions occurred at the level of identity and unity. These were designed to work at a level which is beyond consciousness, both individually and corporately. This is a complex and difficult level to understand and describe. It may include looking at areas such as the use of charismatic leadership, history trips within the organisation, and the use of ritual and celebration.

14

The Xerox journey:

The search for a strategy for keeps

The problem

Background

The Xerox case demonstrates that the problems of change are not restricted to small organisations with modest budgets. Rank Xerox (Xerox) operates in over eighty countries, has over 500 000 customers, large and small, and its revenues for 1992 exceeded A$5 billion. Xerox grew into a large organisation through the pioneering days of photocopier development as the following quotes from Kearns and Nadler (1992) show:

> For the people who were up to the new challenge, the 1960s were incredibly heady times. I have heard plenty of stories about what the climate was like. Everyone felt there was a mission to be accomplished, and so everyone worked late but never complained. The Xerox offices buzzed with energy and purpose. Senior managers believed they were making the world a little better by bringing about the democratisation of information. Steadily a culture was nourished of pioneers building something destined to be immensely powerful yet also something dedicated to the greater good. That was the conviction that Joe Wilson inculcated in people. He recorded an orientation film that got played thousands of times for new recruits and succinctly summed up the ambitions of the company:
>
> 'We think we are creating a power, a power of finance, a power of marketing, a power of research and development, and, above all, a power of people . . . This means you are part of one of the strongest enterprises in North America. Welcome' (page 37).

> . . . By 1970, the shape of the modern Xerox had become clear. The corporation had grown to a large enterprise with its roots in many places . . . the company had built a twenty-nine-story skyscraper headquarters . . . Xerox was now becoming multinational . . . Xerox felt it was going big time (page 49).

Yet with 'big time' comes problems which the skills and abilities of pioneering and enthusiasm alone won't match. So, a layer of top management, mostly with financial and engineering backgrounds ('the Ford Men'), were brought in to Xerox. And now we see how important the human element is and how the power of a change of values can override the logic of skills and abilities.

> The old timers didn't feel the auto people should share the same values. The eager Ford Men had manifest ambition but they were not copier men . . . Their language was the peculiar mumbo jumbo of financial wizards. Among other things, the Ford Men introduced rigid controls and a sense of authoritarianism that didn't exist before. A very hierarchical structure was put into place that had been unknown and to some extent was unfortunate . . . As a result, a rather severe culture clash, which would grow in intensity, developed between the Ford Men and the Xerox people (page 64).

No matter how much a leading edge an organisation has, and no matter how much market share it has, there will always be someone coming up the ranks to challenge. In the case of Xerox, IBM was up and coming, the Japanese were coming, and the world would become a harder place in terms of keeping market share. Kearns and Nadler (1992:3) tell the story about the reshaping of Xerox's future. They tell about the concept of 'retrofit'.

> In fact retrofit and good retrofit almost became a company value and as such, part of its culture. An ingenious group of Xerox inventors, at the "skunkworks" could correct, retrospectively, almost anything. The Xerox platform had always been one of ease of use. Speed was another important issue. Good prompt service to iron out problems was another . . . the Japanese, need not rely on retrofit. Their products were 'snap fit' and did not need the help of a mallet to finish the fit.

> Part of our difficulty was unquestionably our mindset. Certain beliefs would become part of Xerox thinking and there was almost no way to shake free of them.

Xerox learned that the Japanese were able to carry six to eight times less inventory. They matched quality of incoming parts by 99.5 to Xerox's 95 per cent, with half as much overheads. 'In category after category the difference wasn't 50 per cent better or anything like that; it was almost always over 100 per cent.' It sometimes takes that sort of environmental shock to galvanise organisations into action and Xerox was no exception.

The Xerox game changed. A new approach, centred around a continuous process of measuring its products, services and practices against its toughest competitors or those companies renowned as leaders, was to shape the new Xerox mission. The business was to be expressed in terms of superior quality, product reliability and levels of cost. Mindsets were also on the agenda for change — in particular the mindset so well demonstrated by the Japanese, which was to set high expectations of themselves and somehow find a way of meeting them.

Xerox installed many manufacturing and market changes: strategic business units, customer satisfaction, management systems, benchmarking and new cost systems. However, the 'people decisions' were arguably the most radical.

Employee involvement was Xerox's key to future success. People at all levels were allowed to take part in decision making which affected their lives. Most important of all, Xerox became committed to the idea of adopting a *total quality* approach as a vehicle for change.

Leadership through quality?

After being developed in 1983, Leadership Through Quality was launched in 1984 and its lessons began cascading down through all levels of the corporation. The behaviour and actions of management ensured that the management team at all levels of the corporation not only provided the necessary leadership for the successful implementation of Leadership Through Quality, but also practised the principles day in and day out. In other words, managers must walk as they talked.

By 1985, all middle and senior managers had been trained in the use of quality tools and, by 1986, 2500 Quality Improvement Teams were in place. By the end of 1988, *all* Xerox people worldwide had been trained and were using quality improvement tools. The central business priorities for training were:

- customer satisfaction;
- employee motivation and satisfaction;
- market share;
- return on assets.

Xerox was in the same position as any organisation. However helpful the ideas and examples of others, at the end of the day any organisation is unique. It has its own culture, values and philosophy. It has its own business opportunities and challenges. It has its own products and businesses. Also, like all successful organisations, Xerox recognised the two essential ingredients for success: ownership of the quality values, structures systems and processes by *all* organisational members and unequivocal support for the change process by senior management.

How did this begin? In 1983, twenty-five senior operating executives from around the world, working as a team, designed Leadership Through Quality. They hammered out a Xerox quality policy and the broad outlines of a quality strategy and implementation plan. The policy says simply, but powerfully:

> Xerox is a quality company. Quality is the basic business principle for Xerox. Quality means providing our external and internal customers with innovative products and services that fully satisfy their requirements. Quality improvement is the job of every Xerox employee.

The management team took great pains to define precisely what it meant by quality. It noted that quality as referred to in Leadership Through Quality differs from the conventional view of quality in at least four respects.

1 Whereas the conventional definition of quality reminds us of words like 'goodness' and 'luxury', Xerox defines quality as 'conformance to customer requirements'.
2 Whereas the conventional performance standard for quality is some acceptable level of defects or errors, the quality performance standard in Xerox is 'products and services that fully satisfy the requirements of our customers'.

3 Whereas the conventional system of achieving quality is to detect and correct products after they have been completed, Xerox emphasises the 'prevention of errors'.
4 Whereas the conventional system for measurement of quality relies on indices, Xerox measures quality by the 'costs we incur when we do not satisfy customer requirements'.

The management team realised that implanting this view of quality into the Xerox culture would require massive change. It was equally cognisant that change of this magnitude required that Xerox people work with and not against the new systems. Finally, the senior management team articulated some very precise objectives for what it wanted to accomplish through Leadership Through Quality. These included:

- to install quality as the basic business principle in Xerox and to ensure that quality improvement becomes the job of every Xerox person;
- to ensure that Xerox people, individually and collectively, provide external and internal customers with innovative products and services that fully satisfy their existing and latent requirements;
- to establish as a way of life management and work processes that enable all Xerox people to continuously pursue quality improvement in meeting customer requirements.

Such massive cultural change and ambitious objectives required thoughtful planning. After senior management developed its broad plan to help the company achieve its quality objectives, a Quality Implementation Team (QIT) was formed with representatives from each operating unit and corporate headquarters. The QIT assisted in implementing the strategy and managing the transition. The team, with the support of senior management and a Quality Training Task Force, used the 'borad plan' to develop the detailed strategy for Leadership Through Quality. The strategy required a transition team and those mechanisms (below) for change that continue to be used today at Xerox.

Standards and measurements

These provide all Xerox people with new ways of assessing and performing their work, solving problems and improving quality. Tools to do this include a six-step and a nine-step quality improvement process; competitive benchmarking; an emphasis on error prevention and doing things right the first time; problem-solving process; and techniques for determining the cost of quality.

Recognition and reward

These ensure that Xerox people are encouraged and motivated to practise the behaviours of Leadership Through Quality. Both individuals and groups are recognised for their quality improvements whether that takes the form of a simple thank you or a cash bonus.

Communications

This ensures that all Xerox people are kept informed of the objectives and priorities of the corporation in general and their work group in particular, and how they are doing in meeting these priorities. Communications include both formal media, such as magazines, films and communications events, as well as informal means, such as staff meetings.

Training

This provides every Xerox person worldwide with an understanding of Leadership Through Quality and a working knowledge of the tools and techniques for quality improvement. Training is delivered in 'family groups' consisting of a manager and his/her direct reporting staff. The manager, assisted by a professional trainer, conducts the week-long problem-solving and quality-improvement training.

During the course of the week, the group selects a problem or project for application of the quality process and tools. After training, the manager guides the family group in the use of the quality process. Once the project is under way, members of the family group work with a professional trainer to deliver the week-long training to their own subordinates, who then choose their own application project.

This method of training top managers first and having them participate in the training of their subordinates is called a training 'cascade'. It is designed to ensure that managers are trained in and understand the quality process and are actively involved in the training of their family groups. This enables the management chain to practise the 'learn, use, lead, inspect' sequence to reinforce the quality improvement objectives of the training. This happened at the highest levels as the CEO and his direct reporting staff participated in quality improvement projects as part of their own training. Their projects included improving the effectiveness of corporate management committee meetings and streamlining the quarterly operations reviews held with operating units. Their projects required the use of the quality improvement process and the problem-solving process.

The effect of Leadership Through Quality was not immediately measurable. But as each day and each month passed, Xerox began to benefit from its quality process. Xerox people worked as a team. The quality of products improved. Customers were more satisfied. Revenues and profits began to increase, and Xerox won back some of its lost market share. Revenues from Business Products and Systems increased from $8.7 billion in 1984 to $12.4 billion in 1989. Meanwhile, return on assets grew from 10.2 per cent in 1984 to 12.4 per cent in 1989. At the same time, the company's good work was recognised and rewarded by others. After winning the Deming award in Japan in 1980, other Xerox divisions won quality awards in France in 1987, England in 1983 and 1985, and the Netherlands in 1984.

In forming an application team for the prestigious Baldrige National Quality Award, and putting together its application in 1988, Xerox learned more about its products and services as seen through the eyes of the customer. Xerox also learned that it could improve on its quality efforts, a finding that served as the basis for an intensification of the company's quality efforts. The Baldrige Award application required Xerox to provide information for seven categories: leadership, information and analysis, planning for quality, human resource utilisation, quality assurance, quality results and customer satisfaction.

Some of the achievements are described here. Machine performance during the first 30 days after installation, showed an average of 40 per cent improvement from 1985 to 1988. Xerox copy quality was recognised as the best in the world. The 10 Series of copiers, introduced between 1982 and 1986, was 5 per cent to 20 per cent more reliable than its predecessors. Customer satisfaction increased 38 per cent between 1984 and 1988; labour overhead was trimmed 50 per cent from 1984 to 1988; and materials overhead was reduced 40 per cent from 1984 to 1988. Among vendors, Xerox trimmed its supplier base from 5000 in 1980 to less than 500 at statistical process control and just-in-time manufacturing. The Baldrige examination found that the number of defective parts was reduced from about 10 000 parts per million in 1980 to 325 parts per million at the end of the 1980s.

> Given the past successes, what might you visualise as key goals to pursue in future in terms of (a) people development and (b) maintenance of the competitive market position?

The outcome

Two major tools which help *people development* are Policy Deployment and Business Excellence certification.

Policy deployment is both a diagnostic tool and a process for setting objectives. A key principle is that a director limits his/her objectives to a vital few actions. These are then cascaded down the organisation with people at each level agreeing to their own list of actions. The end result, of course, is that all employees have set group and personal objectives, each person being involved in the organisation in a way relevant to the business. 'Self' is very important at Xerox.

The Business Excellence Certification is a method of self-assessment that allows each operating unit to measure itself against six performance criteria, which are in turn broken into 40 subelements. Self-assessments are then validated by an assessor from another unit within the company. Where necessary, improvement plans and actions are agreed and implemented, and then each unit is certified annually, again by a Xerox assessor. Again, where necessary, improvement plans and actions are agreed and implemented, and then each unit is certified, again by a Xerox assessor. A significant factor is that the validation is seen as a coaching opportunity for managers rather than an inspection exercise for quality experts. This is how Xerox expresses its goal setting for people development, through continuity rather than new fads. That is not to say that people will not have new challenges and new achievable steps along the quality journey. The very satisfied category of customer satisfaction, rather than the satisfied category, presents a challenge and one which leads directly to bottom line rewards.

In terms of extending its business competitiveness, Xerox set its sight on goals further afield than in the West. It did this by actively seeking to understand and do business with the very nation who, by its competition on the quality front, presented its greatest challenge

— Japan. Xerox has worked to further develop ties and relationships in South-East Asia and the Pacific basin. Xerox was fortunate as a corporation to have a direct window into Japan Inc. through its partnership with Fuji Xerox Australia. In a competitive environment where the Japanese are as tough on themselves as they ask others to be, Xerox will need to remain focused on quality as a mindset and as a reality for every employee. When operating in Asian cultures, Xerox will never be far removed from the task of managing change. Therefore, new change issues will need to be practically defined, fact-based and clearly analysed.

Fuji Xerox Australia

with David Stringfellow, Managing Director

The problem

Fuji Xerox Australia, previously Rank Xerox for many of its foundation years, has grown with the history of its parent Xerox in USA and Fuji Xerox in Japan. The Australian subsidiary has been operating since 1961 and employs over 1000 staff with a turnover which exceeds A$300 million. Fuji Xerox Australia operates as a major sales and service business unit with direct operations in all capital cities and exclusive indirect Strategic Network Partners — Xerox shops — in non-metro Australia.

> In Fuji Xerox Australia, and of course, the Total Quality Management movement, we have slowly — all too slowly for the competitive stance of Australia — learnt that Total Quality is a basic philosophy and not a programme, injection or short term initiative. After several years of implementing a change management culture, we can now appreciate its impact on learning, business process improvement and of course, productivity and the elimination of waste. It is now moving us into an era of added real value by full use of the contributions of our

> employees and not just financial benefits of business growth so prevalent in managing in the '70s and '80s. This real value is to the benefit of the three stakeholders related to a business, the customers, the investors and the employees.
>
> David Stringfellow, KPMG Newsletter

David goes on to share some important observations for managers. The Total Quality Management culture is not an easy one to manage. However, taking this approach helps learning the areas of coaching and the development of people, information management and communications, teamwork, team spirit and the use of diversity to meet organisational goals. Quality is a journey, not a destination, which is firmly focused on the customer as a business team goal. Management is about working *on* the system rather than *in* the system and, in particular, about enlisting the full assistance of those who work in it. Continuous measurement of customer satisfaction, employee motivation and management practices, as well as revenue, costs, activities and profits are important.

David tells how Xerox, the parent, had given Fuji Xerox Australia a local advantage through recognising the symptoms and diagnosing the problems which faced many organisations worldwide — a loss of focus on the customer, and blurring of the requirements to have a competitive edge in leadership/key business processes/operating standards and methods. Xerox passed on a vision — to become a Total Quality company. Also passed on were objectives, methods and tools to support and enable a total cultural transformation which would embrace management and employee work practices alike. Through Xerox, the cultural transformation was legitimated. However, Australia is not America and there was still the need to develop a cultural fit, and a simple conceptual framework that was both logical and compelling that would drive the use of the Quality tools as a 'natural imperative'. This became the *Crusade for Customer Loyalty* to help the mission of becoming *Market Leader in Customer Satisfaction*. Managers at the highest level became involved. Godfathers — our directors — each adopted one state: spreading the message, reviewing plans, exhorting and supporting issue resolution and initiative at the lowest possible levels. Recognition was crucial — for Company/Divisional/Branch Customer Satisfaction/Query — complaint resolution improvement; for outstanding individual and small group contributions (Branch and National Awards) and for 'Champion' Branch Management Teams. Role modelling became a central tool at Fuji Xerox.

'Walk like we Talk' became the task of managers as they were coached, reinforced and recognised and, in turn, adopted the same throughout their staff. **L**earn **U**se **T**each **I**nspect was used throughout the 'family groups' (of a line manager and his/her directly reporting staff). *In the line by the line* training has been made faster by the use of additional facilitator support and training all new hires during induction.

Striving for excellence can sometimes produce interesting understanding and learning opportunities. Take the case of two quality systems: Prevention/Root Cause analysis and Inspection.

A production line was being used to remanufacture previously used copiers. This put a second life to work in the assets. However, copiers were not noted for their reliability and hence it was decided to include a Pre-Delivery Inspection (PDI) function at the end of the production line to ensure no faulty products left the plant for customer installation. The PDI was planned to need six to seven work hours on a two-station line following initial manufacture and it was, in fact, a model 'production' inspection and correction process.

> Is there any danger that you can foresee as the PDI function pursues the Xerox Excellence in Quality drive, getting better and better all the time?

The outcome

In a sense the inspection function had become too successful; so much so that the production line could depend on it.

After only six months the PDI was re-evaluated to find the work time had become 12 work hours per machine and a longer line of inspection. It was only six months more before it became 20 work hours per machine — exactly 40 per cent of the initial remanufacture time. The real issue was that the company had put a 'catcher' system into place which permitted initial build faults rather than root cause analysis and hence prevention. The lesson to be learned was that people are not machines and they will respond very much to the broad environment and culture (in this case a culture of Inspection) they work within. From a management (and a Quality) point of view the lesson is clear: 'Do it right the first time and don't accept fault rates'. Quality is zero defects. Everything else is the cost of poor quality.

The benefit of a culture change is that, if internalised by the people involved, dismantling systems which seem not to be working for the mission is achievable. Why? Because there is an element of empowerment in the continuous improvement ethic. Empowerment to change where recognised must be automatic (ask not 'why', ask 'why not?' instead). Change action, then, *must happen*. Advice from David is that it should also happen in small, bite-sized steps, everywhere with a clear focus of 'seeing it through' and then to ensure maintenance of controls of improved outputs at new levels. In the case of the PDI section, for example, new levels of operation would include asking some tough questions about the root cause of problems rather than developing a reputation as excellent 'catchers' of them at the inspection stage.

Questions to consider

1 Even though Xerox and Fuji Xerox Australia have come a long way in changing from inward looking to outward looking, how can the organisation maintain responsiveness to technological change where, conceivably, 'copying' could be replaced by technologies such as e-mail?
2 How could Fuji Xerox Australia capitalise on its position as the gateway to Asia for the parent Xerox?
3 How would Fuji Xerox set about acculturating both Japanese partners and Australian employees in each others' cultures, using Hofstede's ideas on national culture?

15

Tubemakers of Australia Ltd

Kembla Grange Plant

with Robin Buckham

The problem

Like Xerox, the 1960s were good to Tubemakers, Kembla Grange Plant. In the 1970s and 1980s the company was busy consolidating. There was a workforce core of skilled workers. These included fitters, electricians and so on. The company manufactured varieties on a theme of one product — pipe. Very often the product was customised and challenging in terms of design and specification. There was a good share of the local market.

Once a contract was procured, the organisational system would react. Capital and manpower were geared up to meet the challenge of the new order. This could, and often did, mean for the workforce overnight doubling of shifts and going flat out to meet the occasion. Predictably with a peaks-and-troughs system, this high of heavy activity would be followed by a low of inactivity and sometimes uncertainty. It was accepted that just as the fat times could be enjoyed, so the lean times had to be endured. The organisation had to find a way to make it possible to lift the game. The view that 'that's the way the business is: seasonal and contract-linked work' needed to be accepted, but also matched by people's willingness to develop flexible systems to meet this business context.

The vision and mission

Part of Kembla Grange's evolving vision concerned the labour force. This was 'to suit the business; a lean group with flexibility varying to suit capacity'.

There was also a conscious effort to stabilise the work situation, to depart from the vagaries of the immediate marketplace for one main product, and to reposition Kembla Grange Plant (the Plant) as pipe line systems as opposed to pipe line suppliers. There was to be a search for fewer troughs and peaks and a more controllable and proactive situation.

The vision required that a culture be developed which included the following values:

- Everyone treats the business as though it is his/hers.
- Everyone shares the vision and knows how he/she can help achieve it.
- Everyone welcomes appropriate change.
- Everyone looks for ways to improve things.
- Everyone is well educated in his/her own speciality as well as having an understanding of the whole business.
- All activities add value to the business.

The mission is 'to be the leading supplier of pipeline systems for oil, gas, petroleum products and mineral slurries in Australia and designated offshore markets'.

Achieving the vision and values, and the mission, has presented many challenges to the management, employees and unions at the Kembla Grange Plant. All stakeholding groups found that making a determined effort to be competitive meant hard work. A lean but permanent organisation rather than a core and influx model was chosen. The challenge was to achieve more productivity with fewer people. This put a heavy burden on the human resource situation for all involved.

All parties were aware that the mission would be achieved only through the best use of the resources available. Such reasoning is usually made clearer to management than to workers. Because of the history of Taylor-like models of what workers should be, there was not a tradition of including workers in such areas as strategic planning, market opportunities and threats, organisational structuring and restructuring. Such items as structuring were usually negotiated on behalf of workers by their unions, and pride in the work was achieved through the culture of the craft. Demarcation was the way to demonstrate the boundaries of good craftsmanship. A major element of the proposed change was the ability to convince workers that there was, in fact, a need for change and that their ideas were a welcome part of that change. See Figure 15.1.

Some of the ideas for achieving the vision included innovations/changes such as an annualised salary, performance appraisal with key

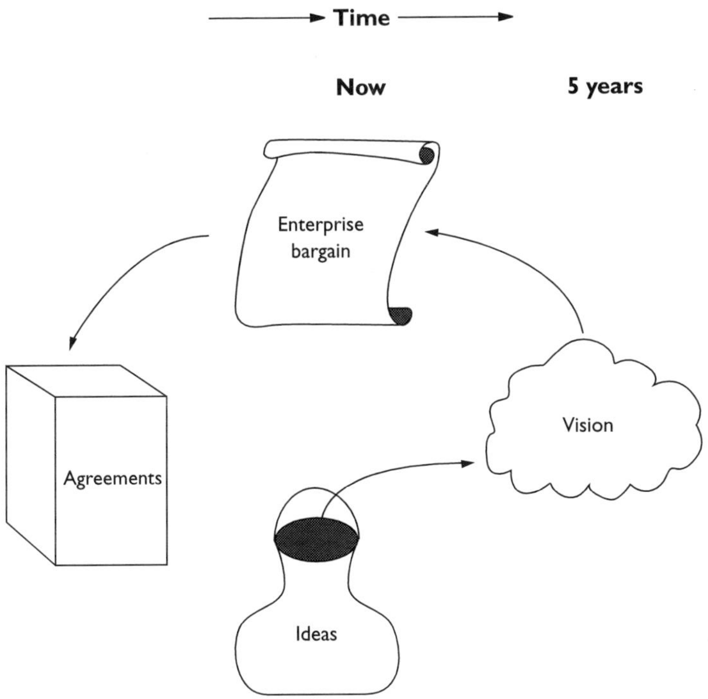

Figure 15.1 *Ideas lead to agreements*

performance indicators, flexible work hours and security of employment with outsourcing where needed. The aim was to have a homogenised workforce with a learning (versus training and skilling) mindset and teams which were to be cellular and non-directed. Structural change was necessary for this environment and the consultative committee structure was chosen. Representatives from the major trade unions, together with one staff and one manager made up a committee of seven.

Quality platform

A very natural platform for change where skilled work is concerned is *quality*. The Plant adopted the quality platform. Figure 15.2 shows how achieving Quality Accreditation fits into the concept of continual improvement.

The organisation is also committed to the quality approach of benchmarking, particularly international benchmarking, and how the idea of bringing workers in on decisions which affect them has been introduced and reinforced by successful companies.

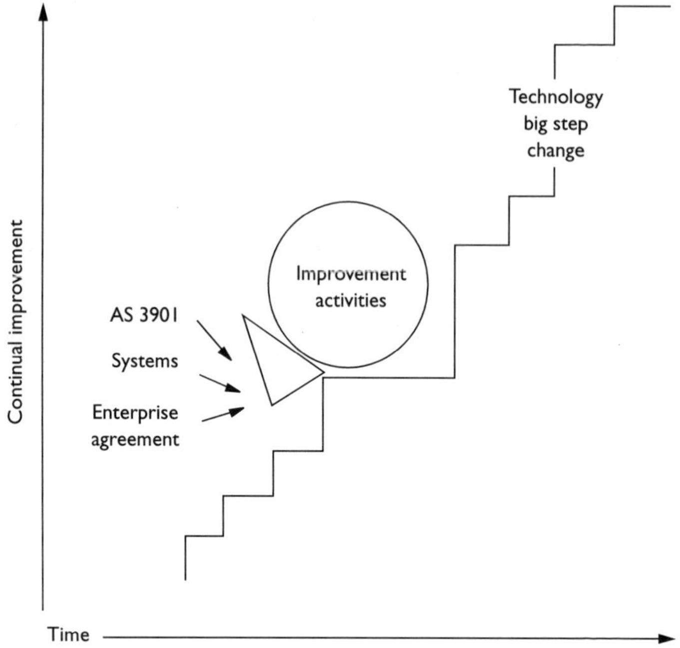

Figure 15.2 *Continual improvement timeline*

An essential component of the quality approach is information or evidence. The Plant engaged in surveys which gathered evidence about customers, markets, competitors and suppliers (see 'The outcome'). The latter resulted in a Supply Agreement with BHP Steel, a major supplier. Inside the Plant, at the manufacturing level, more objective methods replaced natural and intuitive methods previously used. This made it possible to go for reliability and consistency. However, taking a technical approach alone would not achieve the 'softening of attitude' and the growth and development of employees necessary to support a flexible and adaptable response to the lure of international markets. So, the sort of 'soft information' the plant personnel needed was necessary to blend with and complement the technical skills which, in a skilled technical environment, were already well developed and easily grasped.

Socio-technical approach

The system chosen was socio-technical systems (STS) (Lippitt 1982; Emery 1993). The interesting thing about the socio-technical approach is that it causes a new look at tasks. Instead of being looked at as technical operations only, this approach looks at the work as a process: a process in which people and their social interactions play a key part. A socio-technical analysis will look at the technical and environmental requirements, together with the social structures and processes of a task, the goal being to develop an optimal relationship between the two. This relationship between technical and social systems becomes a system itself. The social system, unlike the technical system, requires a particular sort of people environment in which to flourish.

As Robin Buckham (then Kembla Grange Works Manager) said, 'Workplace involvement forms the basis of our people program where we push responsibility down the organisation, and use the ideas as well as the hands of our employees . . . The organisational structure has been extensively flattened since 1990. We have removed an unnecessary supervisory layer, so the plant is now run by leading hands who report directly to the production manager.' (Whitford 1992) The ideas being communicated were to push responsibility down the (now flatter) hierarchy, to enable people to use personal authority, and to have open and two-way communication, including times when things went wrong. There was the need to facilitate an extremely high trust environment and an allegiance to open lines of information and open communication systems as well as a blurring of craft boundaries.

Assisted by STS analysts, both a technical and a social analysis was undertaken. The technical analysis was well received and went smoothly. Not so with the social side. Even though there was an atmosphere of empowerment, expressed in the organisational structure and ideas above, the actual status quo of employees, who had before defined themselves and their abilities through their craft, was challenged. Kanter, Stein and Jick (1992:374) says, 'A manager need not do anything as drastic as laying off workers to trigger intense reactions within an organisation. Realigning a company's change of command, shifting resources from one part of an organisation to another . . . can result in temporary chaos' and Argyris (1985) says 'almost anything which disturbs the organisational status quo or represents a threat to an individual's habitual way of doing things is likely to produce defensive, and often unproductive, behaviors'. Bearing this in mind it was understandable that while people were happy to talk about technical problems they would not talk about social issues for fear of perceived job losses.

> Let's say that what happened at Tubemakers, Kembla Grange Plant, was that there was an unrealised need for more commitment and so on , or maybe a different approach to STS. Let's say that the difficulties of building trust were not fully appreciated. Maybe the traditional Australian 'them and us' meant that more was needed in terms of time, the personal compromises required and preparedness to accept lapses. Let's say that some potentially downheartening experiences had happened recently which could cast a shadow over the new vision and mission (to which the Plant personnel and management were nevertheless committed). What would you do to revitalise the situation and restore enthusiasm and commitment?

The outcome

Two things sustained Kembla Grange in the face of socio-technical systems (STS) not being accepted as planned. These were benchmarking for workplace change, discussed below, and training with a role for the Trade Union Training Association (TUTA).

The benchmarking process is a familiar theme in this case section. You can see by now that there are many ways of going about benchmarking. The Plant followed this procedure:

1. Select the Best Practice organisation to benchmark.
2. Identify measures and develop a questionnaire.
3. Identify partners.
4. Measure performance.
5. Measure partner's performance.
6. Compare with partner's performance.

Within each step ideas and pointers were generated. The three steps outlined below (select an organisation, identify measures and develop a questionnaire, and measure partner's performance) serve to show the Plant's approach.

Select the Best Practice organisation to benchmark

Pointers were:

- Don't try to change things you can't.
- Benchmark practices are critical.
- Don't have too broad or too narrow a scope.

Priority areas were:

- job security;
- consultation and communication to make change effective;
- increasing the level and utilisation of skills.

Identify measures and develop a questionnaire

- Seek information in the form of hard data on the partner's measures.
- Seek information on such things as how results are achieved.
- Look at the sort of general questions used to establish the background.

  Examples of headings and questions used would be:

General background

- How old is the Plant and how old or new is equipment?
- What are the ownership details, number of employees, profile of age, length of service, ethnic mix, families?
- What is the structure/teams and are production and maintenance tied together?
- What is the union situation? How involved are officials and how much autonomy does management have? What are the *big problems* here?

Job security

- Is job security an issue, and why/why not?
- Have numbers had to be reduced for workplace change? When and how was forced retrenchment effected?
- What mechanisms were used to achieve security, for example labour agreement?
- Did the partner get rid of seniority and how?
- Does the partner do employee surveys and are the results relevant?

Consultation and communication to make change effective

- Do workers really understand why change is necessary and where they are going?
- What procedures are there to make changes? Is there training in communication skills?
- How do you *involve* people in change and are they committed to change?
- How were these changes accepted? If they were not, how was this handled and what happened to those who hated them? What problems have you had along the way with communication and consultation?
- What mechanisms are in place for consultation, how do they work and are they effective?
- What mechanisms are there for communication, how do they work and are they effective? Do people feel comfortable talking to management? Do they have a social club and activities outside work?
- Does the partner have systems such as TQM/5 Star Safety?

Increasing level and utilisation of skills, developing a career structure, rewarding people

- What training is in place: TAFE, in-house, Accredited?
- Is there a training plan? How was it developed? Did you do a skills audit (what you have and what you need)? Do you think that employees skills are being utilised and do you have an individual training plan? How do you measure the effectiveness of training and how do you work it?
- Is there a career structure and on what is it based?
- Do you have incentives other than pay, for example profit sharing, superannuation, freebies, bonus, or rewards related to skills and performance?

Measure partner's performance

Members of the Kembla Grange Plant attended seminars as well as visiting a diverse range of organisations. These included Kellogg (Aust) Pty Ltd, Hendersons Automotive, Exicon, Coates, Goninans and Bendix Mindex.

What did the Tubemakers groups look for when going on a visit and what were their tips to themselves? These included being prepared to share, never going alone, taking a gift of appreciation, being aware of cultural and language differences when asking questions, and not expecting people to be automatically interested in them and going down into the organisational structure for answers. This means 'walk the floor'. Ask the organisation where the strengths and weaknesses are. Use the questionnaire as a guide but use it rigorously. Reconvene back at work to develop the master set of data.

Questions to consider

1 The 'compare performance to the partner's' dimension of benchmarking is currently in the process of being achieved. There is a problem in that there is much information but it is hard to use. Why would that be and how would you resolve it?
2 The comparing activity may, in practice, be serving as awareness raising rather than actual performance comparisons. What would you do if this were found to be the case?
3 Achievements to date include success in enterprise bargaining and work redesign. How would you use these successes as part of the communication process and particularly as part of your culture-building and culture-binding endeavour?

16

P.I.C.S. (WA)

A case study of a professional photographic supply business

by John Kelmar

You are James Marston, a marketing manager with Metric Holdings, an Asian group of companies with its headquarters in Hong Kong.

You have just dined with your golfing friend, Peter White. Peter was scheduled to be in Hong Kong for a full week's business and golf but, as he explained, he had to make this a flying visit, adding — half in jest — 'or else I might just end up in jail'.

His story was interesting and you have heard many like it in Hong Kong. Peter once literally saved your life and he has asked for your advice on:

- how to understand the different cultures and values that his company, which he runs with his friend, Edward, and P.I.C.S. (Sydney) obviously have; and
- what to do next.

Here is the story.

Background

When the bailiff delivered the summons Peter and Edward, his business partner, began to wonder whether this would spell the end to their business venture.

Three years previously, Peter and Edward had discussed the possibility of running their own business, supplying equipment to the Perth professional photographic market. At the time, they were both employed as sales representatives with Park Pty Ltd. Park had, over the past 30 years, developed a multifarious photographic business. The division in which Peter and Edward were involved operated as the professional distributorship arm of Park Pty Ltd, trading as P.I.C.S. (WA), under an agency agreement with the Sydney-based importer, P.I.C.S. Pty Ltd.

The Perth photographic market had been, until this time, characterised by customer demarcation such that the retail shops generally served the amateur customers, while the professional outlets catered for the professional, industrial and education/government market segments. This segmentation was dictated by the range of stock that each outlet sold, which, in the case of the professional outlets, was stipulated by the agency agreements they were able to secure from the official importers in Sydney and Melbourne. The Perth market was characterised by the local distributors/agents operating under a gentlemen's agreement not to obtain supplies of each other's agency lines.

Peter and Edward discussed their ideas with the general manager of Park Pty Ltd, before they approached Mr Park. The general manager agreed that the combination of experience would reduce the possibility of failure — Edward had left school at 15 and had spent 10 years employed in the photographic trade in Perth, including being senior salesman with Park Pty Ltd; Peter had developed his experience in the sales and marketing fields, over the past 6 years, in the pharmaceutical and office products industries. Peter, being 3 years older than Edward, had also managed to study part-time and had acquired degrees in science (chemistry) and commerce (management and marketing) from the University of Western Australia, and had just commenced studies for his MBA degree.

Mr Park agreed to finance Peter and Edward in setting up Petard Pty Ltd in order to purchase the stock and the trading name of the P.I.C.S. (WA) division. Mr Park realised that currently the division was not returning the profit levels of the other divisions. In fact, due to the accounting system in use, P.I.C.S. (WA) was trading at a loss, but Peter and Edward were not privileged to know the extent of this loss. The information that was available showed that P.I.C.S. (WA) had annual sales of $250 000, which had been constant for the past three years, and that the mark-up on cost averaged 30 per cent. Mr Park in agreeing to finance the purchase of the division, set an interest rate of 1 per cent above the prime interest rate, for a period of five years, with monthly repayments.

Establishment of the business

With a goodwill figure of $15 000, stock valued at $85 000 and plant valued at $3000, Petard Pty Ltd commenced operations, renting the same showroom from Mr Park as the division had occupied previously.

Fortunately, Peter and Edward were able to delay a number of sales until they had set up their own operations, which gave them an immediate positive cash flow. They were surprised at how receptive their customers were to their new status — Peter as managing director and Edward as chairman of directors. The customers preferred to deal with the owners of the business, who were able to make immediate decisions on pricing, availability and credit without referring back to head office. This assisted the new business in capturing an increasing proportion of the market share.

Peter and Edward also came to realise the extent to which Mr Park had previously been a liability to their selling potential. This was because Mr Park, in striving to increase the size of his business interests, had managed to alienate himself from many of the professional photographers in Perth. This problem still existed because of the location of P.I.C.S. (WA) in premises owned by Mr Park, but it had been reduced considerably.

The suppliers, however, felt somewhat differently regarding the prospect of the two new business proprietors, with no track record and who were undercapitalised, succeeding in an environment in which a number of other businesses were failing each year. In fact, there had been two recent bankruptcies, and three more which were considered to be current high risks. Thus, it became difficult for Petard to obtain large quantities of stock on credit, and they were not in a position to expand on a COD basis.

Expansion program

It was fortunate that Peter's and Edward's assessment of the market proved correct in the first year, for they were able to increase their sales to just over $550 000. This was primarily achieved using Peter's approach of calling on as many customers as possible and personally asking them to increase their purchases from P.I.C.S. (WA). At times, a little encouragement was needed by way of reduced prices. Peter reasoned that all customers required a regular supply of consumable (film, paper and chemistry) and if it became easier for the customer to purchase from P.I.C.S. (WA), the overall sales should increase even at lower profit margins. Edward was happy with this argument as he preferred to remain in the showroom and conduct business with those customers whom he had known for many years. Edward also specialised in handling the demand for the more sophisticated studio and laboratory equipment, with which he had a number of years experience. This approach enabled Peter and Edward to maintain their present customer base, and it also provided the opportunity to develop an expansion program.

Initially, this expansion program centred on capturing a greater number of customers but, in achieving this, Peter and Edward discovered that, due to the agency agreements, there were a number of products that these new customers requested which were not in their present product line-up.

The opportunity to expand their product range appeared when Peter and Edward were in Sydney for a trade show. The Managing Director of P.I.C.S. Pty Ltd expected that all their agents and distributors would be spending time on his stand in order to promote and experience his new products. Peter felt that since Petard Pty Ltd were covering the costs of the trip to Sydney, he would be spending most of his time in developing a knowledge of the competitive products. To his surprise, Peter found that the other importers responded well to his approach, as they were eager to expand their own market penetration.

P.I.C.S. (WA)'s competitors had been in existence for a number of years and, with the prevailing recession, were more interested in maintaining their scale and profit margins, than in securing new customers or attempting to break into new markets. This allowed P.I.C.S. (WA) to expand their efforts into market segments that their competitors felt were doubtful, or which were generating low-profit margins.

Despite the increase in sales, P.I.C.S. (WA) found that their cash flow situation was deteriorating to such an extent that many of their accounts were being paid on the basis of 60–90 days. Peter and Edward were able to pay themselves only for nine out of the twelve months for that first year. However, they were fortunate to both have wives in full-time outside employment, and so this situation did not prove too critical. Edward found the situation more difficult to take as he still needed to make mortgage payments on a monthly basis, and did not imagine that as a business owner his time of working would increase from 35 to 60 hours each week. Edward also felt that the position of chairman of directors entitled him to at least one day off each week to play golf.

Peter was anxious to develop the business to a much greater extent. He proposed the introduction of new agency lines and longer operating hours: open at 8.30 a.m. and close at 6.00 p.m. Peter subsequently discovered that by offering longer operating hours he was able to tap into a new market niche which had not been defined previously — that of the part-time professional photographer who had a regular full-time job and only took photographs in his spare time. Once this market niche was attracted, it was a simple matter to encourage photographers to purchase their hardware items as well as consumable from P.I.C.S. (WA), by offering lower prices, longer trading hours and an increased stock range.

However, Peter also discovered that there was a considerable percentage of customers who were purchasing their basic hardware items in Singapore and Hong Kong. As he had travelled to these destinations, he was able to offer purchasing advice to these customers. This attitude was in direct contrast to their competition, who were interested only in making the sale and completely refused to assist any photographer who did not support their store. Peter reasoned that these photographers were not willing to purchase in Australia, but would need to purchase consumable and accessories on their return. The advice that he offered was also extended to assisting the photographers in setting up their businesses so that they became more profitable, again with the reasoning that if the customer was more profitable, then his disposal income would increase.

The professional outlets were more prestigious due to the type of customer, higher turnover and margins, and the range of quality of equipment that was sold. Many retailers wished to develop professional customers, but were unable to achieve this because of the high cost of entry for the specialised stock. The professional outlets generally were not too interested in the retail customer as they were considered to be low volume and time wasters. Peter's approach was to differentiate between the amateur photographer and the part-time professional, and it was this market that proved profitable.

Problems

This above description indicates the direction in which P.I.C.S. (WA) was heading. The Sydney importer — P.I.C.S. Pty Ltd — was becoming dissatisfied with the declining purchases of their Western

Australian agent. The Sydney company was pursuing a strategy of supplying the top end of the hardware market ($10 000 to $15 000 individual sales), whereas Peter and Edward were designing their business to accommodate the increased demand in consumable. This emphasis was as a result of the prevailing recessive trends in the industry.

P.I.C.S. Pty Ltd felt that it was in a commanding position as it assumed that its Western Australian agent relied on it for the majority of its supplies. This was certainly the situation prior to Peter's entering the industry, and this was being maintained by the other P.I.C.S. Pty Ltd branches throughout Australia. Peter and Edward realised that they would not be able to survive on the consumable market alone, and that they required the support of a substantial hardware supplier in order to promote their image as a professional distributor. This image was critical in defining their market niche strategy as against any approaches that the many retail photographic outlets may pursue.

Edward, being good friends with the Managing Director of P.I.C.S. Pty Ltd, was in a quandary — he realised that business was booming with Peter's approach, but not in the sales of P.I.C.S. Pty Ltd's goods. The Sydney company began to exert increasing pressure on Edward to achieve performance targets, with the threat that the agency agreement would be rescinded due to lack of performance. Peter's response was that he would run the Western Australian operations how he wished, not as demanded by any Sydney importer.

It was now two years since Petard Pty Ltd had commenced operations, and supplies from P.I.C.S. Pty Ltd were becoming more difficult to obtain. There was often the excuse that the stock was not immediately available, that the account was in query or that the order was incomprehensible. P.I.C.S. Pty Ltd had changed their computer accounting system, and because they had not correctly credited stock returns and invoiced goods that had not been sent, the new system was showing the Petard Pty Ltd account in arrears. This, in itself, resulted in many delays in obtaining stock, as P.I.C.S. Pty Ltd were unwilling to invoice and supply stock until the matter had been cleared up — some items took over six months to correct. On one particular occasion, Petard was sent an expensive slide copier machine ($17 500) to be delivered on government contract. The machine was ordered as new, but P.I.C.S. Pty Ltd delivered a four-year-old demonstration model. Peter firmly rejected the goods, but found that P.I.C.S. Pty Ltd initially would not accept the goods for return. This problem was finally resolved after nearly one year, when Peter loaded the goods onto a carrier to be delivered to Sydney, and then ordered the latest model direct from the American factory. P.I.C.S. Pty Ltd were incensed at this audacity, and immediately cut off all credit facilities.

Edward was particularly worried as he was in the process of securing an order for Petard's second one-hour film-processing laboratory, valued at $120 000. They had sold the previous laboratory to an inner-city pharmacy over a year ago, and were now preparing for a second order for the pharmacy's new location. Edward felt that this order would resolve many of the problems that had developed between Petard Pty Ltd and P.I.C.S. Pty Ltd.

The summons for an outstanding account of $23 000 arrived that afternoon. This was the result of the non-crediting of the slide copier by P.I.C.S. Pty Ltd, as well as the invoicing of goods not supplied. At the same time, Edward received a phone call from the pharmacist stating that he had been told by P.I.C.S. Pty Ltd that the only way he could obtain delivery of the new one-hour film-processing laboratory was to order it direct from Sydney.

Peter and Edward knew that a decision was required within ten days, as a reply to the summons was required to be lodged with the court by that time.

Returning to the conversation with James in Hong Kong, how would you do the following?

1 Explain the different cultures and values which P.I.C.S. (WA) has as compared with P.I.C.S. Pty Ltd (Sydney and Melbourne).
2 Advise Peter on a way forward which could bring the two into a fruitful business relationship.

The outcome

In this case the company P.I.C.S. (WA) decided the gap was too great. Following talks with friends such as James and some deep soul-searching P.I.C.S. (WA) decided to move its assets into a new company. The receipt of the summons from P.I.C.S. in Sydney clinched the decision. This new company then ensured that all debts from P.I.C.S. (WA) were paid, except for the amount of the summons from P.I.C.S. Sydney.

This move was accompanied by a personal discussion with all accounts to ensure that they were aware of the circumstance of the move, so that no one would feel they were being put into a compromising situation.

P.I.C.S. Sydney eventually dropped the summons when P.I.C.S. (WA) counterclaimed for $300 000, being the loss of business incurred as a direct result of the inability of P.I.C.S. Sydney to operate its business in an efficient and effective manner.

P.I.C.S. (WA), under their new name, went on to develop its business into one with a turnover of $2 million within the next two years.

17

The Mass Transit Railway Corporation

Cultivating a customer-service culture to create competitive advantage

by Sara Tang, Manager, Management Development and
Patrick Maule, Personnel Director

The problem

Hong Kong has one of the most elaborate public transport systems of any major city with trams, ferries, taxis, a light rail, suburban trains, public light buses and a massive fleet of double-decker buses. Private cars account for only 12 per cent of the average number of people-trips made per day. Despite significantly higher fares than any other modes, the Mass Transit Railway Corporation (MTRC) has steadily gained market share by 5.2 per cent per annum over the past five years with its existing system. Notwithstanding the several competitive modes of transport, MTRC is perceived by many customers as a monopoly, since for them there is no acceptable alternative. The MTRC set out to achieve demonstrable excellence without the aid of its reputation as a monopoly and by its own efforts as an organisation to articulate and realise its vision of excellence.

> Every excellent company we studied is clear on what it stands for, and takes the process of value shaping seriously. In fact, we wonder whether it is possible to be an excellent company, without clarity on values and without having the right sorts of values.
>
> Peters and Waterman 1982

Experience elsewhere has indicated that truly excellent companies abide by a small number of fundamental values which are fully understood and endorsed by employees at all levels. Like these excellent companies, the management of the MTRC is committed to promoting three sets of core values in order to achieve a desirable organisational culture: customer service, respect for the individual, and on time and within budget.

Customer service
The corporation aims to be the most customer-oriented railway in the world, to provide by far the most reliable service and to strive for continuous improvements to meet or exceed the needs of fare-paying passengers.

Respect for the individual
In all dealings with and between its employees, the corporation will ensure that high standards of fairness, equality, objectivity and empathy will be observed and that the needs, opinions and aspirations of all parties are mutually respected.

On time and within budget
The corporation has responsibilities to shareholders, lenders, customers and staff to operate professionally and in a financially prudent way to achieve the most effective and timely use of resources.

The MTRC's three core values reinforce one another. The first, customer service, emphasises the importance of providing excellent service to MTRC's customers. Over two million passengers use the MTR every day. It is the company's responsibility to provide a superior yet cost-effective service both now and far into the future.

The objective is to make the customers feel safe and be convinced that they can depend upon the reliability of every aspect of the service. According to H.T. Mathers, Chairman of the MTRC, 'Service and how it is perceived is the life-blood of our business — delivering and maintaining an excellent level of service, in all its facets, must therefore be our *raison d'être*, our ultimate achievement and commitment.'

Front-line staff who serve the customers are encouraged to provide their best service. Other internal support staff are also asked to hold the same service attitude towards their internal customers, as they would to an external customer.

The second value, respect for the individual, is an essential element of the first. An organisation can achieve results only when its employees are committed and happy, and feel proud of their work. The company believes that only when it treats its employees with respect and empathy can it expect loyalty, commitment and a customer-focused attitude from them.

The final core value, on time and within budget, conveys to all staff the importance of meeting targets and achieving results with high efficiency and cost-effectiveness. As many subsidised railways around the world have discovered, financial success is a vital ingredient, if safety and service standards are to be maintained over the long term. This is, therefore, a critical value that supports the customer-service strategy of providing a reliable and efficient transport system for the community of Hong Kong.

Shaping the culture

When the corporation first set out in 1985 to develop a culture, the then Chairman, Sir Wilfred Newton, was quite clear about his vision of the perpetuity of quality standards. 'If I were to return in 20 or 50 years' time,' he said, 'I want to see that the standards of safety and reliability we are achieving today have not been allowed to slip as a result of lack of funding or commitment.'

Based on this vision, the directors and senior managers embarked upon the process of shaping the values and developing the strategies and objectives in order to effect changes in the corporation's systems, practices and behaviour of its employees. See Figure 17.1. These all had to align if it was to achieve superior transport service for the people of Hong Kong and the competitive edge that leads to financial success.

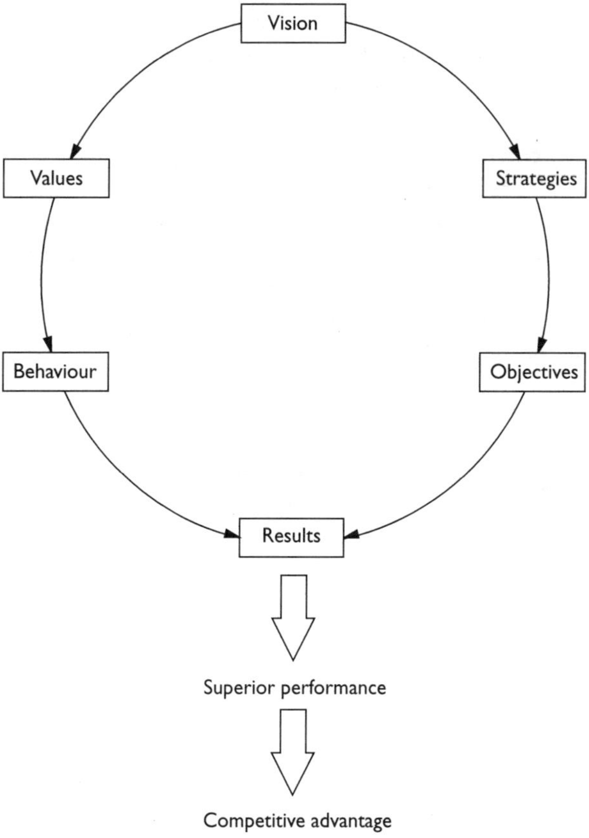

Figure 17.1 *Achieving results through culture change*

Values formation

Determining the appropriate values proved to be a long and intensive process. During 1985 and 1986 the directors and senior managers participated in a number of brainstorming programs that re-examined the established beliefs, role concepts and practices against the changing needs of business. They searched for the most appropriate set of values that could act as the guiding principles for future behaviour.

In retrospect, what emerged appears almost obvious. However, the involvement of many sets of values, and the rejecting of worthy contenders for the few explicitly expressed, simple to understand and inspirational values finally adopted proved tougher than expected. Those involved felt that the greater the effort, the stronger would be the commitment to the results. The three core values of customer service, respect for the individual and on time and within budget were finally adopted with confidence in the process.

Diffusing the vision and values

Once the core values were defined, an intensive communication program was designed to launch them through the corporation. The messages that explained their meaning and their importance were disseminated in a dramatic and creative manner through company dinners that included husbands and wives, videos, songs, handbooks and many other family events (see Figure 17.2).

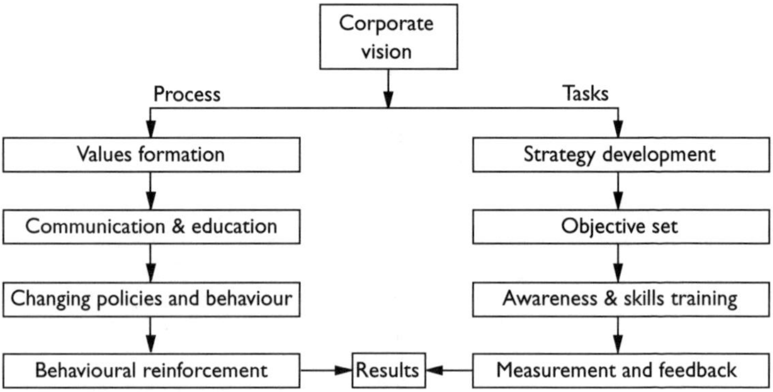

Figure 17.2 *Diffusion of vision*

Strategy development

After the successful launch of the values in 1987, the executive directors took part in another intensive brainstorming session to clarify the MTRC strategies and objectives.

Today the corporation's strategy framework consists of three separate elements: purpose, corporate strategies and business strategies (see Figure 17.3).

The primary purpose is to serve the transport needs of the people of Hong Kong. This is supported by well-defined corporate strategies covering four important areas, namely the customers, human resource management, finance and the corporation's relationship with government (its sole shareholder). The corporate strategies ensure that the revenue-generating business strategies are viable and achievable.

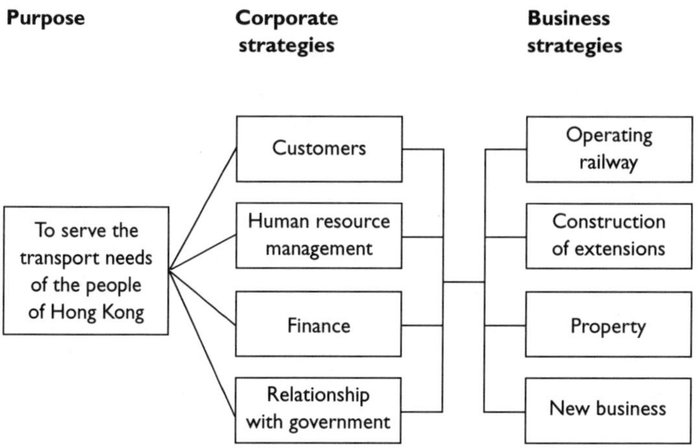

Figure 17.3 *The MTRC strategy framework*

Changing behaviour

A training strategy designed to cascade down the organisation was adopted in 1988. The objective was to ensure that every staff member was equipped with the right attitude, knowledge and skills to support the corporation's commitment to its customers. In the same year, the first management training course on customer service was conducted.

In 1990, the first program for supervisors was run. With the completion of these managerial and supervisory training programs, a new series of attitude-shaping events was conducted for the MTRC's 3000 front-line and supporting staff. By March 1992 every employee had completed such training in customer service.

In total the MTRC ran 14 managerial programs attended by 200 managers, 70 supervisory programs for 1700 supervisors, and 20 one-day programs called 'Vision Day' aimed at obtaining commitment to service excellence from its front-line and junior support staff. For staff who had to interact with customers directly, an intensive skills training workshop was provided where they learned and practised the essential delivery and recovery skills needed in handling customers.

In parallel with these training courses on customer service, specifically designed training programs on the other two core values — respect for the individual and on time and within budget — were also organised. In 1992 the three core values training programs were integrated into a single intensive 5-day residential program. All newly recruited or promoted managers and supervisors are required to participate in these programs, the main objective of which is to ensure that they understand and are committed to the implementation of such values. To make the core values programs more interesting, multimedia presentations and experiential learning methods are used. Videos showing real cases of staff interactions with customers have been produced for in-depth analysis and discussion during the courses. In addition, simulated incidents are used for skills practice. Executive directors, line managers and supervisors are heavily involved as guest speakers and facilitators in all training events.

In the same year, 1992, a new program called 'Focus Day' was organised to promote the concept of internal customer service. This internal customer focus was considered as an essential (but often forgotten) element in the complete service chain (see Figure 17.4).

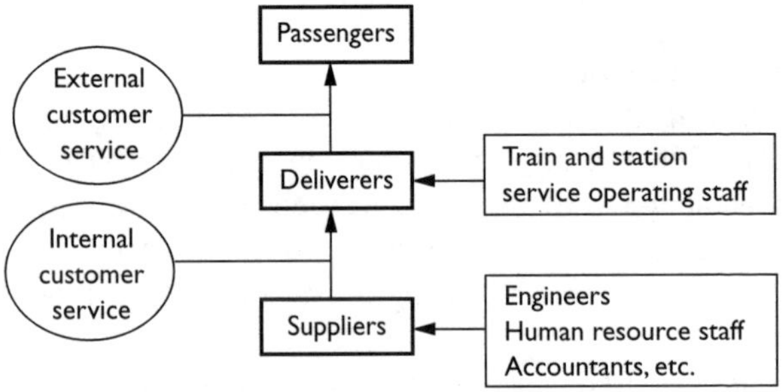

Figure 17.4 *Customer service chain*

Prior to the running of the Focus Day, an internal customer-service survey was conducted to enable each internal service department to understand the needs and priorities of its customers and how they rated the service performance they were receiving.

Sixteen teams were formed on the Focus Day, bringing together service suppliers with their customers to examine the survey results. Opportunities for performance improvement were highlighted by the importance–performance matrices (see Figure 17.5).

During the day and with the aid of trained facilitators, these teams held in-depth discussions to formulate their initial action plans aimed at effecting improvements. Over the subsequent weeks, these teams continued to meet to expand and improve on their agreed plans of action and to follow-up on implementation.

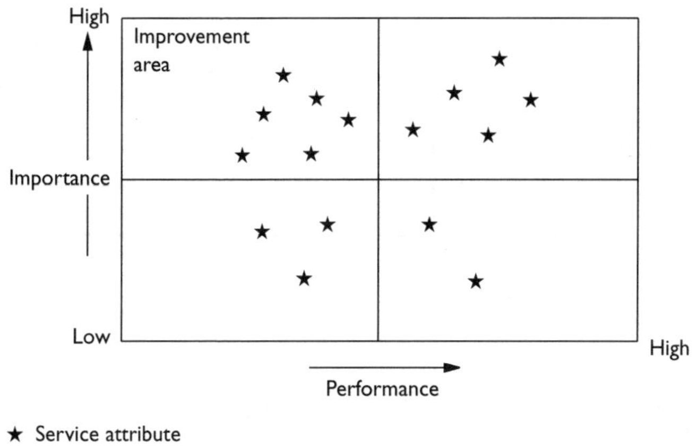

Figure 17.5 *Importance–performance matrix*

The customer-service task force

The MTRC believes that training and development activities should be integrated with other organisational change activities in order to achieve better results and to overcome the problem of transfer from training situations to reality. A customer-service task force has been formed to examine the customer-service targets, and organisational systems and procedures, which support the training initiatives, as well as to implement the strategy. The task force is the 'engine' of the customer-service drive as it ensures that the best ideas which emerge from the training courses or elsewhere are actually implemented and that progress is made.

Targets and standards

A comprehensive set of internal and external customer-service targets and standards have been set to ensure that employees have a clear understanding of the customer needs and management expectations of performance. These targets and standards also enable the corporation to measure and monitor its performance achievements and trends. They are reviewed and modified annually to make sure that they are responsive to the changing needs of the customers and the environment.

If you were working in an organisation such as the MTRC and you had been given the story so far as background, how would you go about the following?

1 Setting internal targets and standards
2 Avoiding the 'success breeds complacency' syndrome

The outcome

Setting internal targets and standards

In setting the internal targets and standards, both internal suppliers and deliverers are involved. They cover all the major activities that support the delivery of service to the final customers. These targets and standards need to be simple, adaptable, achievable and understood by all members of staff. Quality standards are based on the international standard (ISO 9000) and the spirit of 'continuous improvement but with safety standards' dominates.

In setting targets and standards for external customer service, the corporation considers its previous performance, the customers' expectations and the potential for improvement. Over 180 surveys covering 700 000 respondents have been conducted to ascertain the needs, expectation and satisfaction level of the customers. Targets have been set, measured and monitored in eleven key areas.

Customer-service areas

1. Safety
2. Reliability
3. Public announcement
4. Malfunctioned ticket handling
5. Accessibility
6. Air-conditioning
7. Cleanliness
8. Station lighting
9. Availability of station facilities
10. Friendliness
11. Train ride quality

The current major customer-service projects include additional trains to improve service frequencies, the development of high-coercivity tickets (for example, early bird tickets) to improve performance reliability, upgrading train public announcements by digital recordings and enhancing escalator maintenance. To ensure that these and many other smaller projects are actually implemented, the corporation has committed sufficient additional resources of staff, money and equipment.

Accomplishing competitive advantage

It is, of course, difficult to quantify precisely the contribution made by this and other change programs that the corporation has embarked upon. But there is no denying that the overall results are impressive. Most fundamental of the results is the steadily rising market share which now stands at 27.1 per cent of total public transport passenger movements.

Passenger surveys show that in terms of value for money, MTRC stands second only to the extremely cheap tram system and first in terms of overall service. This would directly account for the growth in market share and is clear evidence of a competitive advantage.

Financially and notwithstanding outstanding debts of HK$18 billion, the corporation has in 1992 shown a net profit of HK$400 million after interest and depreciation, and anticipates retiring its debt by the year 2001. It is the only credit-rated public transport company in Hong Kong with an investment grade credit rating, which enables the corporation to borrow at competitive cost margins.

In employee relations terms, the corporation enjoys relatively low turnover at 7.9 per cent in 1992 compared with a Hong Kong average of 25 per cent (HKIPM Survey 1992), and a comparatively low absence rate of 3.6 days total absence per person per annum (Employers' Federation Survey 1992). The latest Staff Attitude Survey (1992) reveals that 74 per cent of all employees consider the corporation to be a good employer. This is despite major work pattern changes that have been created by initiatives to improve productivity, safety management and quality management. Work improvement teams are thriving and growing rapidly in numbers, and the widescale system of elected staff representation reveals no evidence of major discontent.

This leads to enhanced ability to attract and retain high-calibre staff as the corporation's positive reputation as an employer gains ground, aided by being the winner for two years running of the Hong Kong Management Association's Award for Excellence in Training. The corporation and its chairman were also awarded the coveted Communicator of the Year Award in 1992 by the International Association of Business Communicators, largely as a result of its campaign to notify the public of its customer-service performance targets and achievements.

Competitive advantage and reputation are most quickly and easily damaged by accidents and incidents that interrupt services. While safety performance can be difficult to compare from one country to another, the corporation's rate of 1.06 accidents per million passengers compares very favourably with other railways in UK and USA at 4.53 and 1.92 respectively (two railways each). These facts all add incrementally to high credibility, a favourable reputation and, ultimately, to real competitive advantage.

What next?

The corporation has come a very long way in a relatively short time. The changes in attitude and practices have been dramatic and the response by the people of Hong Kong has been ample reward for all the effort. The MTRC has won many accolades at home, from the many visitors from abroad, and from other overseas railways. So much so, that there is a real danger of overconfidence and complacency. Some employees wonder why the corporation still puts so much effort into the ethos of 'continuous improvement' when it is told it is doing so well already.

Accordingly, what MTRC needs is a new, more ambitious, more challenging vision that will inspire its people to stretch that little bit further in the quest for improvements. What is emerging is a vision of leadership — 'To be a leader among mass transit railways throughout the world'. And, the authors say, the debate therefore begins again. The cycle is repeated. The eyes are lifted higher as MTRC sees a new mountain peak beyond the one its people have just ascended.

Questions to consider

Managers realise that there are always contradictions surrounding any strategies and interventions. As the case history developed the authors had to wrestle with questions such as the following which they have shared with you.

1 While each of the three core values discussed brings benefits to the organisation, they may be perceived by staff as contradicting each other. For example, customer service and respect for the individual may not be seen as compatible. Staff may feel that the company treats the customers better than their employees, and some customers may even abuse the staff who under the spirit of customer service have to accept such abuse. Comment on whether such perceptions are correct and suggest ways to make the three values compatible. How can you convince the staff that all three values are achievable without conflict?
2 Compare the vision and the human resource strategy. Comment on whether the strategy is in alignment with the vision.
3 Critically evaluate the appropriateness and effectiveness of the various programs on changing behaviour.
4 By setting targets and standards, the company provides a clear direction and guidelines to staff members. However, the company also wants to promote participation and empowerment. Discuss whether the two initiatives contradict or support each other. Why?
5 Facing the various challenges in the future, suggest a strategic plan to ensure that current excellence will be maintained and continued.

References

Adams, J. S. (1965) 'Inequity in Social Exchanges', in L. Berkowitz (ed.) *Advances in Experimental Social Psychology*, New York: Academic Press.

Argyris, C. (1985) *Strategy, Change, and Defensive Routines*, Boston: Pitman.

Argyris, C. (1992) 'A Leadership Dilemma: Skilled Incompetence', in G. Salaman (ed.), *Human Resource Strategy*, London: Sage.

Argyris, C. (1993) *Knowledge for Action*, San Francisco: Jossey-Bass.

Argyris, C. and Schon, D. A. (1974) *Theory in Practice: Increasing Personal Effectiveness*, San Francisco: Jossey-Bass.

Bennis W. G. (1966) *Changing Organizations: Essays on the Development and Evolution of Human Organization*, Bombay: Tata McGraw-Hill.

Berquist, W. (1993) *The Postmodern Organisation: Mastering the Art of Irreversible Change*, San Francisco: Jossey-Bass.

Bion, W. R. (1961) *Experiences in Groups*, London: Tavistock.

Bolman, L. G. and Deal, T. E. (1991) *Reframing Organisations: Artistry, Choice and Leadership*, San Francisco: Jossey-Bass.

Bond, M. H. (ed.) (1989) *The Psychology of the Chinese People*, Hong Kong: Oxford University Press.

Burns, R. (1993) *Managing People in Changing Times*, Sydney: Allen & Unwin.

Byham, W. C. and Cox, J. (1988) *Zapp: The Lightening of Empowerment*, New York: Fawcett Columbine, Ch. 17, p. 123.

Byrne, J. (1993) 'The Horizontal Corporation', *Business Week*, 20 Dec., p. 44.

Byrt, W. J. and Pickett, L. (eds) (1971) *Personnel Management in Australian Industry and Commerce*, Sydney: Institute of Personnel Management.

Carlzon, J. (1987) *Moments of Truth: New Strategies for Today's Customer-Driven Economy*, Sydney: Harper & Row.

Cascio, W. F. (1992) *Managing Human Resources: Productivity Quality of Work Life Profits*, 3rd edn, New York: McGraw-Hill.

Chung, K. and Ferris, M. (1981) 'An Enquiry of the National Group Process', *Academy of Management Journal* 55, pp. 520–4.

Clegg, S. (1992) 'Modernist and Postmodernist Organisation', in G. Salaman (ed.), *Human Resource Strategy*, London: Sage.

Cohen, L. and Manion, L. (1981) *Perspectives on Classrooms and Schools*, London: Cassell, p. 77.

Covey, S. (1989) *The Seven Habits of Highly Effective People: Restoring the Character Ethic*, New York: Simon & Schuster.

Covey, S. (1992) *Principle-Centred Leadership*, London: Simon & Schuster, p. 15.

Dalmau, T. and Dick, B. (1991) *A Diagnostic Model . . . for Selecting Interventions for Community and Organisational Change*, Chapel Hill, Qld: Interchange.

Deal, T. and Kennedy, A. (1982) *Corporate Culture: The Rites and Rituals of Corporate Life*, London: Penguin, p. 3.

Deiner, E. (1980) 'Deindividuation: The Absence of Self-awareness and Self-regulation in Group Members', in P. B. Pailus (ed.), *Psychology of Group Influence*, Hillsdale, NJ: Erlbaum.

Delbecq, A. Van de Ven, A. and Gustafson, D. (1975) *Group Techniques for Program Planning: A Guide to Nominal Group and Delphi Processes*, Glenview, Ill.: Scott Foresman.

Dick, B. (1991) *Helping Groups to Be Effective*, 2nd edn, Chapel Hill, Qld: Interchange.

Douglas, M. (1986) *How Organisations Think*, Syracuse, NY: Syracuse University Press.

Dreher, H. V. and Siu T. (1990) 'Towards a Generalised Framework for GDSS', *Proceedings of the 10th ASOR National Conference*, Perth, WA.

Drucker, P. (1992) 'The Coming of the New Organisation', in G. Salaman (ed.), *Human Resource Strategies*, London: Sage.

Dumaine, B. (1992) 'Creating a New Company Culture', in P. Frost, V. Mitchell and W. R. Nord (eds), *Organizational Reality: Reports from the Firing Line*, 4th edn, New York: HarperCollins.

Dunford, R. W. (1992) *Organisational Behaviour: An Organisational Analysis Perspective*, Sydney: Addison-Wesley.

Emery, F. E. (1978), 'Characteristics of Socio-Technical Systems', in F. Emery, *The Emergence of a New Paradigm of Work*, Canberra: Centre for Continuing Education, Australian National University.

Emery, M. (ed.) (1993) *Participative Design for Participative Democracy*, Canberra: Centre for Continuing Education, Australian National University.

Etzioni, A. (1971) *A Comparative Analysis of Complex Organisations*, New York: Free Press.

Ferris, G. R., Rowland, K. M. and Buckley, M. R. (1990) *Human Resource Management Perspectives and Issues*, 2nd edn, Sydney: Allyn and Bacon.

Flower, F. and Brown, H. (1983) 'The Industrial Tutor: A Discussion Paper', *Coombe Lodge Report* (UK) 15, 1.

Frost, P. Mitchell, V. and Nord, W. R. (eds) (1992) *Organisational Reality: Reports from the Firing Line*, 4th edn, New York: HarperCollins.

Frost, P. Moore, L.F., Louis, M.R., Lundberg, C. C., Martin, J. (eds) (1991) *Reframing Organisational Culture*, Newbury Park: Sage.

Goffman, E. (1969) *The Presentation of Self in Everyday Life*, London: Allen Lane.

Gregory, J. R. and Weichmann, J. E. (1991) *Marketing Corporate Image: The Company as Your Number One Product*, Lincolnwood, Ill.: NTC Business Books.

Hackman, J. R. and Oldham, E. R. (1980) *Work Redesign*, Reading, Mass.: Addison-Wesley.

Halal, W. E., Geranmayer, A. and Pourdehnad, J. (1993) *Internal Markets: Bringing the Power of Free Enterprise INSIDE Your Organisation*, New York: Wiley.

Hampden-Turner, C. (1990) *Charting the Corporate Mind: From Dilemma to Strategy*, Oxford: Basil.

Handy, C. (1985) *Understanding Organisations*, London: Penguin.

Heron, J. (1989) *The Facilitators Handbook*, New York: Nichols Publishing.

Herzberg, F., Mausner, B. and Synderman, B. (1959) *The Motivation to Work*, New York: John Wiley.

Hofstede, G. (1980) *Culture's Consequences: International Differences in Work-related Values*, Beverley Hills: Sage.

IBIS (1993) Business Papers — the Asia Pacific, Melbourne: IBIS Business Information Services.

Janis, I. (1981) *Group Think*, Boston: Houghton-Mifflin.

Kanter, R. (1984) *The Change Masters: Innovations for Productivity in the American Corporation*, London: Allen & Unwin.

Kanter, R., Frost, P. and Lippett, G. L. (1982) *Organisational Renewal: A Holistic Approach to Organisational Development*, 2nd edn, London: Prentice-Hall.

Kanter, R. M., Stein, B. A. and Jick, T. D. (1992) *The Challenge of Organisational Change: How Companies Experience It and Leaders Guide It*, New York: The Free Press.

Kearns, D. T. and Nadler, D. A. (1992) *Prophets in the Dark: How Xerox Reinvented Itself and Beat Back the Japanese*, New York: Harper Business.

Kelley, H. H. (1972) 'Attribution in Social Interaction', in E. Jones et al., *Attribution: Perceiving the Causes of Behaviour*, Morristown, NJ: General Learning Press.

Kotter, J. P. and Heskett, J. L. (1992) *Corporate Culture and Performance*, New York: The Free Press.

Krugman, P. (1994) 'Does Third World Growth Hurt First World Prosperity', *Harvard Business Review*, July–August 1994.

Kuhn, T. S. and Buss, A. (1986) 'The Structure of Scientific Revolution', in Hampden-Turner, *Maps of the Mind*, London: Mitchell Beazley.

Latane, B., Williams, K. and Harkins, S. 'Many Hands Make Light Work: The Causes and Consequences of Social Loafing', *Journal of Personality and Social Psychology* 37, pp. 822–32.

Latour, B. (1986) *Social Anthropology*, Oxford: Oxford University Press.

Legge, K. (1988) *Personnel Management in Recession and Recovery: A Comparative Analysis of What the Surveys Say*, Manchester: MCB University Press Ltd.

Lessem, R. (1990) 'Existential Strategy' (Foreword) in C. Hampden-Turner, *Charting the Corporate Mind: From Dilemma to Strategy*, Oxford: Basil.

Lewin, K., (1947) 'Frontiers in Human Dynamics', *Human Relations*, 1, 1.

Lewis, L. (1987) 'A Decision Support System for Face-to-Face Groups', *Journal of Information Science* 13, pp. 211–19.

Lewis, L. and Whiteley, A. (1992) 'Initial Perceptions of Professional Facilitators Regarding GDSS Impacts: A Study Using the Grounded Theory Approach', Hawaiian International Computer Systems Science Conference, Hawaii: University of Hawaii.

Limerick, D. (1992) 'The Shape of New Organisation: Implications for Human Resource Management', *Selected Papers from IPMA Conference*, pp. 49–50.

Lippit, R. and White, R. K. (1939) 'The "Social" Climate of Childrens' Groups', in R. G. Barker, J. S. Kounin and H. F. Wright (eds), *Child Behaviors and Development*, London: McGraw-Hill, ch. XXVIII.

Lippitt, G. L. (1982) *Organization Renewal: A Holistic Approach to Organizational Development*, 2nd edn, Englewood Cliffs, NJ: Prentice-Hall.

Lundberg, C. (1990) 'Surfacing Organisational Culture', *Journal of Management Psychology* 5, 4, pp.19–26.

Lundberg, C. (1991) 'Musings on Self, Culture and Enquiry', in P. Frost, L. F. Moore, M. R. Louis, C. C. Lundberg and J. Martin, *Reframing Organisational Culture*, Newbury Park: Sage.

Maier, N. R. F. and Hoffman, L. (1960) 'Quality of First and Second Solution in Group Problemsolving', *Journal of Applied Psychology* 44, pp.278–83.

Maslow, A. H. (1970) *Motivation and Personality*, 2nd edn, New York: Harper and Row.

Mayo, E. (1945) *The Social Problems of an Industrial Civilisation*, Harvard University Press: Cambridge, Mass.

McCabe, M. and Hawke, B. (1993) Interview on Waterfront Reform, carried out in Sydney.

McCarrey, L. E., MacKinnon, C. W., Leonhardt, P. J. and Unsworth, P. J. (1993) *Agent for Reform: Report of the Independent Commission to Review Public Sector Finances by Western Australia Independent Commission to Review Public Sector Finances*, Perth, WA: The Commission.

McGregor, D. (1960) *The Human Side of Enterprise*, New York: McGraw-Hill.

McKenzie (1992) 'Critical Thinking in Health Care Supervision', *The Health Care Supervisor* 10, 4, p. 2.

McLennan, R. (1989) *Managing Organisational Change*, Englewood Cliffs, NJ: Prentice Hall Inc.

Meek, L. (1988) 'Organisational Culture: Origins and Weaknesses', *Organisational Studies* 9, 4, pp. 453–73.

Mondy, R. W. and Noe III, R. M. (1987) *Personnel: The Management of Human Resources*, 3rd edn, Sydney: Allyn and Bacon.

Mumford, A. (1991) 'Writing on Revans R.: Learning in Action', *Personnel Management*, July pp. 34–7.

Osborn, A. (1963) *Applied Imagination*, New York: Scribners.

Pascale, R. T. (1990) *Managing on the Edge*, New York: Simon & Schuster.

Pavlov, I. P. (1902) *The Work of the Digestive Glands*, trans. W. H. Thompson, London: Charles Griffin.

Pedlar, M., Burgoyne J. and Boydell, T. (1986) *A Manager's Guide to Self Development*, 3rd edn, London: McGraw-Hill, p. 4.

Peters, T. and Austin, N. (1985) *A Passion for Excellence*, New York: Random House.

Peters, T. and Waterman, Jr, R. (1982) *In Search of Excellence: Lessons from America's Best-run Companies*, New York: Harper & Row.

Pondy, L. R., Frost, P. J., Morgan, G. and Dandridge, T. (1983) *Organisational Symbolism*, Greenwich, Conn.: JAI Press.

Quinton, A. (1977) 'Existentialism', in A. Bullock and O. Stallybrass, *The Fontana Dictionary of Modern Thought*, London: Fontana Books.

Rist, R. G. (1970) 'Student Social Class and Teacher Expectations: the Self-fulfilling Prophecy in Ghetto Education', *Harvard Business Review* 40, pp. 411–51.

Robbins, S. (1988) *Management: Concepts and Applications*, 2nd edn, Englewood Cliffs, NJ: Prentice Hall Inc.

Robbins, S. (1992) *Essentials of Organisational Behaviour*, 3rd edn, Englewood Cliffs, NJ: Prentice Hall Inc., p. 97.

Robbins, S. (1993a) *Management: Concepts and Applications*, 3rd edn, Englewood Cliffs, NJ: Prentice Hall Inc.

Robbins, S. (1993b) *Organisational Behaviour*, 6th edn, Englewood Cliffs, NJ: Prentice Hall International Inc.

Roethlisberger, F. J. and Dickson, W. J. (1939) *Management and the Worker*, Cambridge, Mass.: Harvard University Press.

Schein, E. (ed.) (1985a) *The Art of Managing Human Resources*, New York: Oxford University Press, p. 249.

Schein, E. (1985b) *Organisational Culture and Leadership*, San Francisco: Jossey-Bass, pp. 52, 56.

Schein, E. (1991) 'What is Culture', in P. Frost, L. F. Moore, M. R. Louis, C. C. Lundberg and J. Martin (eds), *Reframing Organisational Culture*, Newbury Park: Sage, p. 244.

Semler, R. (1992) 'Managing Without Managers', in P. Frost, V. Mitchell and W. R. Nord *Organisational Reality: Reports from the Firing Line*, 4th edn, New York: HarperCollins.

Semler, R. (1993) *Maverick! The Success Story behind the World's Most Unusual Workplace*, New York: Warner Books.

Senge, P. M. (1990) 'The Leaders New York: Building Learning Organisations', *Sloan Management Review*, Fall edition, p. 9.

Senge, P. M. (1992) 'Mental Models', *Planning Review* 20, 2, pp. 4–10.

Shani, A. B. and Pasmore, W. A. (1985) 'Organisation Enquiry: Towards A New Model of the Action Research Process, in D. D. Warrick (ed.), *Contemporary Organisation Development: Current Thinking and Application*, Glenview: Scott and Foresman: pp. 438–48.

Skinner, B. F. (1971) *Contingencies of Reinforcement*, East Newark, Conn.: Appleton-Century-Crofts.

Smith, J. K. (1993) 'Quantitative Versus Qualitative Research: An Attempt to Clarify the Issue', *Educational Researcher*, Mar., p. 7.

Spencer, L. (1989) *Winning Through Participation*, Dubuque Iowa: Kendall/Hunt Publishing.

Tang, S. F. K. and Whiteley, A. M. (1991) *Management Cases in Hong Kong*, Hong Kong: Longmans.

Taylor, F. W. (1929) *Principles of Scientific Management*, New York: Harper and Row.

Trist, E. L. and Bamforth, K. W. (1951) 'Some Social and Psychological Consequences of the Longwall Method of Goal-getting', *Human Relations* 4, pp. 3–38.

Tyson, T. (1989) *Working with Groups*, Melbourne, Vic.: Macmillan, p. 49.

Van de Berghe (1963) 'Dialectic and Functionalism: Towards a Theoretical Synthesis', *American Sociological Review* 28, pp. 695–705.

Vocational Education Employment Training Advisory Committee (VEETAC) (1992) 'Nationally Recognised Training Bringing it Together', Canberra: ACT Accreditation Agency.

Walker, J. W. (1992) *Human Resource Strategy*, Sydney: McGraw-Hill.

Weber, M. (1992) 'Economy and Society: An Outline of Interpretive Sociology', in G. Salaman (ed.), *Human Resource Strategy*, London: Sage.

Wellins, R. S., Byham, W. C. and Wilson, J. M. (1991) *Empowered Teams: Creating Self-directed Work Groups that Improve Quality, Productivity and Participation*, San Francisco: Jossey-Bass.

Western Australia, Parliament (1994) *Acts Amendments (Public Sector Management Act 1994)*, Perth, WA: Government Printer.

Whetton, D. and Cameron, K. S. (1991) *Developing Management Skills*, 2nd edn, New York: Harper Row.

Whitehead, A. K. and Baruch, L. (1981) *People and Employment*, London: Butterworths.

Whiteley, A. M. (1987) The Low Achiever in YTS, PhD thesis, University of Newcastle-upon-Tyne.

Whiteley, A. M. (1991) 'Suggested Strategies for Effective Cultural Interventions to Meet 1997 in Hong Kong', *Proceedings of the Thirteenth Symposium of Asian Studies*, Hong Kong: Asian Research Service.

Whiteley, A. M. (1992a) 'Action Learning in a Traditional Educational Setting', *Journal of Teaching in International Business* 3, 3.

Whiteley, A. M. (1992b) 'Expanding the Horizons of HRM Teaching: Organisational Culture and the Core Values Model', *Second International Organisational Behaviour Teaching Conference*, Perth, WA: Curtin University.

Whiteley, A. M. and Jordan, E. (1990) 'Behavioural Aspects of Introducing Change in Information Systems', *Australia Computer Journal* 22, 2, pp.59–68.

Whiteley, A. M. and Levantard, M. (1994) *Critical Thinking Skills: A Meta Model for Cognitive Development in Management Education*, Perth: Edith Cowan University Teaching Learning Forum.

Whitford, B. (1992) *Success Through Excellence: How Companies in Australia are Seeking and Attaining Excellence*, New York: Prentice Hall.

Wilkie, W. (1990) *Consumer Behaviour*, 2nd edn, New York: John Wiley.

Wilson, H. S. and Hutchinson, S. A. (1991) 'Pearls, Piths and Provocation: Heideggerian Hermanentics and Grounded Theory', *Qualitative Health Research* 1, 2, p. 265.

Woodcock, M. and Francis, D. (1989) *Clarifying Organizational Values*, Aldershot, U. K.: Gower.

Index

absenteeism: disassociation from reality, 26; symbolic meaning, 86–7
achievement recognition, use of rituals, 93
action research: characteristics and process, 111–12; employee values, 53–4; managers as facilitators, 71; participative design, 97
activity, cultural modes of, 122
Allyn, S.C., 94–5
ambiguity, threat of, 124
anonymity, in group decision-making, 107–8
anthropology, organisational context, viii
anxiety, created by change, 34–5
Argyris, C., quoted on single- and double-loop learning, 188–9
Asian countries. *See also* Hong Kong; Japan; Singapore; competition, 4; international dimensions of culture, 122; use of rituals, 92–3; Xerox case study, 228–9
attitudes: constant change dynamic, 62–3; distiguished from values, 39–40
attribution, concept of, 119–20
Australia: low power distance, 123; national values, 39; public sector paradigm, 117–18; public sector values, 37–8
autocratic structures, 98
autonomy, organisational value, 59

bank: case study, 208–20; corporate values, 40
barriers: dimensions of cultures, 124; use of rituals, 92–3
behaviour: attribution theory, 119–20; cultural values about, 58; culture building, 14–16; employees as consumers, 67–70; expressing values as, 75–6; office 'character,' 96; organisational code of, 19; stimulus, response, reward conditioning, 154; symbolic, 86–90
beliefs: constructing reality, 24–6; distinguished from values, 39–40
Bell, Peter, BHP Iron Ore Mobile Equipment Workshop case study, 142–50
benchmarking: BHP Iron Ore Mobile Equipment Workshop case study, 142–50; Gas Cylinders case study, 160–1; Tubemakers of Australia Ltd case study, 239–41
best practice approach, BHP Iron Ore Mobile Equipment Workshop case study, 142–50
BHP Iron Ore: corporate values, 40; Mobile Equipment Workshop case study, 142–50
Buckham, Robin, Tubemakers of Australia Ltd case study, 233–41
bureaucracy: Australian public sector, 37–8; concept of paradigm, 116; modernism, 5, 7; values of control and impersonality, 37
business success: impact of corporate culture, 20; manager/employee relations, 36; P.I.C.S. case study, 242–9; role of values, 40–1
business we are in, defining, 45–6
buying into/out of the job, employee's, 69–70
Byrne, J., quoted on the horizontal corporation, 85–6

calculative contract of employment, 6
Cameron, K.S., quoted on congruent values, 37
case studies: BHP Iron Ore Mobile Equipment Workshop, 142–50;

Commonwealth Industrial Gases Ltd Gas Cylinders Division, 158–76; DuPont (Australia) Ltd, 177–90; how to use, 133–41; introduction, 129–41; Kellogg (Aust) Pty Ltd, 191–207; lecturers' notes, 140; managers' notes, 139; Mass Transit Railway Corporation, 250–61; method, 130–1; P.I.C.S. (WA), 242–9; problem-solving example, 134–7; regional bank, 208–20; step-by-step approach, 137–9; supervisors' notes, 140; trainers' notes, 140; Tubemakers of Australia Ltd Kembla Grange Plant, 233–41; Underground Chemicals Ltd, 151–7; Xerox, 221–32

change: anxiety about, 34–5; away from traditional mindsets, 55–65; constant *versus* forced, 62–3; episodic *versus* continuous, 185–6; history preceding, 81–2; negotiating shared maning, 34–6; strategic *versus* tactical, 133–4; strategists, implementers and recipients, 35; three-step management process, 20–1; useful concepts, 109–15

Clegg, S., quoted on organisational control, 7

co-operative contract of employment, 6

coercive contract of employment, 5–6

Cohen, L., quoted on self-fulfilling prophecy, 109

collectivism, *versus* individualism, in societies, 122–3

common interest program, 162–4

Commonwealth Industrial Gases Ltd: corporate values, 40; Gas Cylinders Division case study, 158–76

communication: company philosophy, 206; of cultural values, 58–9; preparing for change, 71; selective perception, 30–2, 120–1; skills for culture building, 104; stages in creating shared meaning, 26–9; traditional management system, 83–4

compensation, management mindset, 14

competency-based pay, regional bank case study, 216–18

competitiveness: management mindsets, 3–4; meaning of rituals, 94

computerised facilitation of group communication, 107–8

conflict resolution skills, culture building, 104

constructivism: influence of values, beliefs and norms, 24–6; negotiating workable reality, 26–33; postmodernist philosophy, 23–4; view of behaviour, 87

consumer buying behaviour model, 67–70

contracts of employment, psychological: strategic planning, 54: types of, 5, 6

control: management mindset, 14; organisational values, 37; *versus* performance, 124–5

core values method, 66–80; activities and outcomes, 79; employee as customer, 66–70; manager as facilitator, 70–80; workshop activities, 72–9

core values model, 42–65; components, 42–4; mission, 45–6; policies, 47; strategy, 46–7; vision, 44–5

corporate culture, 18–33. *See also* culture; clash with human culture, 13–15; defined, 18–22; domination by management reality, 32; Dumaine quoted on, xi; effect of management mindsets, 3–5, 14–17; employee's sense of identity, 25; negotiated reality, 22–33

corporate values. *See also* values; change, 34–6; role, 36–41
Covey, Stephen: ecological paradigm, 97; quoted on wasting human resources, *xi*; visions and values, 45–6
critical theory, management thinking, 29–30
criticism skills: culture building, 104; self-development, 114–15
culture: anthropological perspective, *viii*; clash of organisational and work group, 14–15; construction and negotiation of reality, 23; core values model, 44; corporate, 34–41; defined by Schein, 18, 20–2; employee's multiple memberships, 24–6; home, 25; influence of home and school on work, 15–16; international dimenions of, 121–4; traditional mindsets, 55–6, 58
culture binding model, 81–4
culture building: customer collaboration, 21–2; employee inputs, 22; facilitation skills, 105–9; heroes, 90–1; internal tasks, 21; managers as facilitators, 70–1; matching organisational design to, 97–103; model, 81–4; paradigm change, 118–19; rituals, 91–6; staff development, 103–105; stories, 96–7; symbols, 84–90; traditional mindsets, 55–6
customers: conflicting values in a training organisation, 39; core values method, 77–8; core values model, 42–3, 50; customer service case study, 250–61; employees as, 66–70; intervention in organisation, 21–2

Dalmau, T., quoted on loss of meaning, 81
Deal, T., quoted on corporate values, 41
decision support systems, technology for, 107–8
decisions about working, employee's, 69–70
democratic structures, 98
deviance, employee, from management reality, 32
Dick, B., quoted on loss of meaning, 81
doing *versus* thinking, management ideas about, 3–5, 9
Dumaine, B., quoted on organisational culture, *xi*
DuPont (Australia) Ltd: case study, 177–90; corporate values, 40

ecological paradigm, 97
economic performance. *See* business success
education. *See also* training and development; organisational context, *vii*
Emery, Fred and Merrelyn, participative design principles, 97–8
emotional inputs: creating shared vision, 72–3; facilitating, 105
employees: as customers, 66–70; buying into work, 69; core values stakeholders, 42–3; culture building skills development, 103–5; decisions of, impact, 69–70; deviance from management reality, 32–3; dimensions of experience, 69; exploring alternative work, 68–9; feeling need to work, 68; lateness and absenteeism, 26; ownership of decisions, *viii*; preparing for change, 71–2; strategic planning process, 50–4; Theories X and Y, 59, 61, 62, 89; traditional mindsets, 55–6
Etzioni, A., psychological contracts, 5–6
excellence, Mass Transit Railway Corporation case study, 250–1

expectations: psychological contracts, 5–7; self-fulfilling prophecy, 109–11
experience of employment, employee's, 69
exploration, employee's of job alternatives, 68–9

facilitation: by managers, 70–2; culture building skills, 103–9
FADE (focus, analyse, develop and execute) framework, 168–9
feminity/masculinity dimension of culture, 124
filtering, selective perception, 120–1
folklore, culture building, 96–7
Fordism: management mindset, 5, 7; objective reality, 23; values of hierarchical authority, 37; Xerox case study, 222
Francis, D., quoted on management, 3
frozen *versus* dynamic metaphors for cultures, 62–3
Fuji Xerox Australia case study, 229–32
fundamental errors in attribution, 120
future scenarios: for corporate culture, 3–5, 7–8; in creating shared vision, 73

Garcia, Joseph, Underground Chemicals Ltd case study, 151–7
gas industry case study, 158–76
General Electric, 95
Geranmayer, A., quoted on paradigms, 116–17
groups. *See also* teamwork; work groups; decision support systems (GSS/GDSS), 107–8; self-management, 13, 14–16

Halal, W.E., quoted on paradigms, 116–17
Hawthorne Effect: construction of reality, 24–5; management mindset, 11–14
heroes, culture building, 90–1
Heskett, J.L., quoted on culture and performance, 20
hierarchical organisations: culture building, 85; design principles, 101–3; modernism, 7
Hofstede, G., international dimensions of culture, 122, 124
home: core values model, 44; employee's sense of identity, 25; influence on work culture, 15–16
Hong Kong mass transit case study, 250–61
horizontal organisations, culture building, 85–6
human nature, management world views, 10
human resources management: as marketing, 8; employees as customers, 70; incorporation of values, 63–4; regional bank case study, 209–10, 213–14; relationship to other disciplines, *viii*; symbolic behaviours, 86

illumination, stage of problem-solving, 136
imaginal inputs: changing mindsets, 57; creating shared vision, 72–3; facilitating, 105
incubation, stage of problem-solving, 136
individuals: problem-solving with work groups and organisations, 132; *versus* collectivism, in societies, 122–3; world view, 23
industrial relations: DuPont (Australia) Ltd case study, 190; Gas Cylinders case study, 173; international best practice program, 150; Kellogg (Aust) Pty Ltd case study, 192–3
information: changing mindsets, 56–7; encircling model, 207; service function, 203–7; traditional management system, 83

internal market paradigm, 117–18
international best practice approach, 142–50
internationalism, use of symbolic behaviour, 90
interpersonal skills, culture building, 104
interpretivism, view of behaviour, 86–8

Japan: collectivism, 123; management mindset; Xerox case study, 222–3, 228–9
Jick, T.D., change management, 34–6
job: consumer model of employee behaviour, 66–70; evaluation, 215–16; recruitment and selection, 63–4

Kanter, R.M., change management, 34–6
Kearns, D.T., quoted on history of Xerox, 221–3
Kellogg (Aust) Pty Ltd: case study, 191–207; corporate values, 40
Kelmar, John, P.I.C.S. (WA) case study, 242–9
Kennedy, A., quoted on corporate values, 41
key values: core values workshop, 74; definition, 42
knowledge, attitudes, skills, values (KAS and KASVAL), constant change dynamic, 62–3
Kotter, J.P., quoted on culture and performance, 20

labour market, 1960s, *vii*, *viii*
laissez-faire structures, 98
language: customer surveys, 77–8; hierarchical organisations, 85
lateness: disassociation from reality, 26; symbolic meaning, 86–7
leadership: Kellogg's (Aust) Pty Ltd case study, 205–6; role in culture building, 62; training course, 196–202; Xerox case study, 223–7
learning: concepts for culture building, 116–25; contrasted with training, 63; self-fulfilling prophecy, 109–11; single- and double-loop, 188–9
Lee, Peter, Commonwealth Industrial Gases Ltd case study, 158–76
legends, culture building, 96
Lessem, R., developing shared meaning, 27–8
Luxfer Gas Cylinders, 160–1

machine model of organisations, 4–5
making sense: postmodern management, 7–8; role of corporate culture, 19
management: accessibility, 90; by walking about (MBWA), 93, 124; culture building, 14–17; filtering reality, 59–62; first-line and middle, displacement of, 172–3; Hawthorne Effect, 11–14; mindsets: changing, 55–65; traditional, in core values model, 49–65; mindsets and corporate culture, 3–17; modernism, 5–7; participative, 106; postmodernism, 7–9; scientific philosophy of, 9–11; self-development, 113–15; systems, core values, 47–9; theories *versus* paradigms, 116–17
managers: as facilitators, 70–2; case study notes, 139; culture building skills development, 103–9; designers of rituals, 95–6
Manion L., quoted on self-fulfilling prophecy, 109
marketing: employee as customer, 66–7; internal market paradigm, 117–18; organisational context, *vii*–*viii*; postmodern management, 8

marketplace. *See* customers
masculinity/feminity dimension of culture, 124
Mass Transit Railway Corporation case study, 250–61
Matsushita, Konosuke, quoted on Taylorism, 16–17
Maule, Patrick, Mass Transit Railway Corporation case study, 250–61
McBurney, Richard, Commonwealth Industrial Gases Ltd case study, 158–76
McGregor, Douglas, Theories X and Y, 59, 61, 62, 89
meaning: change as negotiation of, 34–6; construction by investigation, 87–8; stages in creating shared meaning, 26–9
mental models. *See also* mindsets; concepts of paradigm, 116–19; construction of reality, 24; critical appraisal of, 29–30; managers', of employee values, 51–4; negotiated and prescribed realities, 61–2; visions as, 48–9
mentoring philosophy, 70–2
Mick the Killer legend, 94
mindsets. *See also* mental models; changing, 55–65; style of management, 3–17; traditional, 49–65
mining industry case studies: best practice, 142–50; safety, 151–7
mission: core values model, 45–51; in culture building model, 81–4
modernism: management mindset, 5–7; negotiated and prescribed realities, 61–2; objective reality, 23
money-making: common interest program, 162–4; competency-based pay, 216–18; Hawthorne Effect, 12–14; scientific management mindset, 11
motivation cycle, 68–70

Nadler, D.A., quoted on history of Xerox, 221–3
Napoli, David: performance *versus* control, 124–5; regional bank case study, 208–20
National Cash Register (NCR) Corporation, 94–5
national cultures: social implications for organisations, 121–4; values, 39
need for a job, employee's, 68
negotiation: culture building skills, 104; process of change, 34–6; reality, in core values model, 59–65; shared workable reality, 26–33
newcomer rituals, 94–5
norms: constructing reality, 24–6; dominance and deviance, 32; work groups, 13

objectivism: modernist mindset, 23; view of behaviour, 86–7
OKX model, 72–3, 113, 115
organisational design, matching with culture building, 97–103
organisational structures: core values, 47–9; symbolism, 85–66; types of, 98
organisations. *See also* corporate culture; future of, 3–5, 7, 8; machine model, 4–5
ownership, employees', of decisions, viii

P.I.C.S. (WA) case study, 242–9
paradigm, concept of, 116–19
participative design principles, culture building, 97–103
participative management, facilitation, 106
Pascale, R.T.: changes facing managers, 4–5; quoted on managerial mindsets, 51–2
perception: concept of, 120–1; construction of reality, 22; manager's, of work, 26; selective, 30–1, 121
performance. *See also* behaviour; business success; attribution

theory, 119–20; management, bank case study, 218–19; *versus* control, 124–5
Peters, T., quoted on excellence, 250
photocopier manufacturing case study, 221–32
photographic supply business case study, 242–9
pipe manufacturing case study, 233–41
policy, core values model, 46–8
positivist view of behaviour, 86–8
postmodernism: construction of reality, 23–4; management mindset, 7–9; negotiated and prescribed realities, 61–2
Pourdehnad, J., quoted on paradigms, 116–17
power distance dimension of culture, 123
preparation stage of problem-solving, 136
prescribed reality, traditional management mindset, 59–65
prescribed tasks, employee values, 53
problem-solving: case studies, 133–7; stages, 136–7
productivity: common interest program, 162–4; Hawthorne Effect, 12–14; symbolic meaning, 86–7, use of rituals, 92
profit-centre principle: internal market paradigm, 118; use of rituals, 91–2
psychological contracts of employment: strategic planning, 54: types of, 5–6
public sector: mass transit case study, 250–61; new paradigm in, 117–18; values, 37–8

quality management: Gas Cylinders case study, 168–70; postmodernism, 8; Tubemakers of Australia Ltd case study, 235–6; use of symbolic behaviour, 90; Xerox case study, 223–32

Rank Xerox. *See* Xerox reality: constructivism, 22–4; influence of values, beliefs and norms, 24–6; negotiated, in core values model, 59–65; prescribed, in traditional management mindset, 59–65; workable, 26–44
recruitment: case study problem-solving, 134–7; incorporating core values into, 63–4
redundancy, in organisational design, 98–100
research. *See* action research
retrofit, Xerox case study, 222
Richards, Bill, Kellogg (Aust) Pty Ltd case study, 191–207
rite of passage, 94–5
rituals: culture building, 91–6; managers as designers, 95–6
Robbins, S.: action research process, 112; quoted on group principles, 13; quoted on perceived reality, 22

safety case study, 151–7
Schein, E., definition of culture, 18, 20–2
Schon, D.A., quoted on single- and double-loop learning, 188–9
school, influence on work culture, 15–16
scientific management: mindset, 9–11; objective reality, 23
selection of staff: case study problem-solving, 134–7; incorporating core values into, 63–4
selective perception, 30–1, 121
self and others: self-fulfilling prophecy, 110–11; stages in creating shared meaning, 26–9
self-development, part of management development, 113–15
self-fulfilling prophecy, in learning, 109–11
self-managing work teams, 165–7
Semco. *See* Semler, Richard

Semler, Richard: management mindsets, 3–4; manager/employee relations, 35–6
Senge, P.M., quoted on failure of ideas in practice, 49
sense. *See* making sense
shared vision: culture building model, 81–4; methods for creating, 72–3, 78–80
sickness, symbolic meaning, 86–7
Singapore, national values, 39
skills: constant change dynamic, 62–3; culture building, 103–6; self development, 114
social events, use of rituals, 92–4
social systems, traditional mindsets, 55–8
socio-technical systems: definition, 98; regional bank case study, 214–15, 219; Tubemakers of Australia Ltd case study, 236–8
space, in national cultures, 122
Spencer, L., quoted on participative management, 106
status symbols, culture building, 84–5
Stein, B.A., change management, 34–6
stimulus, response, reward conditioning, 154
stories, culture building, 96–7
strategy: core values, 47–9; core values model, 46–54; use of symbolic behaviour, 89–90
Stringfellow, David: Fuji Xerox Australia case study, 229–32; quoted on anxiety about change, 34
structural symbols, culture building, 85–6
subcultures, core values model, 54
suboptimisation, strategic planning, 51
success. *See* business success
supervisors: case study notes, 140; contrasting styles, 10; culture building skills development, 103–9
surveys, language of, 77–8
symbols: culture building, 84–90; defining corporate culture, 19–20; traditional mindsets, 57
synergy, creating shared meaning, 29

Tang, Sara F.K.: Mass Transit Railway Corporation case study, 250–61; quoted on management, 3
tasks: one task-one person syndrome, 100; traditional mindsets, 55–7
Taylorism: Hawthorne Effect, 12–14; management mindset, 9–11; psychological contracts, 5; values of mechanising, controlling and organising, 37
teamwork: culture building skills, 104; expressing value as behaviour, 75–6; incorporating values into recruitment and selection, 63–4; self-managing work teams, 165–7
Theories X and Y, 59, 61–2, 89
thinking *versus* doing, management ideas about, 3–5, 9
time orientation, 122
total quality management (TQM). *See* quality traditional management style: communication system, 83–4; core values, 49–65; overview, 4–5
training and development: case study notes, 140; contrasted with learning, 63; culture building skills, 103–9; facilitation skills, 105–9; group cohesion, 96–7; in core values method, 77; leadership in management course, 196–202; safety case study, 151–7; self-development, 113–15; self-fulfilling prophecy, 109–11
training organisation, example of conflicting values in, 38–9

transport organisation: case study, 250–61; vision and values workshop, 74–8
Tubemakers of Australia Ltd Kembla Grange Plant case study, 233–41

uncertainty avoidance dimension of culture, 124
Underground Chemicals Ltd case study, 151–7
unions. *See* industrial relations

values: Australian, 37–8, 122; changing corporate values, 34–41; Confucian, 122; congruence of employees' and managers', 37; constructing reality, 24–6; core values method, 66–80; core values model, 42–65; dominance and deviance, 32; examples of, 37–9; importance to companies, 40–1; key, distinguished from core, 42, 74; management systems, 47–9; national values, 39, 122; nature of, 39–40; organisational structure, 47–9; role of, 36–41; strategy, 47–9; understanding values, 36–7
verification stage of problem-solving, 136
vision: core values model, 44–54; shared: in culture building model, 81–4; methods for creating, 72–3, 78–80

Warburton, Richard, interviewed about workplace culture, 177–82
Waterman, R., quoted on excellence, 250
Weber, Max, theory of bureaucracy, 116
Western Electric Co., Hawthorne Effect, 12
Whetton, D., quoted on congruent values, 37
White, Bill, 93
Whiteley, A.M., quoted on management, 3
Woodcock, M., quoted on management, 3
work experience, marketing of, viii
work groups: core values model, 44, 50–1, 54; employee's sense of identity, 244–6; Hawthorne Effect, 11–14; problem-solving with individuals and organisations, 132; self-managing, 165–7
world view: individual, 23; positivist and interpretivist approaches, 88

Xerox: case study, 221–32; core values method, 77